MATRILINY TO PATRILINY
A Study of the Rabha Society

MATRILINY TO PATRILINY
A Study of the Rabha Society

MANIS KUMAR RAHA

GIAN PUBLISHING HOUSE
NEW DELHI-110002

GIAN PUBLISHING HOUSE
4348, Madan Mohan Street
4-C Ansari Road, Darya Ganj,
New Delhi-110002

ISBN 81—212—0244—2

PRINTED IN INDIA

Published by Mrs. Gayatri Garg for Gian Publishing House, New Delhi
and Printed at Godwall Printers, Delhi.

To
Late Professor T.C. Das
and
Late Professor M.N. Basu
who inspired me to
undertake this study

PREFACE

The Rabhas, like many other tribal groups of West Bengal, are one of the Scheduled Tribes inhabiting mostly in Jalpaiguri and Cooch Behar districts of West Bengal. I got interested to study these people not because they were a Scheduled Tribe and little-known, but because they had a peculiar social system the matrilineal system which persisted significantly among a section of them who inhabited in the settlements inside the reserve forests while the same system was steadily declining among the other section of this ethnic group, the village dwelling ones, for their keen urge to get a place in the local Hindu society thereby inheriting a new social system, patriliny. Friend-Pereira's observation in 1911 that, 'they are in a stage of transition from matriarchal to patriarchal form of life,' inspired me to examine the Rabha society in West Bengal to see whether they were also following the same path of transformation i.e. shifting from one social system to another as did their congeners in Assam in the past. Surprisingly enough that what Friend Pareira marked among the Rabhas of Assam as early as 1911 still holds good among the present day Rabhas of West Bengal. My preliminary investigation has eonfirmed my hypothesis that the matrilineal Rabhas of West Bengal, due to different external and/or internal factors, have kept their journey on to form a new patrilineal society.

My study shows that of the two ecological sections of the Rabhas, the forest inhabiting ones (the Forest Rabhas), has still preserved their traditional matriliny to a great extent (though no doubt they are also changing), but their village dwelling brethren have discarded many of their traditional matrilineal traits to give place to the patrilineal Hindu cultural traits. This type of change, though unique, it is most probably present among almost all matrilineal societies of India, the nature and extent of such change may, of course, vary slightly from one such group to another. I have studied this type of change among the Rabhas of West Bengal with the idea that it may throw new light on the study of culture change in the Indian society with particular reference to the culture change among the tribal society of India. I firmly believe that the students of anthropology and allied disciplines will get new ideas from this study and may be interested to undertake research work among other matrilineal societies in an identical way.

M.K. RAHA

ACKNOWLEDGEMENT

From the very start of the work to the publication of a book an author requires to take help and assistance from different individuals and institutions. I am no exception. From the very beginning I had to take help from the persons of different walks of life and for this I express my deep sense of gratitude to all of them. I particularly refer to my teachers, Late Professor T.C. Das and Late Professor M.N. Basu who once inspired me to undertake such study. I shall remain ever grateful to them. I am taking this opportunity to remember my deep indebtedness to Dr. Amal Kumar Das, Director, Cultural Research Institute, Govt. of West Bengal, for his valuable advice, suggestions and help. It is my privilege to gratefully remember all the help, assistance and co-operation extended to me by the authorities of the Divisional Forest Offices of Cooch Behar and of Buxa, the Block Development office at Kumargram, in the district of Jalpaiguri and also the offices of the Special Officer, Scheduled Castes and Scheduled Tribes Welfare, Jalpaiguri and also of Cooch Behar. I am also indebted to Dr. Aloke Kumar Ghosh for his constant help and valuable suggestions. I have incorporated some good photographs. These have been supplied to me by the authority of the Indian Museum and also by Shri Sunil Paul of Kamakhyaguri village, Jalpaiguri. I am really thankful to them. Shri Paul in addition, helped me in varied ways while I was in the field and also while I was in my place of work. In fact he is still helping me by enlightening me about the latest situation in the Rabha area and also the condition of the Rabhas. The help he rendered and is still rendering to me cannot be measured. My sincerest thanks are due to him. Shri L.M. Dhyani, Smt. Mala Mukherjee, Shri Sudip De, Smt. Vimla, Miss Geeta, Shri Pitambaru and Shri Anand Minj helped me in typing out the manuscript of this book. I am indebted to all of them. Shri Swapan Das has helped me in comparing the manuscript. I am thankful to him. But I specially mention Shri Palash Chandra Coomar, my colleague, who rendered all possible help to me in finalising the book. I owe my indebtedness to him for his all out help and co-operation. Thanks are also due to my numerous friends and well wishers for whose help and advice this work has been made to success. Last and not the least with a deep sense of gratitude I remember all the inhabitants of the villages and forest *bastees* I surveyed, particularly the Rabhas of these settlements who did not hesitate to pay all their loving attention to my personal comfort, to co-operate with me very sympathetically all through and to render ungrudging help to me in the collection of data.

CONTENTS

LIST OF ILLUSTRATIONS

Introduction

INTRODUCTION

It was a rainy morning of Mid-August of 1962 when I first entered the Rabha land of the district of Jalpaiguri. In the midst of heavy downpour I got down from the metre-gauze train on the platform of a tiny station of Kamakhyaguri. It was all over muddy as rain water had covered many places. Croaking of frogs from the rain soaked bushes of the Western Duars could be heard all around. With great difficulty I could reach the dilapidated Dak bungalow near the market place. Hearing of my visit some local people came to meet me and one of them was Sri Dabendra Nath Das, the undisputed Rabha leader, the first Rabha I met.

I could not meet any other Rabha for the next two days as I had to keep myself confined for two days in the Dak-Bungalow because of the non-stop heavy downpour. After the stoppage of rain I heard the very disheartening news of the floods. The rivers like the Raidak, the Ghorumara, the Torsa had flooded many areas, and the flood water had reached only a few miles away from Kamakhyaguri. This was my first independent field work outside Calcutta. I was all alone. In that forest clad, animal infested, malarious and flood stricken area and in that dreadful rainy season I felt, in a natural course, very much disheartened and perturbed.

But I had no way to flee. Rail connection was disrupted because of the flood. I halted in that Dak-Bungalow for two more days, and I gradually stabilized my mind and regained my courage and determination of undertaking research work among these people. Then one morning I moved to Dakshin Manasi, a village where a good number of the Rabhas live, crossing at many places, knee-deep water and slush. I settled myself ultimately in the out-house of a very generous Rajbansi started my work.

My first visit to the settlement of the Forest Rabhas (The terms "the Forest Rabha" and "the Village Rabha" have been used for the convenience of the study and to distinguish between the two sections of the Rabhas of West Bengal. See also Das & Raha, 1967 : Introduction) was, in the same way very interesting. Purodha *bastee*, the first Forest Rabha settlement I visited, was within the Reserve Forest. The area is under dense forest full of wild animals. The peculiar and mysterious environment of the reserve forest gave me a very new feeling—a feeling mixed with fear, joy, delightfulness and adventure. Thereafter I spent a total of eighteen months in various Rabha settlements—in the Forest *bastees* in the midst of the Reserve Forests full of wild animals, and the villages in the neighbourhood of the reserve forests.

Before my first visit to the Rabha land, I had acquainted myself with almost all the published literature about the Rabhas which threw much light on their past culture. I framed up a problem before I undertook my field work as I realised that a modern scientific study generally began with a problem which constituted its geneneral objective. Social scientists like Radcliffe-Brown (Fortes, 1949 : VII), Leach (1962: 1), Fortes (1949: VII) and others, have favoured hypothesis as the starting point of studies in social science. Getting a clue from the past records, I built up the hypothesis that the Rabha society was changing from one social system to another—from matrilineal social system to another—from matrilineal social system to patrilineal one, for various factors. I got very much interested in this type of change among the Rabhas, accordingly planned to undertake a research study among them, with the hope to see the same type of change if any, among the present day Rabhas of West Bengal. In a later phase I found that my hope had been fulfilled. My first few field trips among both forest and village dwelling Rabhas in both Jalpaiguri and

Cooch Behar districts, proved my hypothesis that the Rabha society was moving from matriliny to patriliny.

The present day Rabha society of the State of West Bengal reflects a curious co-existence of two different social systems, matriliny and patriliny, one being supplanted by the other. One section still preserves their traditional matriliny to a great extent while the other section seeks to replace it with the patrilineal system borrowed from the local Hindus. Of course, some other forces also helped them in this regard.

The studies on the Rabhas of West-Bengal show that both the ecological groups belong to the Koch Rabha section, and are directly divided into a number of exogamous clans known as the *husuk*, some of which are totemic in nature (Das and Raha, 1967 ; Raha, 1970 : 104-112 ; Raha, 1977). Many of these clans have sub-clans which probably might have developed in later period. Though the Forest and the Village Rabhas have some common features as described above, yet in certain respects they bear great diversities, which may be found in the institutions and structure framing their respective social organisation. The differences are noticeable in various aspects of the family organisation, economy, political organization etc.

The Khasis and the Garos, the typical matrilineal communities of Eastern and North-East India attracted many scholars who have studied different aspects of their culture. A few other communities in the northern part of West Bengal and mainly in Assam, also show matrilineal features. They include the Pnar, the Lyngngam, the Pani-Koch, the Lalung, the Rabha and others. In connection with the Pnars, Banerjee states, "They are mother-right people like the Khasi" (1963 : 165). Ehrenfels his article marks both Lyngngam and the Pnars as the matrilineal tribes (1955 : 308-319). Fereira also postulates that the Lyngngam and the Lalung acquired their matrilineal features from the Khasi (1965 : 231). Among the Pani-Koch both Martin (1938 - 540) and Rowney (1982 : 146-147) observe quite a high frequency of matrilineal elements. Majumdar also finds the existence of matrilineal elements to a great extent among the Koch of Garo Hills (1967 : 65-71). The same thing may be said in connection with the Rabhas. Early accounts give evidence of the matrilineal features being present among them. Sunder, in his account on the Rabhas, marks that among these people the "relationship is traced in the female line. Property descends to the widow. Male members get nothing. If there is no widow, property passes on to the daughter" (1895 : 72). It is also revealed that :

> "at some remote period of time that the matriarchate was in full vigour, is apparent from the story of Dahan...where Dahan, the leader of the people, is really the maternal uncle and natural guardian of Toba Rani the chieftainess or the queen of the tribe" (Friend-Pereira, 1912 : 142 ; Das, B.M., 1960 : 119 : 121).
>
> "Their society is based on the matriarchal system like the Garos and the Khasis of Assam ... Among the Rabhas the daughter inherits the property.... The bride-groom has to go to the bride's house after marriage leaving his parent's house for ever. The wife is all in all in the family",

observes Barua (1951 : 35). "The *bar* (clan) is matrilineal. The children take the *bar* name after the mother (Das, B.M., 1960 : 10).

On an analysis of the social organization of the two sections of the Rabhas of West Bengal it is found that the two sections, namely the Forest Rabhas and the Village Rabhas, show somewhat different pattern. While differences are noticed in certain aspects of the culture of these two ecological groups, similarities are also found in several other aspects.

The first thing that needs to be mentioned is the affinity between the two sections of the Rabhas. These two sections of Rabhas are basically of one group. Both of them belong to the Rabha community and members of one section treat those of the other as their congener. The two villages, Madhya and Dakshin Manasi, were once like the present Purodha and other forest *bastees* ecologically. They were thinly populated and covered with dense forests. The aged Rabhas of these two villages say that in their boyhood days they had the same culture as that practised by the Forest Rabhas of the present day. Purodha and the other forest *bastee* areas were later on declared as reserve forests where the local inhabitants (who were the Rabhas and other tribals) were allowed to stay. Manasi villages remained as villages and were mainly peopled by the Rajbansis, a dominant Scheduled caste. There were also the Rabhas who have been living side by side for several generations. The long and intimate contact and the inter-dependence of these two ethnic groups brought about two-fold changes in the Rabha culture of the two villages. The Village Rabhas started borrowing the cultural norms and aspirations from their neighbouring Rajbansi caste people. Their present-day cultural pattern shows some distinct changes. They have progressed from little to the greater tradition, from tribalism to Hinduism. Secondly, the waves of Hinduism have been progressively helping them changing their culture from matriliny to patriliny.

A number of authors has stated that the Koches became Rajbansis after they became Hinduised (Martin, 1838 : 538, Boileau, 1891 : 20 ; O'Dannel, 1891 : 262 ; Boverly, 1872 : 130; Risley, 1891 : 492 ;Gait: 99; Grierson, 1903 : 95; Porter, 1931 : 473 : Sanyal, 1965 : 13). Thereafter in the first quarter of this century the Kshatrization movement started among the Rajbansis. This movement was later on accelerated by late Panchanan Burman, the famous Rajbansi leader and reformer. As a result of this movement, a large number of the Rajbansis became Kshatriyas (Sanyal, 1965 : 17-19 ; 1963 : 1-21). The Rajbansi Kshatriyas consider themselves a little superior in the ladder of social hierarchy to the ordinary Rajbansi.

In the pre-independence period the two villages, Madhya and Dakshin Manasi were mainly peopled by the Rabhas and the Rajbansis. Most of the *jotedars* (land-owners) were the Rajbansis and the Rabhas were mainly the *adhiars*(share-croppers). So the Rabhas were economically dependent on the Rajbansis. What was initially economic dependence was later on turned into a social dependence for the Rabhas. The Rajbansis exerted influence on the Rabhas and created an image of their superiority over them. The Village Rabhas have also witnessed the Kshatrization movement under which the Rajbansis acquired a superior position and identified themselves with the Hindus. They started imbibing the cultural traits from their neighbouring Hindu masters, the Rajbansis. The adoption of Hindu cultural elements was considered by them as 'the sole criterion to ascend the ladder of caste hierarchy' (Srinivas, 1952 : 30). This aspiration to become Hindus gained momentum in the wake of the support of some political parties like the Hindu Mahasabha and the Indian National Congress. Later on, in 1930 they started the Kshatrization movement and in this they were inspired by some political and religious leaders. They 'made' themselves *kshatriya* by performing some religious rites and by observing some social restrictions and rigidities.

Their strong desire to become the Hindus in order to elevate their social position, has paved the way to their Hinduization. As a result of the cultural absorption the present day Rabha culture of the villages has little difference with the Rajbansi culture of the same area.

A different pattern is observed in the Forest Rabha culture of Purodha, Nalgarh and Kamala *bastees*. The Rabhas of these settlements live in an insulated world of their own. Their contact with the Hindu caste people (e.g. the Rajbansi and others) is very meagre. Generally, no Hindu excepting a few Nepalis, live in these forest *bastee*. The Reserve Forest Laws also prevent others from entering into these *bastees* and live there. The Rabhas, in their turn, go to the weekly market once or twice in a fortnight and very seldom visit the town areas. They have little chance of coming in close association with the Hindu caste people. Their culture therefore, shows less infiltration of the Hindu cultural elements. They have been able to preserve their tradition to a great extent.

It is not that the Rabha society of West Bengal is only changing. Every thing in this universe changes. And likewise "all cultures are in a constant state of change" (Linton, 1940 : 468). This process of change is noticeable in human society and culture everywhere. The idea of a dynamic society and changing universe went on taking shape amidst strong opposition from the conservative forces in different periods. In the nineteenth century this ideology found wide acceptance following the revolutionary theories prescribed by Darwin which were later on strongly supported by many eminent personalities like Huxley, Haeckel and others.

In India studies of this kind started only in the second quarter of the twentieth century when

> "striking refinements and innovations in the anthropological approach to the study of culture based on a combination of the historical and functional methods, which has resulted in a renewed emphasis on a field of anthropology known as Cultural Dynamics and Acculturation in particular, flourished in Europe and America" (Dutta-Majumdar, 1956 : 5).

The change of culture in a society depends on various factors. The main factor is contact—contact in different spheres. When two societies or two cultures come in contact, it is expected that the weaker culture will borrow elements from the dominant one. Sometimes a few individuals from one culture, can exert influence over another culture of society and cause change in the latter. "The fundamental processes of culture change are concerned with the modification in the knowledge, attitudes and behaviours of the individuals...who composed a society." (Linton, *op. cit.*).

In India, as stated earlier, the tribal societies are also changing. This change in culture is largely the result of their contact with the Hindu people. The tribal people of this subcontinent are living for centuries in close contact with the numerous dominant Hindu caste people on whom they depend economically. Tney felt a strong desire to unify themselves with the cultural matrix of the dominant Hindus only to upgrade their position in the ladder of the Hindu social hierarchy.

For a long time the tribals of India were trying to improve their conditions on economic, social, religious, ethical and other aspects with the help of some external agencies. The religious ideologies like the Christianity and the Hinduism helped them in this regard. During the pre-independence period a large number of the tribal people of different parts of India, were baptised to Christianity. The interest of these people for Hinduism expedited their movement towards Hinduism. A steady growth of Hinduism among the tribal populace of this country can thus be found. That a very large number of the tribal people have leaned towards Hinduism, is evident from the figures of the census reports of different periods where more and more tribal people are found to have declared themselves as the Hindus. Even the studies on different tribal communities of India have borne this out.

The Pati Rabhas, a section of the Rabhas of Assam, for example, follow Hinduism to a great extent. According to Friend-Pereira, "They are the most advanced section of the tribe, for they have adopted the Hindu customs" (Friend-Pereira, *op. cit.*). Buchanon-Hamilton in 1810 and Dalton in 1872 found the Pati Rabhas adopting Hindu doctrine. (Martin, 1838 : 546 ; Dalton, 1872 : 87). Domant also marks that 'the Pati Rabhas have become to a great extent, Hinduised (1880 : 233). Besides the Pati and the Koch sections of the Rabhas the different tribal groups have accepted this change. For example, the Hos, the Santals, the Mundas, the Oraons, the Khasis, the Garos, the Kols, the Bhils, and many others have adopted this course of progress for their respective societies. In his book Majumdar described the changes among the Ho, following their contact with different agencies like the Hindus, the Christian Missionaries etc. The wealthier section of this community has embraced Hinduism to be able to raise its social prestige (Majumdar, D.N., 1937). Datta-Majumdar (1956 : 109-129) marked these changes among the Santals,

> "As a result of contact with the impinging forces of Hinduism, British Government, Christianity, Santiniketan and Sriniketan...the traditional Santal culture has everywhere been undergoing transformation" (1956 : 109).

The Bhumijas of Bihar, Orissa and West Bengal have also had such changes. A large number of them has been Hinduised over a period of the time (Sinha, 1953 : 148-164 ; Sinha, 1956 ; Sinha, 1957a : 23-37 ; Sinha, 1957b : 93-118 ; Raha, 1964b : 361-368). Both Christianity and Hinduism exercised great influence on the life of the Oraons of Chota Nagpur (Sachchidananda, 1964 : 95-99 ; Bose, 1967a : 204-205 ; Roy, 1928 : 316-352). In Sunderban area (southern part of West Bengal) marked impact of Hinduism is found in the Oraon culture (Das and Raha, 1963 ; Raha, 1964b : 361-368). Similarly, the Munda culture of Chota Nagpur (Sachchidananda, 1964: 87-90; Bose, 1967 : 204-205 ; Roy, 1912 : 284-285, 325-343) and of southern Bengal (Choudhuri, 1961 : 1-175 ; Raha, 1964b : 361-368) has changed. Likewise among different tribes of Central India Griffith noticed the change of culture (1964 : 275-278). Due to the contact with the Hindus, the culture of the Malpaharias has also changed (Das, et al, 1966 : 1-166).

In the peninsular India among the tribes of Nilgiri Hills, both Emeneau (1938 : 101-121) and Mandelbaum (1941 : 19-26) noticed the changes in the life of the Todas, the Badagas and the Kotas. Marked changes have also been observed in the culture of both the Chenchus (Fürer-Haimendorf, 1943 : 284-318) and the Reddis (Fürer-Haimendorf, 1947) by Fürer-Haimendorf. In his book on the Iravas of Malabar, Aiyappan has shown the nature and extent of changes in this community (Aiyappan, 1944). Besides the above communities, in north-eastern part of India among the Garos (Bose, J.K., 1947 : 97-107 ; Burling, 1963a : 289-322 ; Nakane, 1961 : 90) and the Khasis (Chattopadhyay, 1960 : 35-37) cultural changes of different degrees have taken place for the Hinduism and the Christianity. The Koches also at present 'have adopted such an amount of sanskritisation that they have definitely come under the fold of the 'Hinduism' (Majumdar, 1967 : 70). The culture of the Purum Kukis shows 'undeniable traces of loans from their Hindu neighbours' (Das, T.C., 1945 : 188).

The present tribal culture of this country has shown marked changes. Though these changes are due to the action of various forces, the role of Hinduism is dominant.

> "The Hinduization of the primitive tribes will eventually lead to their becoming a part of the Hindu social system and then being integrated into its lower strata and becoming regarded by the Hindus as out-caste or Scheduled classes" (Griffith, 1946 : 277).

The other type of changes among the Rabhas is the process of patriarchalization among them i.e. their movement from matriliny towards patriliny.

Though the matrilineal system was much more widely distributed in India (Hutton, 1951:150), the matrilineal communities and communities bearing matrilineal elements are chiefly found in the north-east (Khasi and Garo Hills) and in the south-west (Kerala) of modern India (Ehrenfels, 1941 : 5, 12). In this country there are still some communities such as the Garos (Playfair, 1909 : 1-180 ; Burling, 1963a : 1-377), the Khasis, Gurdon, 1914 : 1-209 ; Nakane, 1961 : 102-123), the Nayars (Iyer, 1909 : II : 47 ; Nakane : 1963 : 23-28 l, Gough, 1962 : 293-404) and others where full-fledged matriliny is found to be prevalent. There are some others such as the Uralis (Thurston and Rangachari, 1909 : VII ; 242 ; Mukherjee, 1954 : 113 ; Mukherjee, 1961 : 216), the Kanikkars (Thurston and Rangachari, 1909 : III : 138-162 ; Mukherjee, 1961 : 216-217), the Muthuvans (*op. cit.*) the Mala Pantarams (*op. cit.*) and others who embrace partial matriliny i.e. matrilineal and patrilineal traits co-exist. This co-existence of the two diverse cultural patterns among the cultural tradition of these communities of India, has been possible because of the contact of the indigenous matrilineal civilization of India and the later immigrant patrilineal cultural complexes (Ehrenfels, 1941 : 3).

The Rabha culture also shows similar features. The community, as Friend-Pereira sees, once had a full-fledged matrilineal base but now "they are in a stage of transition from matriarchal form of life" (Friend-Pereira, 1912 : 142). This tribe which was once matrilineal, has imbibed patrilineal features, and is now in the process of patriarchalization.

The present day Rabha culture, especially that of the Village Rabhas, may be said to be in a transitional stage from matriliny to patriliny. Many traits which are matrilineal among the Forest Rabhas, are patrilineal among the village Rabhas. Again there may be cases among the village Rabhas where the old matriliny still persists. While in one section of the Rabhas (the Forest Rabhas) the traditional matriliny still persists to a great extent, the other section (the Village Rabhas) shows a strong inclination to seek a new path and to form a new masculine society. This change among the Village Rabhas is the result of contact and interactions with the patrilineal Rajbansis who have imbued these Rabhas with the patrilineal Hindu cultural elements. They have thus hammered on the root of their traditional culture and have paved the way for change. The impact of modernization, urbanisation, market and cash economy etc. have only forced the pace of change in the Rabha culture.

Due to the easy communication system the tentacles of the urban civilization have already penetrated in their traditional culture. Many of them are looking for amenities of urban living. The present political situation is also having an impact on them. Some of the enlightened Village Rabhas are taking active part in the modern politics. All these have influenced the process of culture change and have motivated them to secure a new pattern of social system.

Under the influence of the dominant patrilineal culture, some matrilineal tribes have also adopted patrilineal cultural elements in a similar way. Some families among the Garos of Jalpaiguri have already started passing on the land to their sons, against the Garo Laws (Nakane, 1961 : 89-90).

> "Christianity with its patriarchal bias and its emphasis on the family as a sacred unit has influenced the Garo into adopting a more patriarchal system and a patrilineal trait much in evidence among the Garos of Boko" (Mehra, 1954 : 13).

Bose also marks a strong force growing among the Garos of Mymensing (now in Bangladesh) which may hasten the pace of patrilocal residence in the near future. The young Garos are demanding the right of inheritance of property by the Garo males due to the influence of the local Hindus (Bose, J.K., 1947 : 107-1-5). The Koches of the Garo Hills represent 'a stage of transition from the norms of a matrilineally biased society to those of patrilineally biased society' due to the 'gradual adoption of Hindu practices' (Majumdar, 1967 : 68). In the case of the matrilineal Nayars also 'the increase in the establishment of paternal elementary families gradually split *tarward* (matrilineal joint family) into pieces, lessening the function of *tarward* though among the Nayars it may not be a shift 'to a patrilineal system but may be patrinominal system with a kind of bilateral arrangement' (Nakane, 1963 : 24-28). "Neolocal residence in elementary families or small patrilocal grand-families, occasionally with divorced or widowed sister have thus become the dominant forms of domestic grouping" among the present-day matrilineal Tiyyars of North Kerala (Gough, 1962b : 645-646). Even among a non-Indian community like the Minangkabau of Sumatra, 'the social and the political organizations of the people are at present, a bewildering intermixture of pagan matrilineate and Hindu and Mohammadan patrilineate (Loeb, 1934 : 27).

In other non-Indian matrilineal communities, cultural changes in different aspects are also visible. But factors responsible for such changes may be different. The

> 'recent literature has accumulated evidence to show that under economic changes brought about by contact with western industrial nations, matrilineal descent groups (of different countries) gradually disintegrate' (Gough. *op. cit.* 631).

With the development of the cash-crop farming and accumulation of wealth, there is a tendency for matrilineal groups among a section of the Tonga 'to break down into small bodies of uterine siblings and their immediate descendants through females' and those who are deeply embedded in the new economy, 'desire a shift to familial inheritance' (Colson, 1962 : 95). Among the Ndembu, Turner marks the similar tendencies due to the adoption of cash-crop farming and wagework. Under these new economic systems they spend their earnings mainly for the member of their own elementary family thus depriving their own matrilineal kins (Turner, 1957 : 24, 133-136, 218-221) of the right. Among the matrilineal Bemba tribe Richard marks the 'immeasurable' increase of father's power and his rights over his children for the modern economic conditions (1951 : 175). He also notes the breakdown of the matrilineal descent groups and traditional grand-families and the increase of the autonomy of the elementary family (Richard, 1940 : 76-77). A number of changes in the Hopi matrilineal system also have been reported by Eggan. Among them, at present, the features that a man's personally acquired property is divided within his children particularly the sons, the houses are occupied by the elementary families, and owned by the males etc., show their inclination towards patriliny. Their emphasis on the patrilineal inheritance and patrilocal residence is gradually becoming prominent (Eggan, 1950 : 58, 134-138). Such types of changes are found among many other matrilineal societies.

Thus it is seen that

> 'the matrilineal principle was universally regarded as obsolescent. In its place the elementary family was rapidly becoming the effective unit of residence, economic cooperation, legal responsibility, and socialization (Gough, 1962b : 647).

It may be hypothesised that the social organization of the Rabhas shows some peculiarities in terms of two dimensional changes : one is the movement towards Hinduism to secure a higher social status, and the other is the movement from matriliny to patriliny. The former type of change has led to a great extent to the other type of change. And I have tried to deal with these changes.

For the purpose of this research project I visited a number of forest *bastees* in both Buxa and Cooch Behar Forest Divisions resided mostly by the Rabhas as well as a number of villages in the districts of Jalpaiguri and Cooch Behar where the Rabhas live in good number along with various caste groups tribes and others (as there is no village in West Bengal which is wholly peopled by the Rabhas or the Rabhas are numerically dominant group there). In all these settlements I undertook preliminary study among the Rabhas in the beginning of my field work. Finally I selected five settlements—three forest *bastees* and two villages in the district of Jalpaiguri. I selected all these settlements from the district of Jalpaiguri, as this district had the highest concentration of the Rabhas according to 1961 Census, and only in this district both the Forest and the Village Rabhas are found to reside. The three selected forest bastees are Purodha, Nalagarh and Kamala and the two villagcs, Madhya Manasi and Dakshin Manasi. I have used pseudonym for all these settlements for obvious reason. All the five settlements hold the largest number of the Rabhas.

Among the Rabhas the largest social unit is tribe and the smallest one is the *nogou* or household. In between these two social units come the social units which are the wider kin groups. These units are the *husuk* i.e. clan organisation and the *ningosa* and the *juku* i.e. relations developed through marriage, blood or some other ways. But undoubtedly the most active and important social unit is the *nogou* or household. The relationships or the kin affiliations grow from this point, as this social unit is formed due to marriage, and from marriage blood relation originates. That means this social unit gives birth to relationships developed through marriage and blood. Upto this comes the structural aspects of the Rabha society. Then comes the funcitonal aspects. Most of the activities of the Rabhas have their origin at this level. Be it social control or religious practices or many life-cycle ceremonies or even the economic activities, all these move round the household though no doubt all these activities have their linkages with the wider kingroups. While these have direct relations with each and every member of the tribe, clan and other kin groups, the members of the household have more concern with these. Participation of the members of the household is a must, and the outcome of these activities is received by the members of the household. Judging from this angle of the Rabha social system I have arranged the chapters of my book accordingly. The whole of the Rabha life and activities have been spread over in eleven chapters of this book. The first chapter though deals with the Rabhas and their physical and ethnic environment, it also gives a brief idea about the Rabha as a tribe or ethnic group, its origin, affiliation, population growth etc. in brief. The next chapter deals with the wider kin-group i.e. clan or *husuk* organization. In Chapter III, I have discussed about the kinship system and its activities. The household and its activities have been dealt in Chapter

IV. The crises of life have been covered by chapters V, VI and VII. The birth and infancy have been dealt in Chapter V and marriage has taken its position in Chapter VI. Chapter VII highlights the death rituals. One of the most important aspects of human life and thereby of the Rabha life, is their economic activities and livelihood pattern which I have analysed in Chapter \ III. The social control and political activities have been placed in Chapter IX. No doubt religion is very important in the life of the Rabhas and Chapter X takes care of it. The last chapter i.e. Chapter XI has summed up the life and activities of Rabhas through a comparison between the two ecological groups of the Rabhas—the Forest Rabhas and the Village Rabhas showing the mobility of the Rabha towards patriarchalization i.e. patrilineal form of the society while their congeners living in the reserved forests, have retained traditional matriliny to a considerable extent. It is important to mention here that in all chapters from Chapter II to Chapter X comparison has been made between the two ecological divisions of the Rabhas to examine the process of change of their social system from matriliny to patriliny.

The Backdrop : The People and Their Environs

1

THE BACKDROP : THE PEOPLE AND THEIR ENVIRONS

The Place

In the state of West Bengal the Rabhas are mostly found to reside in the districts of Jalpaiguri and Cooch Behar. These two districts have important historical tradition. In the distant past the district of Jalpaiguri was a part of the kingdom of Pragjyotisha or Kamrupa. Raja Jolpeswar constructed a temple at Jalpes and established the Jalpes *lingam*. Both the Pal dynasty and the Khen rajas included this district into their kingdom. The city of Kamtapur at Cooch Behar was established by Niladhwaj—a Khen Raja. It was subsequently included into the Koch kingdom founded by Biswa Singh. Later on the western part of this kingdom was annexed by the Mughals. It formed a part of the frontier faujdari (magisterial jurisdiction) of Fakirkundi or Rangpur after the conquest by the Muhammadans. It came under East India Company with the cessation of the Diwani in 1765. Later on the Bhotias occupied duars or low land passes. "They exercised predominant influence over the whole tract from the frontier of Sikkim as far east as Darrang, and frequently enforced claims of suzerainty over the enfeebled state of Cooch Behar ..." as stated in the Imperial Gazetteer of India (1908 : 32-33). By a treaty of 1773 Cooch Behar was delivered from the Bhotia. The Bhutan war of 1865 resulted in annexation of the whole of Duars from the hand of the Bhotias and came under the authority of the East India Company. While the Eastern Duars was incorporated with the district of Goalpara, Assam, the western Duars was partly included with Darjeeling district and partly with Jalpaiguri district.

The territory of modern Cooch Behar was once part of the ancient kingdom of Kamarupa and had no separate existence of its own as a district and as such the early history of this district is therefore embedded in the wider history of Kamarupa.

At present both Jalpaiguri and Cooch Behar districts come under Jalpaiguri division. The district of Jalpaiguri with its headquarters at Jalpaiguri town, is subdivided into two sub-divisions with eleven police stations. The district of Cooch Behar with head quarters at Cooch Behar town on the other hand, is divided into five subdivisions and eight police stations.

The district of Jalpaiguri which derived its name from *jalpai* an olive tree and *guri*, a place, meaning thereby the 'place of *olive* trees' (Gruning, 1911 : i) is situated in the northern region of the Jalpaiguri Division. It has a rectangular shape lying lengthwise in the east west direction. The district headquarters that is Jalpaiguri town is situated on the bank of the river, Teesta. The district has an area of 2,407 sq. miles (6,234 sq. km) according to the Surveyor General of India. According to 1971 Census there is a total of 1750, 159 souls residing in this district with 927, 707 males and 822, 452 females. There are, 428, 595 sheduled tribe population forming 24.49% of the total population of the district.

The district of Cooch Behar which was a princely state during pre-independence era, is situated on the northern part of Jalpaiguri division with its headquarters at Cooch Behar town, the territory derived its name, Cooch Behar in the 16th century when this territory was occupied by the Koch kings, "The name Cooch Behar is a compound of two words—'Cooch, and 'Behar'. The term Cooch is a corrupted form of Coch or

Koch, being the name of a race of people, inhabiting a large tract of country to the north-east of Bengal and Behar and more properly *vihara* denotes abode or sport" (Mitra, 1953b : v). The district has an area of 1289.0 sq. miles or 3386.4 sq. kms where 1414, 183 persons with 737, 931 males and 676, 252 females live (1971 Census).

Ethnic Composition

The district of Jalpaiguri in West Bengal in its area of 6,245 sq. kilometres, has given shelter to 17,50,159 souls according to 1971 Census (2214, 871 according to 1981 census). This population includes a large number of castes and communities including Scheduled Tribes and Castes and also many religious groups. The earlier census returns indicate the thin population density in the district as most part of the district was under dense forest, full of wild life and tea gardens. But the growth of population in the district took place in successive phases when waves of immigrants came to this region from different parts of the country. As a result, the present day Jalpaiguri district is peopled with different ethnic groups who may be classified into three different categories :

i. *Original Settlers*—they are here either from the beginning or settled here long back, e.g. the Rajbansi, the Rabha, the Garo, the Mech, the Muslim and others.

ii. *Intermediate Immigrants*—they came along with the establishment and development of the tea-industry, e. g. the Oraon, the Munda, the Santal, the Malpaharia and others.

iii. *Later Immigrants*—they came to this tract after independence in 1947 e. g. various Hindu castes like the Brahman, the Kayastha, the Mahishya, the Jugi, the Napit, the Saha, the Kaibarta and others.

As a result of the influx of the refugees from East Bengal (at present Bangladesh) into Jalpaiguri district, different functional castes, such as the Brahman (priests), the Napit (barbers), the Tanti and the Jugi (weavers), the Malo and Jelia Kaibarta (fishermen), the Dhobi (washerman), the Saha (traders and businessmen), the Kumar (potters), the Teli (oilmen) and such others were added. But even about sixty years back Gruning observed the absence of the functional castes. "There are no village servants — barbers, washermen and sweepers..." (Gruning, 1911 : 102). So the incoming of the successive waves of the immigrants, particularly after independence, may be considered as the turning point in the social and cultural life of the people of Jalpaiguri district.

Settlement Pattern

The Rabha settlements in the district of Jalpaiguri can be divided into two types on the basis of the ecology of their habitat. The first one is the forest *bastee* situated within or outside the Reserve Forests. The *bastees* or colonies are owned by the Forest Department of the Government of West Bengal. The houses used for various purposes are built either by the Forest authority or by the inhabitants themselves, though in the latter case the materials are supplied by the Forest authority. Most of the Forest *bastees* inhabited by the Rabhas, are usually uni-ethnic in nature though in some *bastees* some other tribal people or some Nepali caste people are found to reside. But in no Forest *bastee* inhabited by the Rabhas, the Hindu (Bengalee) caste people are found to dwell. In their settlements the Rabhas like to live in one place grouped together. Further, the Reserve Forest protection and preservation laws also bar the entrance of outsiders in these *bastees*.

The other type of Rabha settlement is the village, where these people are found to reside in the neighbourhood of several other ethnic groups, particularly various Bengalee (Hindu) caste people. Before independence the Rabhas used to live in these villages with the numerically and socio-economically dominant Rajbansi caste. But after independence this area, like other parts of West Bengal, received a large number of Hindu refugees from the then East Bengal (now Bangladesh). As a result, the Rabhas got as new neighbours, various caste groups such as the Namasudra, the Jugi, the Saha, the Kaibarta the Bairagi, the Brahman the Kayastha and other. As such their contact, which had hitherto been confined to a few ethnic groups like the Rajbansi, the Mech, the Oraon and others, was considerably widened.

A typical forest *bastee* consists of a number of huts vertically arranged on one or both sides of a central road which sometimes become broad enough within the *bastee* to serve as a common courtyard. A small courtyard is kept in the front and the kitchen garden behind. As the area of homestead is very short, the houses are very close to each other ; these are seen to be huddled together in rows. A number of individually and group owned store houses and cattle-sheds are found here and there, but close to the *bastee*. The bachelors' dormitory (*naksa*) is situated in the middle. The place of worship of the community (*baidam nogou*) is situated in the west of the *bastee* within the forest where a number of miniature temples are constructed for various deities and spirits. The cremation ground (*morgandi*) lies in the north of the *bastee*. One or two wells or tubewells are found which are common to all. A primary school also exists in some *bastees*.

In the village, on the other hand, the Rabha houses are scattered here and there though sometimes these are arranged lineally in a locality or hamlet (*para*). As stated earlier, various caste people, Muslim and also the tribals are found to reside close to them. Their hamlets are connected with the main motorable road by means of a number of lanes and bye-lanes. Buses ply on the main road. The common place of worship is not found everywhere, individual temple is found near the house. Schooling facility is not in every village. The cremation ground is situated on the bank of a river or canal, and not far off from the village. In almost all the villages, a big house of a big landowner (*jotedar*), encircled by some small houses of his relatives and share-croppers (*adhiar* or *halua*), forms a social unit by itself.

> "The Village community can scarcely be said to exist in Jalpaiguri district. The country is divided into small farms, each with its central homestead, the residence of the tenant farmer (*jotedar*), surrounded by the homes of his relations and farm labourers perhaps a few under tenants" (Gruning, 1911 : 102). Half a century ago or even later the *jote* was 'the social unit' in this district 'and not the village'.

Settlement Studies

All the five settlements (three forest *bastees* and two

villages) selected for the study, are situated within Alipurduar sub-division (popularly called the Western Duars) under the district of Jalpaiguri.

Of the three forest *bastees*, Purodha is situated under Paro Beat of the Damanpur Range within Buxa Forest Division. Nalgrah *bastee* is under the Bania Beat and Kamala *bastee* in under Kodal Beat of the Chilapata Range within Cooch Behar Forest Division. Purodha and Kamala *bastees* are under Kalchini Police station while the other is under Alipurduar Police station.

The two villages, Madhya Manasi and Dakshin Manasi are situated under Kumargram Police station and Kumargram Block.

Forest Bastees

Purodha *bastee* is situated about 12 km. south east of the Damanpur railway station and about 18 km. south east of Alipur junction. The nearest metalled road, the Alipurduar-Jalpaiguri road, is about 10 km. with which Purodha is connected by means of a narrow unmetalled forest road. The Lateral Road under the National Highway project, passes very close to the *bastee.*

Nalgarh *bastee* is situated very close to the Chilapata Range office. This *bastee* is about 35 km. west of Alipurduar town and 38 km. north of Cooch Behar town. Though Hasimara is the nearest railway station about 25 km. from this place, due to lack of communication, people go to the railway station at Cooch Behar or Alipurduar town. The nearest bus route is at Sonarpur, about 10 km. south of this *bastee* connected by a metalled road, which links Hasimara at one end and Sonapur on the other. Sonapur has connection with Cooch Behar town and Alipurduar and other parts of the Jalpaiguri district.

Kamala *bastee* is situated on the Sonarpur Hasimara road, about 15 km, north of Nalgarh *bastee.* The nearest railway station and bus route are at Hasimara about 10 km. north-east of this *bastee.* The famous Jaldapara Game Sanctuary is adjacent to this *bastee.*

Villages

The Villages, Madhya and Dakshin Manasi, are situated on

the old Alipurduar-Kumargram road. Practically this road runs through the heart of the former village, and there was a regular bus service on this road. The nearest railway station, Kamakhyaguri, is within a distance of 5 km. The Post Office, Health Centre, Anchal Panchayat Office, Scheduled Castes and Tribes Welfare Centre, Eri-silk Training-cum-Production Centre, other Government Offices, Cinema hall (temporary), High School, market (bi-weekly and daily), all are present at Uttar Manasi village. The Sub-divisional town, Alipurduar and the Thana Head Quarters, Kumargram are situated 30 km. east and 35 km. north respectively of these villages.

Ethnic Composition and Population of the Settlement

As stated earlier, the forest *bastees* are generally uni-ethnic in nature while the villages inhabited by the Rabhas include a number of tribes, castes and other communities. Of the three forest *bastees*, only one (Kamala) is shared by thirteen Oraon households while the other two (Purodha and Nalgarh) house only the Rabhas (in Purodha there is only one temporary household of a Kami (Nepali) blacksmith, working for the Rabhas). But both villages (Madhya and Dakshin Manasi) have given shelter to various ethnic groups including Scheduled Tribes, Scheduled Castes, other castes and Muslims.

From Table 1 it is evident that while the Rabhas living in the Forest *bastees*, form the overwhelming majority, they become minority within a large number of caste groups (Scheduled Castes and other non-Scheduled Castes) in the villages. Here in the villages the numerically most dominant group is the Rajbansi, a Scheduled Caste which occupies 33.02% of the total households and forms 32.93% of the total population of the villages. They are followed by the Namasudras (16.98% and 16.88% respectively) also a Scheduled Caste, Scheduled Tribes, other Scheduled Castes, non-scheduled castes and Muslims do not have much significant strength, each member of all these groups has a frequency of below 6.00%.

From Table 1 it is also evident that the total Rabha population of five settlements studied is 1,815 : it covers 73.60% of the total Rabha population of the State as per 1971 Census

TABLE 1

Community wise distribution of households and population in different settlements

Communities	All Forest Bastees						All Villages		
	Households		Population				Households		
	No.	%	Male	Famale	Total	%	No.	%	Male
1	2	3	4	5	6	7	8	9	10
Rabha	182	92.86	625	592	12.17	94.56	113	17.94	310
Oraon	13	6.63	37	30	67	5.21	24	3.81	75
Kharia	—	—	—	—	—	—	3	0.48	8
Munda	—	—	—	—	—	—	1	0.16	1
Nagesia	—	—	—	—	—	—	1	0.16	2
Total Sch. Tribe	195	99.49	662	622	1,284	99.77	142	22.55	396
Rajbansi	—	—	—	—	—	—	208	33.02	540
Namasudra	—	—	—	—	—	—	107	16.98	296
Malo	—	—	—	—	—	—	31	4.92	76
Muchi	—	—	—	—	—	—	8	1.27	15
Kami (Nepali)	1	0.51	1	2	3	2.03	—	—	—
Total Sch. Castes	1	0.51	1	2	3	0.23	354	56.19	927
Jogi	—	—	—	—	—	—	29	4.63	78

Haluadas	—	—	—	—	—	—	33	5.23	78
Sutradhar	—	—	—	—	—	—	7	1.11	13
Barujibi (Barui)	—	—	—	—	—	—	9	1.43	28
Bairagi	—	—	—	—	—	—	6	0.95	9
Kumar	—	—	—	—	—	—	2	0.32	5
Kayastha	—	—	—	—	—	—	11	1.74	29
Mahishya	—	—	—	—	—	—	2	0.30	3
Saha	—	—	—	—	—	—	1	0.16	1
Napit	—	—	—	—	—	—	2	0.32	8
Brahmin	—	—	—	—	—	—	1	0.16	2
Muslim	—	—	—	—	—	—	31	4.92	92
Total Other Communities	—	—	—	—	—	—	134	21.26	355
All Communities	196	100.00	663	624	1,287	100.00	630	100.00	1,678

	Population			All Settlements					
				Households		Population			
	Female	Total	%	No.	%	Male	Female	Total	%
	11	12	13	14	15	16	17	18	19
Rabha	288	598	18.39	295	35.72	935	880	1,815	39.99
Oraon	78	153	4.70	37	4.48	112	108	220	4.85
Kharoa	7	15	0.46	3	0.36	8	7	15	0.33
Munda	1	2	0.06	1	0.12	1	1	2	0.04
Nagesia	—	2	0.06	1	0.12	2	—	2	0.04
Total Sch. Tribe	374	770	23.67	337	40.80	1, 058	996	2,054	45.25
Rajbansi	531	1,071	32.93	208	25.18	540	531	1,071	23.60
Namasudra	253	549	16.88	107	12.96	296	253	549	12.10
Malo	69	145	4.46	31	3.75	76	69	145	3.19
Muchi	13	28	0.86	8	0.97	15	13	28	0.62
Kami (Nepali)	—	—	—	1	0.12	1	2	3	0.07
Total Sch. Castes	866	1,793	55.13	355	42.98	928	868	1,796	39.58
Jogi	81	168	5.17	29	3.51	87	81	168	3.70
Haluadas	72	150	4.62	33	4.00	78	72	150	3.30
Sutradhar	18	31	0.96	7	0.85	13	18	31	0.68
Barujsbi (Barui)	28	56	1,72	9	1.09	28	28	56	1,23
Bairagi	9	18	0.55	6	0.73	9	9	18	0.40
Kumar	7	12	0.37	2	0.24		7	12	0.26

Kayastha	37	66	2.03	11	1.33	29	37	66	1.45
Mahishya	1	4	0-12	2	0.24	3	1	4	0.09
Saha	4	5	0.15	1	0.12	1	4	5	0.11
Napit	4	12	0.37	2	0.24	8	4	12	0.26
Brahmin	—	2	0.06	1	0.12	2	—	2	0.04
Muslim	73	165	5.08	31	3.75	92	73	165	3.65
Total Other Communities	344	689	21.20	134	16.22	355	334	689	15.17
All Communities	1,574	3,852	100.00	826	100.00	2,341	2,198	4,539	100.00

(2,466), but only 29.98% of the total Rabha population of West Bengal (6,053) and 43.93% of Jalpaiguri cistrict according to 1961 Census. Out of these, 1,815 souls of the five settlements, 51.52% are males and the rest 48.48% females. This Rabha population forms 39.99% of the total population of those five settlements (4,539). While among the total population of the three Forest *bastees* (1,287), they share 94.56%, they form only 18.39% of the total population of the two villages (3,252). It means that in spite of their overwhelming majority in the forest *bastees*, the Rabhas cover a small part of the population of the village.

The total Rabha population of all the three forest *bastees* is 1,217 of which 51.36% are males and 48.64% females. Again of this total population 42.56% are above 14 years of age, while only 2.55% are above 59 years. On the other hand in all villages studied, the proportion of males and females in the total Rabha population (598), is 51.84% and 48.16% respectively. Of this total Rabha population, 47.83% belong to the age group '14 and below', while only 4.18% in '60 and above.'

As for the duration of settlement of the different communities, of these 21 communities of these two villages, the Rajbansis, the Rabha and thc Muslim are the original settlers though some of the Rajbansis have also come from the then East Pakistan (now Bangladesh) after independence. The remaining communities are immigrants. Of them the Oraon, the Munda, the Nagesia, the Brahmin (Assamese) settled in these villages long before independence (Intermediate Immigrants) while the rest of the caste groups including the Brahmin (Bengalee) and the Napit (Bangalee) came here mainly from the then East Bengal (now Bangladesh) directly after 1947 or migrated from Assam after 1958 (Later immigrants). But the Forest Rabhas of the three *bastee* are the original inhabitants of the said *bastees* or of the neighbouring areas.

The People

The earliest report on the Rabhas is available from the account by Buchanon-Hamilton as early as 1810, which was later on reproduced by Martin (1838 : 546-549). Since then till early fifties a number of short account has been published, some of them are undoubtedly very much scrapy in nature. But the anthropological research work actually started from the middle of fifties of this century when some anthropologists forced their attention towards this ethnic group and brought them to limelight. As a result of the studies undertaken by them a couple of books, one on these people of West Bengal (Das & Raha, 1967 : 1-176) and other on their peers in Assam (Das, 1960 : 1-149). A good number of articles came to the public since that time.

Since 1959 the Rabhas of the State of West Bengal are recognised as the Scheduled Tribe. But prior to 1956 they were considered as the Scheduled Caste or Depressed Caste (Porter, 1933 : 239) or Backward class (D'Malley, 1913 : 183).

Besides their official recognition the Rabhas of the five settlements identify themselves as the Rabhas or Koch Rabhas. When a person asks a Rabha, "*Nug Rabha Na Utung* ?" (Are you a Rabha ?), he spontaneously answers, "*Ang Ban Rabha*." (I am a Rabha). When the Village Rabhas are asked about the racial identity of the Forest Rabhas, they promptly reply that the latter group also belongs to the Rabha or the Koch Rabha group. Similar answer is also received by the Forest Rabhas regarding the Village Rabhas. While saying this they do not hesitate to point out the present day cultural and linguistic differences prevalent among them. About the village Rabhas the Forest Rabhas say that they (the village Rabhas) have become 'Hindus', while the Village Rabhas mark the other group as being somewhat *buno* (backward) practising 'old culture'.

Origin, Migration and Affinity

The details of the origin, migration and affinity of this ethnic group have already been dealt with in an earlier publication (Das & Raha, 1967 : 27-30). As such I shall touch these aspects only very briefly.

Most of the Forest and Village Rabhas of the five settlements are ignorant of the origin of their race. A Rabha legend as told by an aged Rabha woman, runs thus. 'Long after the creation of the earth, God created two human beings, a man and a woman. They lived as brother and sister. When they were grown up, one day they could not help checking their carnal appetite, and as a result of this illegal action, the woman gave birth to several daughters, and from them different sections of the Rabhas originated.' Almost identical story was also written in some early accounts (Friend-Pereira, 1912 : 141-142 ; Playfair, 1908 : 16).

Regarding the origin and migration of the Rangdania section of the Rabhas, Friend-Pereira says,

> "The Rangdania Rabhas have a tradition that in earlier period of their history they dwelt in the Garo hills, and that after many conflicts with the Garo tribes they were finally driven down to the plains which they now occupy. They say the cradle of their race was at Sumsang, which is the Garo name for the modern Someswari river and the valley it waters before its descent into Pargana Shusang in the district of Mymensing." (Friend-Pereira, 1912 : 145)

The legend prevalent among the Garos is that when Husheng was the chief of the powerful Atong clan, he brought the Rabhas into the Someswari valley to till land, because at that time the Garos, being nomad, were not acquainted with more settled method of husbandry. Afterwards when the Brahman minister of the Husheng treacherously slew his master and seized the supreme power, a period of bloodshed and anarchy followed, and the Rabhas were driven out of the valley (*op. cit.*). Rev. Endle states, "Their origin is imperfectly known, but they are said to bc descended from a Hindu father who lost castes by marrying a Kachari woman" (Endle, *op. cit.*). Anderson views that the Rabhas appear to be a Hindu name for the tribe and many of the so-called Rabhas are Kacharis (cf. Grierson, 1903 : 105). Major Playfair believes that most of the tribes belonging to Bodo group such as the Kacharis, the Garos, the Rabhas and the Koches migrated from Tibetan regions. According to him the migration took place from that region to Brahmaputra valley and thence to the hills of Assam in the remote past. He further states that the Rabhas after migrating from Tibetan region occupied the Garo Hills, whereform they came down to the plains (Playfair, *op. cit.*). That their original habitat was the region bordering the northern slopes of the Garo Hills, is also supported by the fact that certain section of the tribe which lives on the border of that district, has no word for the north and south but describe the former by the word *bhota-hi-chu* or Bhutan and the latter by *tura*, the district head quarters of the Garo Hills (Tura) (Playfair, *op. cit*, see also Endle, *ap. cit.* : 83). Studying somatometric and some other genetical characters of the Rabhas and some other tribes of Assam, (Das, 1960) has shown that the Rabhas have more affinities with the Garos than other tribes. Regarding the origin of the Rabhas, he states,

> "Mongolian peoples came in successive waves from the north and north-eastern region. They have partly or wholly absorbed the autochthonous Australoid and later on formed various tribes like the Rabhas, the Garos, etc." (*op. cit* : 117).

The Rabhas of the settlements surveyed, are of the opinion that they are autochthons of this land. They say that the area constituted by the districts of Goalpara of Assam, and Jalpaiguri and Cooch Behar in West Bengal is their cradle land where they are living for generations.

The Rabhas no doubt have, cultural similarities and also ethnic affinity with a number of ethnic groups ; and these similarities have been marked by different persons during different period of time. Buchanon Hamilton (1810) marked similarities in the socio-religious aspects and material culture of the Rabhas with those of the Pani Koch. Dalton on the other hand, treated the Rabhas as a branch of the Kachari race having connection with the Garos (1972 : 87). Hodgson (1880 : 105) and Porter (1933 : 597) found them as belonging to the Great Bodo or Mech family. But Endle (1911 : 83) and Waddel (1900 : 65) had seen their affinity with the Kachari (Datiyal or Border Kachari). Allen's view was that Rabhas were a section of the Bodos and appeared to be an offshoot of the Garo (1903 : 49). Their similarities with the Garos had also been marked by Playfair (1909 : 19-20). He also believed that the Atongs and Rugas (divisions of the Garos) had a common origin with the Rabhas and Koches. Gait in connection with the affinity of this people states,

> "There seems to be a good deal of uncertainty as to what these people really are. In lower Assam it is asserted that they are an off-shoot of the Garos while in Kamrup and Darrang it is thought that they are Kacharis on the road to Hinduism. That they belong to the Great Bodo Family is certain, but it is not equally clear that the Rabhas are more closely ãllied to any one tribe of that group than to another. On the whole, therefore, although some Kacharis and Garos may have become Rabhas just as others have become Koches, it seems probable that the Rabhas in reality are a distinct tribe." (1892 : 232).

Friend Pereira believed that the Atong (a section of the Garos) and the Rangdania Rabhas descended from two sisters, Sae Bonga and Bonga Kata and as such they were related (1912 : 142). Bainos affirmed them to be the Bodo (1912 : 129).

In early days there was some misapprehension about the Rabhas in the mind of the people. Some people misidentified them as the Garos because of their similarity with the Garos (Sunder, 1895 : 72-79 ; Choudhury, 1903 : 600).

The book written by Das and Raha has given in details their affinity with different ethnic groups (1967 : 27-30). But what is most interesting is their relation with the Rajbansis. Domant comments that a Rabha may become a Rajbansi on payment of a small tribute to the priest and promising to conform to the rule of the caste (1880 : 235) Allen also reports, "the rank of the Rajbansi is recruited from the aboriginal tribes such as Mech, Rabha and Kachari..." (1903 : 39). Das and Raha also report the cultural similarities between the Village Rabha and the Rajbansis (1967 : Introduction).

Population

In India the Rabhas are found only in the states of Assam and West Bengal. Out of the total of 1,41,096 Rabhas in India according to 1971 Census, 1,386,30 (98.32%) live in

Assam and the rest 2,466 (1.89%) live in West Bengal. In Assam they are chiefly found in the districts of Goalpara, Kamrup and Darrang, while in West Bengal their main concentration is in the district of Cooch Behar (1,891 or 76.68%). The district of Jalpaiguri which according to 1961 Census held the highest concentration of the Rabhas (68.26%) (Das & Raha, 1967 : 31), has now secured the second position with only 343 (13.9%) Rabhas. It is somewhat surprising to see that the Rabha population has much been reduced from 1961 to 1971. While in West Bengal there were 6,053 Rabhas in 1961, only 2,466 Rabhas are now found to inhabit this state. Further while Jalpaiguri district has 4,132 Rabhas in 1961 there are only 343 Rabhas as reported in 1971 Census. While I enquired about this decrease of the Rabha population from the State as well as from the district of Jalpaiguri, I have been told by the Office of the Director, Census Operation, West Bengal, that in West Bengal 46,829 tribal population have been declared as unclassified. It may be that many Rabhas are included in this category. Further they have also been reported by the Census authority to be present in five more districts, and these are Midnapur (118), 24 Parganas (105), West Dinajpur (6), Calcutta (2) and Bankura (1). The two districts, Midnapur and 24 Parganas also reported 152 and 76 Rabhas in 1961 but the existence of the Rabhas in Midnapur and 24 Parganas districts, is doubtful.

Of the total Rabha population of the district of Jalpaiguri majority (90.29%) live in Alipurduar Sub-division. Again out of the 3,731 Rabhas of this Sub-division, majority (94.53%) are distributed in three police stations, namely, Alipurduar (42.50%) Kalchini (28.19%) and Kumargram (23.75%).

It is interesting to notice the unusually high proportion of females of the Rabha population in Kumargram police station according to 1961 Census there were two males and 884 females in a total Rabha population of 886 which is not practicable.

In Cooch Behar district there were 1,608 Rabha population according to 1961 Census. Of these Rabha population almost all Rabhas (1,600) lived in Tufangunj sub-division which covers Tufanganj Police Station only.

The Census of 1961 made no distinction between the Forest Rabhas and the Village Rabhas ; so no separate figures for the forest and the village dwelling Rabhas are available. But the information supplied by the Divisional Forest Officers, Buxa and Cooch Behar Divisions, show that in 1966 there were 2,982 Rabhas who lived in different forest *bastees* of these two Forest Divisions. Of this population, 1,648 (53.71%) lived in different forest *bastees* of Buxa Division, while 1,334 (46.29%) in Cooch Behar Division. Again this Rabha population of the two Divisions formed 48.04% and 70.62% of the total population of those two forest Divisions respectively (the total population being 3,222 and 1,889 respectively excluding the official staff and their families). In Buxa Division maximum concentration of the Rabha (838 or 54.13%) was found in the Damanpur Range where the Rabha constituted 70.30% of the total population of the Range. Again of the Rabha population of this Range, the Rabhas of Purodha Beat (649 in 1966) constituted 77.45% of the total Rabha population of the Range.

Similarly in Cooch Behar Division highest concentration of the Rabha was at Chilapata Range where there were 908 Rabhas forming 68.07% of the total Rabha population of the Division. Again of the total Rabha population of this Range highest concentration (274 or 30. 18%) was found in Kamala *bastee* under Kodal. Next comes Nalgarh *bastee* (208 or 22.91%) under Bania Beat.

Variation of the Rabha Population

In Table 2 variation of the Rabha population in West Bengal and in Jalpaiguri district from 1911 to 1961 has been shown.

Table 2 clearly depicts that the Rabha population has been increased to a considerable extent from 1911 to 1931 in West Bengal and also in Jalpaiguri district. While in West Bengal as a whole, it suffers from a decrease of population by 1.99% from 1931 to 1941, a considerable number of the Rabha population (878 or 42.29%) has been increased during the lapse of these ten years (1931-1941) in the district of Jalpaiguri. From 1941 to 1951 the reverse picture is seen. During this period the Rabha population in West Bengal has been

TABLE 2

Variation of the Rabha population of West Bengal and Jalpaiguri district, 1911 to 1961

Year	West Bengal			Jalpaiguri district		
	Population	Decade variation	Percentage variation	Population	Decade variation	Percentage variation
1	2	3	4	5	6	7
1911	772	—	—	722	—	—
1931*	3,015	+ 2,293	317.59	2,076	1354	187.53
1941	2,955	— 60	— 1.99	2,954	878	42.29
1951	5,113	+ 2,158	73.03	— 2,869	— 85	— 2.88
1961	6,053	+ 940	18.38	4,132	1263	44.02
1971	2,466	— 3,587	— 59.26	343	— 3,789	— 91.70

*Figures for 1921 are not available.

increased by 73.03%, but in Jalpaiguri district this has been decreased by 2.88%. From 1951 to 1961, increase of the Rabha population is noticed in both West Bengal and Jalpaiguri. But in 1971 there is unusual reduction in the Rabha population in both West Bengal and Jalpaiguri district is seen. It is difficult to explain such an unusual situation if at all that has happened.

Language

The Rabha language, the mother-tongue of the Rabhas, has been classified in the Linguistic Survey of India as belonging to the *bara* or *bodo* group under Assam-Burmese Branch of the Tibeto-Chinese Family of languages. Recently Shafers has included this language under Koch sub-group (1953 : 225-264). Datta's (1969) view is that the Rabha speech should be included in Garo sub-group and especially with Garo of Jalpaiguri.

Though the Census of 1961 returns all the Rabhas of this State as the speakers of the Rabha language but in fact many of the Village Rabhas of the districts of Jalpaiguri and Cooch Behar do not know the Rabha language. The younger generations of the villages have almost forgotten their old mother tongue. At present they speak in local Bengali (Rajbansi) which is mixed with some Rabha words when they speak amongst themselves. The Forest Rabhas of course, have retained the Rabha language as their mother tongue. The males and some females know Bengali.

The change of language of the Rabhas has also been marked by the earlier account writers also. They have found that their language is fast dying out in favour of Bengali or Assamese.

The Husuk Bond : The Wider Kingroups

2

THE HUSUK BOND : THE WIDER KINGROUPS

In West Bengal both the Forest and the Village Rabhas belong to the Koch Rabha group which is a sub-division of the Rabha community (Allen, 1903 : 49-50 ; Endle, 1911 : 83 ; Friend-Pereira, 1912 : 942 ; Das, 1960 : 6). Besides the Koch Rabha with its two ecological sections, the other Rabha sub-divisions, such as Rangdania, Pati, Moitoria, Songa, Bitlia, Dahuria and others of Assam (Martin, 1838 : 546-547 ; Dalton 1872 : 87 ; Doman, 1880 : 232 ; Gait, 1892 : 232 ; Allen 1903 : 49-50 ; Endle, 1911 : 83 ; Friend-Pereira, 1912 : 142 ; Porter, 1933 : 463 ; Das, 1960 : 6) are not present in this district. Of the three different branches of the Rabhas, such as Ringga, Bingga and and Rabha, mentioned by early writers (Buchanon-Hamilton, 1810 ; Martin, 1838 : 546-547), the former two are also not found to exist.

The Husuk System

As already stated the Rabhas are divided into a number of exogamous clans, known as the *husuks*. This social unit exists in both ecological groups of the Rabhas—the Forest Rabhas and the Villages Rabhas and identical *husuks* are present in both. In both cases these are unilateral, exogamous, matrilineal descent groups.

This clan organisation is also present among the Rabhas of Assam. The Rangdania, the Moitoria and the Dahoria sections of the Rabhas of Assam like the Koch Rabhas of West Bengal, have a common set of unilateral Exogamous, matrilineal descent groups, known as the *barai* (Friend-Pereira, 1912 : 142 ; Das, 1955 : 52 ; Majumdar, 1968 : 317). The Pati section living in the eastern region of Assam does not recognise such social division. But its congeners residing in the western part, cover such *barai* organisation (Majumdar, *op. cit*). In this regard, the Rabhas of West Bengal have entirely a different set of matrilineal clans, and excepting a few, most of the clan names are quite different from those of the other sections of the Rabhas inhabiting Assam. Rather, many Rabha clans of West Bengal, according to Majumdar, have similarity in names with those of the Koch of the Garo hills (*op. cit.*).

One striking difference in the clan organisation which exists between the Rabhas of West Bengal and the various other sections of the Rabhas living in Assam like the Rangdania, the Pati (of western region), the Moitoria, the Dahuria and others. is the absence of the *huri* system among the Rabhas of West Bengal. Among the Assam Rabhas two or more *barai* or clans combine together to form a group called the *huri*.

"Clans belonging to the same *huri* are regarded as closely related to each other and, as such, inter-marriage between persons belonging to different clans of the same *huri* are not individually named and their coherence of the clans within the *huri* centres round sharing common magico-religious rites" (*op. cit*).

This *huri* system may be similar to the *neoya husuk* system of the Rabhas of West Bengal. Both the Rabhas and the Garos have exogamous matrilineal clan organisation ; but the Rabha *husuk* differs from the Garo *ma'chang* on some points. Unlike the Rabha *husuks* some Garo *ma'chang* are named after some places such as Banbongre, Adogrc etc. (gre=a village or a hamlet). The Rabha *husuk* is never named after any place. Secondly though some Garo *ma'changs* are named after some animals, plants etc like Do'po (owl), Bolwari (a kind of tree), Gara (a kind of lizard), Chambogong (a kind of wood), Mecheng (an odorous plant), functionally these are not totemic. The members of these clans do not have any emotional or ritual attachments with the respective corresponding animals or plants. They also do not abstain from killing, injuring, hurting, eating or using these animals or plants in any way (Goswami & Majumdar, 1967 : 251). The Rabhas observe clan totem rules quite strictly. Again unlike the *husuks* of the Rabhas of West Bengal, the *ma' chang* of the Garos are grouped in a few broad groups such as the Sangma, the Marak, the Momin, the Sira and the Areng (Das Gupta, 1968 : 133). But in the *husuks* organisation of the Rabhas of West Bengal such grouping do not exist. The only similarity between the Garo and the Rabha clans is the similarity in the name. Both the matrilineal ethnic groups have the following clan names in common : Dalbot or Darboth, Moiji, Nongbok or Lokobok etc.

Identically the War Khasi also have exogamous matrilineal clans like the Rabhas. But like the Garos and unlike the Rabhas of West Bengal their clans are not totemic, though some clans bear the name of some object like Symrem clan, representing a kind of tree or Diengdoh clan which is a wooden log on which meat etc. are chopped. As in the case of the Garos and unlike the Rabhas, the members of these clans do not keep any association with these clan objects and do not refrain from killing, eating or in any way utilising these.

Origin and Development of the Husuk

Very little is known about the origin of different Rabha *husuks*. Only a few, particularly the Forest Rabhas, know these legends. An analysis of these stories shows that in many cases the Rabhas adopted these *husuks* out of repentance for their ill behaviour with objects like animal, plant etc. These objects later on became the totem of their *husuk*. For example, the legends behind the origin and development of Pomrei and Mositak *husuks* can be cited.

The *husuk* Pomrei was originated from killing a *pomrei* or *pani-mach* (tortoise) by a Rabha couple, and the death of the tortoise brought a devastating earthquake in which the crop, domestlc animals etc., of the couple were destroyed. The couple then promised to abstain from catching, killing, and injuring the tortoise. Thus it became as their *husuk*. Mositak *husuk* originated from killing a *mosi* (young deer) by a Rabha woman with a wooden club (*tak*=to thrash). The plaintive cry of the dying deer melted the heart of the woman who made similar promise, and Mositak became their *husuk*.

Neoya Husuk :

Some of the *husuks* are divided into a number of *sub-husuks* known as *neoya husuk* (*neoya*=related). The members of a *husuk* and its sub-*husuks* consider one another as related. For example, I can cite Banda and Moiji *husuks*. The *husuks* Banda has a number of sub-*husuks* such as Bandadhai, Bandasusuk, Bandasang, Bandabantao etc. While the sub-*husuks* of Moiji are Moijidong, Moijipran, Moijisamper, Moijinai, Moijibhog, Moijibhobra etc. The members of Bandadhai *husuk* consider those of Banda, Bandasusuk, Bandasang, Bandabantao etc. as their relatives. In a similar way clansmen of Moiji and its sub-*husuks* claim relation amongst themselves.

Regarding the origin of these *neoya* or sub-*husuks*, it seems to be logical to assume that there were no such sub-*husuks* in the ancient Rabha society, but only the original *husuks*. Later on some original *husuks* suffered from excessive population growth which resulted in the separation (fission) of a fraction of members from the parent *husuk*, and the formation of the sub-*husuk*. The origin of this new type is due to some socio-political or socio-religious reasons. However, we see that the original Banda or Moiji *husuks* is divided into a number of sub or *neoya husuks* which are identified by prefixing or suffixing some word before or after the original *husuk* name. Thus by adding some identifying words like *dhai*, *susuk*, *sang*, *bantao* etc. after the original Banda *husuk* or *dong*, *pran*, *samper*, *nai*, *bhog*, *bhobra* etc. after Moiji *husuk*, the *neoya husuks* of Banda and Moiji are formed.

	Dhai	Bandadhai......*BANDADHAI*
	Susuk	Bandasusuk......*BANDASUSUK*
BANDA	Sang	Bansasang......*BANDASANG*
	Bantao	Bandabantao......*BANDABANTAO*

	Dong	Moijidong......*MOIJIDONG*
	Sampar	Moijisamper......*MOIJISAMPER*
	Nai	Moijinai......*MOIJINAI*
MOIJI	Pran	Moijipran......*MOJIPRAN*
	Bhog	Moijibhog......*MOIJIBHOG*
	Bhobra	Moijibhobra......*MOIJIBHOBRA*
	Nakal	Moijinakal......*MOIJINAKAL*

Similar is the condition with Uni and its sub-*husuk* such as Uni-Brahman, Uni-Chandal, Unichatama, Unichitangbarai etc. Kantran and its sub-*husuk* such as Hedam Kantran and Hasak-Kantran etc.

The socio-political and/or socio-religious factors responsible for segregating these later developed sub-*husuks* from the parent *husuks*, are found to have been rationalised by the members to the respective *husuk* or sub-*husuk*, who gave them shape of legendary stories. Some of these stories run as below :

Unichtangbarai :

This *husuk* was originated from the Uni-*husuk* when some members committed a crime by taking three sacred eggs of a great festival. This created difficulty in worship. The guilty persons confessed their crime, and since then they and their progeny had been placed in a separate *husuk*, Uni-Chitangbarai (*chi*=egg ; *atam*=three).

Bandasusuk :

This *husuk* developed from a greedy Banda couple who stole a jugful of milk of a festival and distributed the milk amongst their kinsmen. This action called the curse of the angry deities. As a result of the curse of the deity, they were taken seriously ill and their progenies became Bandasusuk.

Gobitanji—Nogora :

This *husuk* arose out of a Nogora couple who sacrificed their only son-in-law to appease the supreme deity, (*gobi*= household son-in-law ; *tangi*=to sacrifice).

Moijisamper

The original *husuk* is Moiji. Once a woman while quarrelling with her neighbour, hit the latter with a pestle. The neighbour died For this evil act of her, she was given Moijisamper (*samper*=to thrash with pestle)as her new *husuk* name.

Thus from original *husuks*, new sub-*husuks* (*neoya husuk*) were dcveloped thereby multiplying the number of *husuks* in the Rabha society.

Again it is also seen that under the influence of some Hindu castes new *husuks* had also been developed in the Rabha society. Uni-Brahman and Kaswap are the examples of such new *husuks*. In order to get a higher status in the society (as the Brahman get in the Hindu society), some Uni persons suffixed their *husuk* with the word, Brahman. They claimed higher social status after getting the new *husuks*, Uni-Brahman. Kaswap of course, came from the Rajbansi caste through the marriage with the Rajbansi girl with Kaswap as her *gotra*.

Exogamy is the feature of the *neoya husuks*. They also shun espousing among other *neoya-husuks* of the same original *husuk*. A Hedam-Kantran is forbidden to marry a Kantran or a Hasak-Kantran. Similarly, an Unichitambarai refrains from taking an Uni-Brahman or Uni-Chandal as consort and so on. They look for their mate among other *husuks* which do not fall under any other prohibitory rules.

Saru Husuks

Besides the *neoya husuks*, there is another group of *husuks* among the Rabhas weich they call the *saru husuks* (*saru*=friend). The more Hinduised Village Rabhas call these as the *banhdab husuk/gotra* or *mitar gotra* also (*bandhal*, *nitar*=friend). The members of one of such *husuk* consider others as their friends (*saru* or *bandhab*). They believe that the ancestress of one of such *husuk* established friendship with that of another such *husuk*, and as such, the progenies of one still consider those of other as friends.

The following *husuks* are the *saru-husuks* to one another :

1. Banda : Lombak
2. Pomrei : Lombak
3. Kantran : Lombak
4. Moiji : Lokobak

5.	Kantran	:	Pomrei
6.	Kantran	:	Panchibak
7.	Chinchet	:	Uni-Chandal
8.	Kara	:	Kama
9.	Kara	:	Kencham
10.	Kama	:	Kencham
11.	Kamarasanji	:	Bandasusuk
12.	Kamamochat	:	Bandadhai
13.	Uni-Brahman	:	Bandasusuk
14.	Negenang	:	Sumbri

In each of the above sets, the members of one *husuk* consider those of other as their friends, and as such, the *husuk* of these sets are known to their respective opponents as the *saru husuks* or *bandhab gatro*. For example, Lombak is the *saru-husuk* of Banda, Kantran and Pomrei and vice versa. The members of the Lombak *husuk* believe, on the contrary, that the ancestress of their *husuk* was friend to that of Banda, Kantran and Pomrei *husuk*. But on the other hand, Banda and Kantran, and Banda and Pomrei are not *saru husuks*. Similarly the Kara, Kama and Kenchem *husuks* consider one as the *saru husuk* to other i.e. Kara is *saru* to Kencham and Kama and Kenchan *saru* to both Kama and Kara. Similar is the case with other *saru husuk*.

Marriage between two *saru husuk* also falls under prohibitory degree to i.e, the members of a particular *husuk* do not prefer to marry within *saru husuk*. The reason behind the presence of such prohibitory rule is the prevalence of the friendly bond between these *husuks*. At the time of marriage negotiation in the Rabha society, the negotiator always keeps this in mind along with other marriage rules. Only two cases of marriage within the *saru husuk* could be traced. Of these two cases, one took place at Purodha *bastee* where one Nepti Uni-Brahmin married Rongol Bandasusuk (Uni-Brahman and Bandasusuk) are *saru* to each other. Since this was a love marriage, both of them had to pay fine for violating the rule of *saru* exogamy. The other incidence occurred at Dakshin Manas where marriage took place between Kantran and Pomrei. Here one Bhajahari Kantran married some Jalesari Pomrei. This is also a case of love marriage.

Functions of the Husuk

Like the Garo ma'chong (Goswami & Majumdar, 1967 : 254) the Rabha *husuk* are *par excellence* marriage regulating units. These units prevent the members fram breaking marriage rules prevalent in the society. But like the Garo *chanima* process, (*op. cit.*) the Rabhas do not have any choice for the wife's *husuk* or for any cognate *husuk* at the time of second marriage. Marriage within the *husuk* is considered to be the greatest sin. Similarly, marriage with *neoya* or *saru husuks* is also considered unlawful.

Among the Forest Rabhas the property is held by the *husuk*. Though the individual has actual right on the movable property and assumed right over the immovable property, the right is transmitted to the proper inheritor within the clan in due course. Because of the prevalence of matrilineal descent and inheritance and matrilocal residence the property among the Forest Rabhas always remains within the jurisdiction of one *husuk* and never passes over to another clan, as happens among the Garos (Playfair, 1909 : 71-72 ; Goswami & Majumdar, 1967 : 254). Among the Forest Rabhas the property is customarily owned by the female and inherited by the daughter from the mother. The husband of the heiress only manages and maintains the property. Though the house and the land (in case of the forest labourer) are officially transferred from the deceased father-in-law to the living son-in-law (husband of the heiress who belongs to different husuk), he has still to ask for the consent from his wife and her matri-kins when he wants to repair the old house or build a new one or to lease out a portion of the land to some one for share-cropping etc. So, among the Forest Rabhas property is, in one sense, controlled by the *husuk*.

But among the Village Rabhas, due to the prevalence of matrilineal descent and patrilineal succession and inheritance, the *husuk* has no control over the property. A man gets his mother's *husuk*, but father's property (father has different *husuk* due to rule of exogamy). The property always passes from one *husuk* to another. So, here due to the different pattern of the rules of inheritance and of descent the *husuk* has no control over the property.

Through the marriage, the husuk establishes a bond between the two contracting families and lineages. Though this bond is not so permanent as that of the Garos (*a'kin* bond) among whom the continuity is maintained by the replacement marriage (Playfair, 1909 : 68-69 ; Burling, 1963 : 140-163 ; Goswami & Majumdar, 1967 : 255-256). Nevertheless, in some cases it does not cease to exist even after the death of one of the spouses.

Besides, the *husuk* has some function concerning the magico-religious practices.

Husuk Exogamy and other Prohibitory Rules

The Rabha *husuk* is exogamous. They consider the breach of this rule as very formidable and injurious to the society. If one gets married in one's own clan, the ancestors and the ancestresses will be furious and beshrew which ultimately will spoil the married life with dissatisfaction, disease, unhappiness, still birth and even with death. Moreover, they think that in case of the marriage within the same *husuk*, the couple is not likely to bear any child or if a child is born it will soon be dead. For such an incident the wrath of the ancestors and ancestresses will also fall on the near relatives belonging to the same *husuk*. So marriage with the same *husuk* is prevented with all efforts. Even fornication between the members of the same *husuk* is considered sinful because of the rule of *husuk* exogamy. The prime reason why such rule still exists in the Rabha society is that the members of the same *husuk* recognise one another as brother and sister (Raha, 1970 : 82). As in other tribal societies in the case of the Rabhas too, a person is considered to be related to every one of his or her clan. So, marriage in the same clan is considered incestuous. Marriage is avoided only in the original *husuk* but also within the *neoya husuk*. For example, a Moijidong must not marry a Moijipran. In this case also the same concept of evil operates.

Among the Forest Rabhas, no such incidence of intra-*husuk* marriage has been found. Two cases have been reported from the Village Rabhas-one from Dakshin Manasi and the other from Madhya Manasi. In the former case, marriage took place between two Moijisampers which in other case it was between two Darboths. In the former case the premarital intimacy forced them to marry. In the second case it was the man's employment in the Government service that led him to adopt his father's *husuk*, Pomrei instead of his mother's *husuk*, Darboth. So when he married, he stuck to his father's *husuk* even though it was contrary to the custom.

Like tne Yap as reported by Schneider (1953 : 218) among the Rabhas too, as one gets one's adoptive mother's *husuk*, the adopted child abstains from marrying in adoptive mother's *husuk* as he gets her clan. At the same time, he avoids his real mother's *husuk* also in connection with marriage.

Father's Husuk

The Rabhas generally consider their mother's *husuk* (i.e. their own *husuk*) more important when they go for marriage. They show very little interest in their father's *husuk*. Only recently the Hinduised Rabhas started recognising its importance. There is generally no social bar against marrying in the father's *husuk*. Among the Forest Rabhas marriage in the father's *husuk* is permissible. In fact such marriages are happening in the Forest Rabha society. They do not even mind going in for marriage in the father's *neoya husuk*. Among the Village Rabhas also there is no rule forbidding marriage in one's father's *husu*k. Yet many Village Rabhas, especially the more Hinduised ones, along with observing the prohibition of marrying in the mother's *husuk*, also avoid having spouse in the father's *husuk*.

This tendency of avoiding marriage in the father's *husuk* is of recent development among the Village Rabhas. They have probably followed the practice of the refugee Hindu castes, of not marrying in the father's *gotra*. It is not a Rajbansi influence because the Rajbansis have only one *gotra*, Kaswap. So, the question of avoiding marriage in father's *gotra* does not arise among them. Moreover, this tendency among the Rabhas as also among the Koch of Assam (Majumdar, 1967 : 69) has been noticed during the last twenty years or so. Their earlier generations did not care for the same even 25 years back. They did not think it wrong to marry in their father's *husuk*. So some cases are found in the two villages studied where such marriages had occurred.

From Table 3 it is evident that in both settlements the frequency of the husbands marrying in their father's *husuks* is almost same. In these cases, their father's *husuks* and their fathers-in-law's *husuks* are same. But the picture is different in case of the wives marrying in their fathers *husuks* in those two settlements. While in Purodha 15 wives (10.20%) married in their father's *husuks*, in Madhya Manasi only 2 wives (3.57%) did the same thing. Further, it is also clear that out of a total of 32 cases where marriage has taken place in father's *husuks* in those two settlements, 25 cases (78.13%) are in Purodha Forest *Bastee* and the rest 7 (21.87%) in Madhya Manasi village. In all respects marriage in fathers' *husuks* are more in forest *bastees* than in the villages. The low frequency of such marriages among the Village Rabhas shows that they do not favour such marriage as much as Forest Rabhas do.

Rule of Husuk Descent

The descent of *husuk* is reckoned through female line i.e. the children married or unmarried, receive their mother's *husuk*, and the married children continue to use this even after marriage and so long they remain alive. The same rule was prevalent among the Rabhas of olden days (Sunder, 1895 : 72; Friend-Pereira, 1912 : 142). This rule is similar to what is found among different matrilineal ethnic groups of India. The father's *husuk* is of no importance to the off-springs so far as the descent is concerned. Even if a child is adopted it always gets its adoptive mother's *husuk* and not of its adoptive father's *husuk*. This rule of descent is followed even if the marriage takes place with other communities. When a Rabha marries a non-Rabha or *vice-versa* and the couple lives in the Rabha society, the descent is reckoned through the female line.

Like the Yap among whom the adopted child becomes completely affiliated with *genun* (matrilineal clan) of its adoptive mother (Schneider, 1953 : 218), among the Rabhas also adopted child gets its adoptive mother's *husuk*. If the child is not of Rabha origin, but belongs to some other community, then it follows the Rabha rule of descent. Like the Yap (*op. cit.*)

TABLE 3

Showing the Frequency of Marriages in the Father's Husuk

Name of the Settlement	No. of Surviving Couples	No. of Husbands marrying in their Father's Husuk		No. of Wives marrying in their Father's Husuk		Total Marriage in the Father's Husuk	
		No.	%	No.	%	No.	%
1	2	3(a)	3(b)	4(a)	4(b)	5(a)	4(b)
Purodha	147	12	8.16	13	8.84	25	17.01
Madhya Manasi	56	5	8.93	2	3.57	7	12.50
Total	203	17	8.37	15	7.39	32	15.76

among the Rabhas also, an adopted woman transmits to her children only the affiliation of her adoptive mother's matrilineal clan ; she does not transmit the clan affiliation of her real mother.

Though among the Rabhas in general the descent is reckoned through female line, still some cases are also found where this rule of descent has been violated. The following reasons may explain the acceptance of the Rabha *husuk* by some non-Rabha husbands and rejections by some others.

The non-Rabha husbands before their marriage used to live with their respective father-in-law as share-croppers or were somehow economically dependent on these Rabha people ; later on they are married with the relatives of their masters. Even now the non-Rabha societies (the Mech, the Rajbansi and different other Hindu castes) do not see with favour the marriage with the Rabhas. So they have no alternative but to merge with the Rabha society where these marriages are accepted. And as they start living in the Rabha society, they are to follow the Rabha rule of descent.

As for the rejection, the conditions are quite different. In these cases the husbands who are non-Rabhas, were either economically well off and did not like to be included in the Rabha society or their intention to remain as one in their own society got no objection from their compatriots.

It is evident that the non-Rabhas accept the Rabha social norms only when they are economically depressed and are dependent on their Rabha father-in-law or when they are considered derelicts in their own society.

Both the Forest and Village Rabhas trace their descent through the female line. In no case, it is traced through the male line. The matrilineal descent has a pervasive influence on conduct because it is the basis of the lineage and therefore determines political allegiance, rights of succession and inheritance, the regulation and validation of marriage, and corporate support in such crises as death and economic distress (Fortes, 1949 : 76).

Husuk Population

The Rabha population is not uniformly distributed in

different *husuks*. The population picture from two settlements Purodha and Madhya Manasi shows that there are some *husuks* which bear a good number of population, while some others have a few individuals only. The presence of a good number of *husuks* proves that these are multi-*husuks* in nature. In Table 4 sex-wise distribution of population in different *husuks* in the above two settlements, is given.

Table 4 clearly shows that maximum number of persons of Purodha *bastee* (15.44%) belong to the Chinchet *husuk* while Kantran *husuk* has the highest frequency (12.38%) in Madhya Manasi. In the order of descending frequency in Purodha *brstee* come Karabojidal and Kencham (10.49% each), Uni-Brahman (9.29%), Bandadhri (8,55%), Unichitanbarai (7.94%) and Kantran (7.05%), the other *husuks* cover small number of persons. In Madhya Manasi after Kantran come Chinchet and Darboth having an equal frequency of 11.07% each. Next to these come Lavong (10.10%), Mositak (7.17%) and Banang (6.51%). Other *husuks* are smaller in size and have varied frequencies. The table also reveals that in both settlements there are some clans which have a very small population strength. From genealogies it is revealed that most of these have come to these settlements through married or as an adjunct to a family or by some other means such as service, share-cropping etc. It is also revealed that some *husuks*, such as Bantao, Bandasak, Choudai, Dapar, Lengabarai, Sarjinang etc. which are present in Purodha are absent in Madhya Manasi. On the contrary, Banang, Darboth, Haiphang, Lavong, Moijibhobra, Negenang, Panchibak and some other *husuks* are present at the latter settlement, but absent at the former. It is interesting to note that some Hindu *gotra* and surname such as Kaswap and Saha have crept in Madhya *Manasi* following the marriage with the Hindu people who have such *gotra* and surname. These *gotras* and surnames are conspicuously absent in Purodha *bastee*.

Totemism

Totemism, which is the association of certain groups (usually clans or lineages) which in a tribe with certain classes of animate or inanimate things, several groups being asso-

TABLE 4

Husukwise Distribution of Rabha Population of Purodha Bastee and Madhya Manasi Village

S. No.	Name of the husuks	Frequency of husuk population at Purodha Male	Female	Total	% to the total	Madhya Manasi Male	Female	Total	% to the total
1	2	3	4	5	6	7	8	9	10
1.	Banang	54	23	57	7.55	6	14	20	6.51
2.	Bandadhai	34	23	57	8.55	6	11	17	5.54
3.	Bantao	1	4	5	0.75	—	—	—	—
4.	Soja Bantao	1	3	4	0.60	—	—	—	—
5.	Bandasang	1	—	1	0.15	—	—	—	—
6.	Bandasusuk	5	1	6	0.90	—	—	—	—
7.	Chinchet	47	56	103	15.44	16	18	34	11.07
8.	Choudai	2	—	2	0.30	—	—	—	—
9.	Dalangsa	2	4	6	0.90	—	—	—	—
10.	Darboth	—	—	—	—	17	17	34	11.07
11.	Dapar	2	7	9	1.35	—	—	—	—
12.	Haiphang	—	—	—	—	4	4	8	2.60
13	Hardok	2	—	2	0.30	—	—	—	—
14.	Here	—	—	—	—	1	1	2	0.65
15.	Kamaraba	8	11	19	2.85	—	—	—	—

15.	Kamachikram	2	5	7	1.05	—	—	—	—
17.	Kara	2	3	5	0.75	1	—	1	0.33
18.	Karalombok	3	1	4	0.60	—	—	—	—
19.	Karahatong	—	1	1	0.15	—	—	—	—
20.	Karabojidal	33	37	70	10.49	—	—	—	—
21.	Kas wap (Rajbansi)	—	—	—	—	5	—	5	1.63
22.	Kantran	21	26	47	7.05	24	14	38	12.38
23.	Kencham	31	39	70	10.49	—	—	—	—
24.	Lavong	—	—	—	—	16	15	31	10.10
25.	Lengbari	3	3	6	0.90	—	—	—	—
26.	Lokobak	—	—	—	—	1	—	1	0.33
27.	Lombok	20	17	37	5.55	—	—	—	—
28.	Moijbhobra	—	—	—	—	3	4	7	2.28
29.	Moijipran	15	14	29	4.35	5	11	16	5.21
30.	Moijidong	3	1	4	0.60	12	5	17	5.54
31.	Moijisamper	—	—	—	—	1	1	2	0.65
32.	Moijinakal	1	2	3	0.45	—	—	—	—
33.	Mositak	4	1	5	0:75	13	9	22	7.17
34.	Negenany	—	—	—	—	1	4	5	1.63
35.	Nogman	—	—	—	—	1	—	1	0.33
36.	Nogra	3	—	3	0.45	5	2	7	2.28
37.	Pomrei	15	20	35	5.25	3	7	10	3.26
38.	Pomreimondu	1	—	1	0.15	—	—	—	—

39.	Pauchibak	—	—	—	—	2	—	2	0.65
40.	Serjinang	1	—	1	0.15	—	—	—	—
41.	Kaswap (Saha)	—	—	—	—	1	2	3	0.98
42.	Uni-Brahman	37	25	62	9.29	10	4	14	4.56
43.	Unichitanbarai	28	25	53	7.94	3	2	5	1.63
44.	Uni-Chandal	3	7	10	1.50	1	3	4	1.30
45.	Not identified	—	—	—	—	1	—	1	0.33
		331	336	667	100.00	159	148	307	100.01

ciated with distinct classes (Notes & Queries of Anthropology, 1964 : 192) is featured by a number of *husuks* of the Rabhas living in the forests as well as in the villages. Following Frazer, this totemic system of the Rabhas may be called as exogamous totemism (Frazer, 1910 : IV : 9). Though totemism is found to characterise as much as 35 (43.75%) Rabha clans, there are yet many other clans (56.25%) which do not have any totems. This dual existence of totemic and non-totemic clans among the Rabhas is an interesting feature. How this occurred is a point that needs some discussion. The following possibilities may provide a clue for a clearer understanding :

(1) The totemism is a later development and was borrowed from other eommunities.

(2) A section of the Rabhas changed their totemic character which was once a common feature of all Rabha clans.

(3) From the beginning the Rabha community was maintaining these two systems.

(4) Ferreira suggests (personal communication) that another explanation of two systems co-existing may be found in the combination of two originally different groups fused together which constituted the Rabha society. Of the two fusing groups one is non-totemic and the other totemic.

Postulation—I

In West Bengal the Rabhas live surrounded by the ethnic groups like the Rajbansis, the Meches, the Oraons, the Mundas the Koches and others. The Rajbansis do not have clan organisation and the Meches are non-totemic, but quite different clans. The Oraons and the Mundas have full-fledged tatemic clans. It is open to doubt whether the Rabhas have borrowed the totemic feature from the Oraons, the Mundas and such other tribes, because there are very little cultural interactions between the Rabhas and these groups. It is evident that the Rabhas, especially the Village Rabha section, depend to a great extent, on the Rajbansi group so far as their culture is concerned. They have been depending on the

Rajbansis from a remote past in every sphere of their life. It would be reasonable to suggest that the Rabhas might have borrowed the totemic character from the Rajbansis. But the Rajbansis do not have any totemic clan (Sanyal, 1965 : 89 ; Also personal investigation by the author). Moreover, the Forest Rabhas do not have close connections with the Rajbansis as the Village Rabhas may have.

The other possibility may be that the Rabhas might have adopted the same feature from the Koches who have identical clan organisation (Majumdar, 1967 : 66-67) as that of the Rabhas. But, according to several authorities the Koches were later on converted into the Rajbansis by the process of Hinduization (Martin, 1838 : 538 ; Hodgson, 1849 : 704-706 ; Boverly, 1872 : 130 ; Boileau, 1892 : 20 ; O'Dannel, 1891 : 262 ; Risley, 1891 : 262 ; Risley, 1891 : 491 ; Gait, 1901 : XXXVII ; Grierson, 1903 : 95 ; Porter, 1931 : 473 ; Sanyal, 1965 : 13). Even if the Rabhas have borrowed this system from the Koches or any other 'patriarchal totemic tribes' it must have taken place long, long before the advent of patriarchal Hinduism (and naturally of Westernization) (Ehrenfels, 1941 : 92).

Postulation—II

The second suggestion that a section of the Rabhas who once had totemism in the clan organisation, has relinquished the same, is also not easily acceptable. On enquiry none of these non-totemic clan members could remember the presence of any sort of totemism nor recollect any legend which might signify the existence of totemism with the *husuk* organization. Had there been totemism in the clan organisation of the Rabhas, it would have been reflected in the legends, though the rapid process of Hinduization has somewhat erased the rights and obligations concerning totemism (*op. cit.* 100). And in the Village Rabha society, slackness in observing the restriction and prohibition is also marked among the enlightened and sophisticated Rabha section (Das & Raha, 1967 : 69-70). Even then it is also felt unlikely that living in the same geographic and socio-economic situation, the totemism among section of the Rabhas will degenerate while it is retained in the clan organization of another section.

Postulation—III

The third postulation is also not easily acceptable. According to Niggemeyer, the matriarchal form of totemism (where totem is traced through the female line) in South India as well as in Assam has been developed as a mere product of contract between 'pure mother right and patriarchal totemism as totemism does not occur in the classical mother-right area' (Niggemeyer, 1933 : 585-586 : Ehrenfels, 1941 : 76-77). He further thinks that the matrilineal descent within the totemismic tribes and castes is not original, rather some kind of assimilation of matriarchal elements, and that the patrilineal descent within the totemism in India, is the older and more original form (Niggemeyer, *op. cit.*). Ehrenfel's view is that the totemism and the mother-right in India belong to two different cultural units, and the mother-right in India is older than the totemism, (1941 : 101). In this connection it may be mentioned that among the Rabhas at some remote period of time the matriarchate was in full vigour (Friend-Pereira, 1912 : 142) and the same matrilineal features are still persisting in many aspects of their culture (Raha, 1970). "It is not common for matrilineal tribes to have totems...So far as India is concerned totemism is evidently a patrilineal phenomenon" (Prof. John. V. Ferreira : personal communication). Among the matrilineal Garo (Playfair, 1909 : 65 ; Ferreira, 1965 : 219) and Khasi (Gurdon, 1914 : 66 ; Ferreira, 1965 : 229-230) some clans show totemic trace, and in both of them no respect or reverence is shown to the totemic objects nor do the members abstain from killing, injuring or otherwise hurting them. That means among them too, there are clans which have got no totems.

So, following Niggemeyer, Ehrenfels and Ferreira it may be inferred that totemism is not an original cultural trait among the Rabhas.

Postulation—IV

The last postulation as suggested by Ferreira, is that 'the Rabhas constitute a combination of two originally different groups fused together.' In this connection it may be said that the two ecological group of the Rabhas, the Forest Rabhas and the Village Rabhas, though have great difference, culturally and linguistically, belong to the same ethnic group and have both totemic and non-totemic *husuks*. It is now difficult to trace out the two 'originally different groups' (if any) among the Rabhas. The other group is not surely the Rajbansis or the Meches because the Rajbansis do not have clan system and the Meches have quite different non-totemic clans. The only possibility is the fusion of the Koch community which have identical matrilineal clan organisation (*nikini*). But firm evidence in support of this hypothesis is lacking. Some early authors found sporadic evidence of the Kocharis or the Koch becoming the Rabhas or the Rabhas into Rajbansis. According to some, the Koches, especially the Pani-Koch section, have a considerable resemblance with the Rabhas (Martin, 1838 : 539). But the Pani-Koches are matrilineal tribe. So, it may not be improbable that a patrilineal section of the Koches might have fused with the Rabha community in a remote past.

From the above discussion it can be said that out of the four postulations two (no. II and IV) seem to be probable. Regarding first postulation it may be said that matrilineal tribes like the Khasis and the Garos also have similar dual system and

> "so far as the totemic traces of the matrilineal Khasis and Garo are concerned, these may be attributed to the influence absorbed from the surrounding countryside through contagion" (Ferreira, 1965 : 22).

And the same thing might happen to the Rabhas, if Niggemeyer and Ehrenfel's view that the matriliny and totemism never co-existed in a community in India, is acceptable.

Regarding the fourth postulation there is a possibility that the section of the patrilineal Koches with totemic clan organisation, might have fused with Rabhas society thus introducing totemism in them.

In general the Rabhas show their regards and reverence to the totemic objects by abstaining from eating or otherwise using, domesticating, killing, destroying, maiming, hurting or injuring the totemic object. "But slackness in observing these restrictions and prohibitions may now be present among the enlightened and sophisticated Rabhas" (Das & Raha 1967 : 69-70). Often this section of the Village Rabhas like the Garos (Playfair, 1909 : 65), the Khasis (Gurdon, 1914 : 66) or the Oraons (Das & Raha, 1963 : 92), the Mundas (Raha, 1964b : 363-364) show indifferent attitude towards the totemic objects. Now-a-days they do not think it wrong to break the totemic taboos. A 'modern' Banda person, who was prohibited from using milk and milk product, now milk the cow and sell the milk.

TABLE 5

Distribution of Totemic Husuks as per Totemic Objects

Totemic Objects	*Totemic Husuks* No.	%
A. Single Totem		
1. *Boal* fish	7	20.00
2. *Shol* fish	1	2.86
3. Deer	2	5.71
4. Tortoise	2	5.71
5. Rat	1	2.86
6. *Karna* (Lizard)	1	2.86
7. *Dauk* bird	1	2.86
8. *Kora* bird	1	2.86
9. *Bhati* bird	1	2.86
10. Earthworm	1	2.86
11. *Indi* (insect)	1	2.86
12. Banyan tree	1	2.86
13. *Beth* Creeper	1	2.86
14. Brinjal	3	8.57
15. Ginger	2	5.71
16. *Simla* Aiu (a kind of sweet tuber)	1	2.86
17. Yeast	1	2.86
Total :	28	80.00
B. Double Totem		
18. Peacock and Peahen	2	5.71
19. *Dauk* and *Kora* birds	1	2.86
20. Ginger and *Boal* fish	1	2.86
Total :	4	11.43

C. Multiple totem		
21. Milk and Milk-products	2	5.71
22. Milk, Milk-products and *Indi* (Insect)	1	2.86
Total :	3	8.57
All Total :	35	100.02

The Rabha totemic *husuks* may be grouped into three different categories so far as the number of totemic objects belonging to a particular *husuk* is concerned (Table 5). These three groups are (I) those totemic *husuks* having a single totem, (II) those with double totems and (III) those with multiple totems i.e. more than two totemic objects in each. Of the total totemic *husuks* the first category has the highest frequency (80.02%) followed by second and the third. Some *husuks* have their individual totem for each while others have common totem. For example, while only one *husuk* (Banang) has *karna* (a kind of *lizard*) as its totem object, seven *husuks* (Bandasang, Dalangsa, Kamarsanji, Moijibhobra, Lokobak, Moijidong and Moijipran) have one common totemic object i.e. *Boal* fish. Similarly brinjal and ginger are totemic objects for three and two *husuks* respectively and so on. The presence of double and multiple totem objetcs for a particular *husuk* is also none-the-less interesting. An individual observes totemic restrictions for more than one totemic object.

It is also clear that the Rabhas have chosen mostly, the edible objects as their totems. Of the totemic husuks, 94.28% have such totemic objects which are edible such as fish, reptile, bird, milk and milk-products, fruits, roots apd tubers etc., while the non-edible totemic objects have only a small frequency of 5.71%. Plant and creeper are the only non-edible totemic objects present among the Rabhas.

The Juku and the Ningosa: The Network of Relations

3

THE JUKU AND THE NINGOSA : THE NETWORK OF RELATIONS

The Juku and the Ningosa :

The Rabhas in their multilineage habitat (forest *bastees* or the villages) are connected with one another by blood or by marriage. A lineage in the Rabha society covers more than one household and operates within the legal and social framework of this unit. There is no bar against marriage, and social interaction between the members of the two lineages. Among the Forest Rabhas the lineage members trace their descent from common ancestress through a determinate number of generation. In the Village Rabha society the conception of the lineage membership is not that clear as in the Forest Rabhas. This is because of both matrilineal and patrilineal systems are in existence together. For this reason a Village Rabha despite being a member of the matrilineage, is often found to be closely related with the members of his patrilineage.

The kinship of the *neoya* system among the Rabhas of this district gives rise to two types of kinsman—the *ningosa* and the *juku*. The members of the former group trace their relation through the mother i.e. members of the matrilineage. The members of the *juku* group are related through the father or the members of the patrilineage. Each of the *ningosa* and the *juku* types of kin-groups is 'essentially a unilineally descent group with some corporate functions'. The members of these groups can trace genealogical relationship to each other. The term *ningosa* literally means 'we are same' or "we are one" i. e. those belong to the same lineage group. But the literary meaning of the term *juku* is 'stranger' or 'outsider'. Though there are some common kinship terms which cover relatives from both kin-groups functionally their activities are different. Similarly in different ecological and social situations, the behaviours of the members of different kin-groups are not alike. While the mother and her lineage members in the Forest Rabha society, are considered as the members of a broader family and closely related to one, the father and his lineage members there, are considered as the 'outsiders' to a person. The condition is different in the Village Rabha society. There all the members of one's matrilineage are not considered as close relatives, nor the members of one's patrilineage are treated as distant ones or 'outsiders'. Some of the lineage members from both father's and mother's sides are considered as close relatives, while others become distant ones.

In the life of an unmarried Forest Rabha, male or female, the influence of his *ningosa* is more important. But when a Forest Rabha male gets married and goes to the house of his wife's residence he falls under the hold of his wife's *ningosa* i.e. the maternal relatives of his wife. But in case of a married Forest Rabha woman the condition remains unaltered as she lives under the control of her mother's kin-groups'. In the event of being heiress, her husband's influence and authority get reduced as long as her matrikins and her father remain alive. But as her father dies, her husband becomes the 'owner' of the house and the land, and holds official authority. But in no case the authority of the father's and husband's relatives becomes dominant in a Forest Rabha household.

From his or her childhood, a Forest Rabha finds himself or herself surrounded by both the *jukus* and the *ningosa* due to the preference of the *bastee* endogamy to a great extent. Still he or she realises this influence of his or her matrikins more than that of the patrikins. When his or her natal household is in need or in danger, his or her matrikins come forward first for help. In case of the loan, his or her matri-kins are first of all requested for the same. Similarly he or she moves faster to help his or her matri-kin in danger and need. When a social or religious ceremony takes place in the house of his or her matri-kin, he or she renders the best of his or her co-operation. In the same way he or she also gets the co-operation of the members of his or her matrilineage when any ceremony is celebrated in his or her natal family. When a Forest Rabha male goes to the house of his wife after marriage, he finds himself amidst his wife's parents, unmarried brothers and married or unmarried sisters and sometimes with some maternal relatives. He works for his wife's family and gives his earnings to his parents-in-law for the maintenance of their family. Here whether he becomes, in a later period, the head of his household or not, the members of his own matrilineage, whose influence and authority he has so long felt, has very little influence on him, and instead his wife and her matri-kins have marked authority and influence over the affairs of his family. In connection with his land to be let out for share-cropping to some body or in connection with the selection of partner for his childern he consults more often with his wife's relatives than with his own relatives, and ultimately he is found to respect the view of his wife's relatives.

Another important reason for considering a man and his own relatives as 'outsiders' by his wife's relatives is that in the Rabha society, unlike the Garos (Burling, 1963 a : 140-152, 347-348), it is not binding on the part of both husband's and wife's natal families to supply a mate if either of the couple dies. When a man dies, his parents' family is not bound to supply another man to his widow and vice versa. As a result if either of the partners dies, the relationship or the *neoya* bond between the two families gradually becomes thinner and ultimately ceases to continue. If a man dies his wife and children either live in their own elementary family or go to the house of her mother or sister and settle with them unless she (the widow) remarries. On the other hand, if the wife (non-heiress) dies, the husband usually leaves the wife's house, and either settles after remarriage or starts staying with some of the members of his matrilineage. His children if unmarried, usually stay with their mother's mother's or mother's sister, but in rare cases follow their father. Only in a few cases the man is found to settle with his children of the former wife even after remarriage.

Like the Garos (*op. cit.*: 140), the Forest Rabhas also call the household of the non-heiress sister as an 'off-shoot' of the parental house. Though the establishment of this new household often hampers the smooth running of the economic and social affairs of the parental household, still due to their close connection with the parental household, a somewhat balanced interaction in social, economic and religious spheres continues. Of course, it is also seen that due to the unemployment and want of sufficient land for share-cropping, sometimes a man with his non-heiress wife and children, shifts to some other settlement : that act sometimes weakens the intimate connection with the natal household.

The picture is different among the Village Rabhas. So long as they remain unmarried, they are under the influence of some of their father's as well as mother's relatives i. e. both the *juku* and the *ningosa*. The condition remains unchanged in the life of a Village Rabha male even after his marriage because of the virilocal residence. In case of a married Village Rabha woman the situation is different. After her marriage she usually goes to her husband's house and lives within or around her husband's patri-kins (the *juku*) and sometime matri-kins (the *ningosa*). So, the influence of her hunband's *juku* and *ningosa* is found to exist side by side in her husband's family. The influence of her own *juku* and *ningosa* is very insignificant. In the Village Rabha society a men feels the influence of his *ningosa* and the *juku* from the dawn of his life. Due to the virilocal residence and patrilineal inheritance he gets his *juku* in close quarter. He seeks their advice, help and co-operation in need and similarly offers his strength and cooperation to them. At the same time his mother's relatives, especially the mother's brother play an important role in his life. In every important event of life such as birth, first feeding of rice ceremony, marrriage etc., the presence of mother's brother or mother's father is considered indispensable. This dual authority continues even after marriage. It is important to mention that in the Village Rabha society the influence of the classificatory sisters of the parents is less than that of the brothers of the parents. But in the forest *bastees* the classificatory brothers and sisters of the mother play dominant roles than that played by the classificatory brothers and sisters of the father.

In the Village Rabha society due to the prevalence of somewhat different social pattern, the mode of activities of the *jukus* and the *ningosa* is somewhat different from that of the Forest Rabhas. Here though the descent is matrilineal, but in majority of the cases the inheritance is patrilineal, the residence, virilocal and the household, patri-kin oriented. Here the wife goes to the household of her husband who usually lives with his parents and sometimes with some members of his patrilineage (the *juku*). As a result of all these, a man has to bother more about the members of his own patrilineage (the *juku*) and less about his matri-kins (except the mother's brother and some others) and also matri and patri-kins of wife. They (the *ningosa*) have very little say over the activities of his own family. When a man dies his wife either lives with her children in her deceased husband's house or returns to her own parental house or to her brother's house. But if the wife of a man dies, he lives in his own family with his children. Sometimes he also remarries. If he does not remarry, usually he keeps his children with him or with his father's brother's or mother's brother's or his own brother's house. Here also none of the parties who came under union, takes the initiative of supplying a mate to the living person. So in the Village Rabha society, the *jukus* dominate over the *ningosas*. The relatives of the wife's sides i. e. both the *jukus* and the *ningosas* of the wife have still less influence over his family.

In the villages the Rabha brothers live in an extended household even after marriage so long their father remains alive. After the death of the father, the brothers, who are the owner of the movable and immovable property, usually partition the property and establish separate households. Unlike the Forest Rabhas, they do not move towards their wives' house after marriage but bring the wives to their own house hold. Of course there are cases where a poor Village Rabha male serves his prospective father-in-law in order to marry the latter's daughter and sometimes permanently lives with his father -in-law as *gharjai* (i.e. household son-in-law). In the latter case, he cultivates his father-in-law's land and spends all his earning for his wife's natal house and ultimately looks after his parents-in-law in their old ages, if his wife has no brother. In some cases of eourse, he is found to leave his father-in law and to establish a new household with the help of his wife's father. But in general the Village Rabha males live in or around their paternal house and keep a close connection with their *jukus*.

Kinship Terminologies

Among the two sections of the Rabha (the Forest and the Village Rabha), kinship terminologies are different as apparent from Appendix 4 while the Forest Rabhas use their original kinship terms, the Village Rabhas use both the original and the local Rajbansi terms, but lean more towards the Rajbansi (local Bengali) terms than towards their own. It seems curious that the younger generations have almost forgotten their traditional kinship nomenclature, and they are quite accustomed to use the Rajbansi terms. Except in case of a few, the terms used by the Rajbansis of the area (Sanyal, 1965 : 129-133 ; Mukherjee, 1952 : 47-56) are quite similar to those of the Rajbansi terms used by the Village Rabhas of Madhya and Dakishin Manasi and the neighbouring villages.

In the Rajbansi terms used by the Village Rabhas and also in the original Rabha terms, both classificatory and denotative terms are found. In case of the original Rabha terms, there are some denotative terms which refer to particular relatives such as *aoa* (Fa), *amai* (Mo), *achu* (MoFa), *avebudi* (FaMo), *nousil* (WiYoSi), *bhasur* (HuElBr), *kilang* (DaHu), *namsa*(SoWi) etc. But most of the Rajbansi terms used by the Rabhas are denotative in nature.

Sometimes two and more relatives are known by a singular term. For example, *mama* indicates both MoBr and FaSiHu, *mani* refers to MoBrWi and FaSi. Similarly, the term *etei* is used for both FaElBr and MoFlSiHu, *akay* for FaElBrWi and MoElSi ; *eiti* for FaYoBrWi and MoYoSi, *ada*, for ElBr, MoBrSo, FaElBrSo, FaYoBrSo, FaSiSo and MoSiSo, *aye* for FaBrDa, FaSiDa and MoSiDa, *achusa* for SoSo, and SoDa and so on.

The Rajbansi terms as used by the Village Rabhas include a few classificatory terms also. In this case both FaElBr and MoElSiHu are termed as *jyato* while their respective spouse as *jyatai*. Similarly, ElBrDa, YoBrDa, ElSiDa, YoSiDa, WiBrDa, WiSiDa and HuBrDa have a single term *bhatijhi* and ElBrSo, YoBrSo, ElSiSo, YoSiSo, WiBrSo, WiSiSo and HuBrSo have the only term *bhajya*. In the same way the term *bhagna* refers to ElSiSo, YoSiSo and HuSiSo and the term *bhagini* ElSiDa, YoSiDa and so on. But most of the Rajbansi terms as used by the Village Rabhas are denotative in nature.

There lies wide difference in the kinship nomenclature of the Rabhas of West Bengal and those of the Rabhas (Rangdani) of Assam (Das, 1960 : 128-133). While the Rabhas of the district of Jalpaiguri call only the MoBr and FaSiHu as *mama*, the Rangdani Rabhas of Assam call a number of relatives e.g., FaSiHu, WiBrSo, MoBr, WiFa, YoBrSo (ws), ElBrSo (ws) and HuFa by the same term, *mama*. While the former group of the Rabhas includes only MoBrWi and FaSi within the term *mani*, the latter group includes FaSi, WiBrDa, MoBrWi, YoBrDa (ws) ElBrDa (ws) and HuSiDa. Again while Jalpaiguri Rabhas use two different terms *dadi* and *bongtei* for FaYoBr and MoYoSiHu respectively, the Rangdani Rabhas use only one term *bangbang* for these two relatives. A similar difference is observable in case of the terms for SiSo (ms) and HuSiSo and SiDa (ms) and HuSiDa among these two groups of the Rabha and so on. So, it is clearly indicated that the kinship terminology of the Rabhas of the district of Jalpaiguri differ greatly from those of the Rangdani Rabhas of Assam.

The Rajbansi terms as used by the Village Rabhas have great similarities with those of the Rajbansis of these villages. Those also have great similarities and some differences with those of the Rajbansis as mentioned by Sanyal (1965 : 129-133). The differences lie in case of some terms. While the Village Rabhas and the Rajbansis of Manasi Village call their MoElSi as *jyata* and MoElSiHu as *jyato* Sanyal refers to *boromosi* and *boromousa* for the said relatives respectively among the Rajbansis. Similarly while to a Village Rabha and the Rajbansi of these villages his ElSiHu (ms) is *ano*, to a Rajbansi of Dr. Sanyal he is *bonu* or *bohonai*. Both ElBrSo (ms) and YoBrSo (ms) are termed by the Village Rabhas as *bhajya*, they are *bhatija* to the Rajbansis as mentioned by Sanyal (*op. cit*). Similarly, while a Village Rabha and the Rajbansi of these villages refer to his WiSiSo and WiSiDa as his *bhajya* and *bhatijhi* respectively, a Rajbansi, as stated by Sanyal, mentions them as his *bhagina* and *bhagani* respectively and so on. There is ample evidence to show that kinship nomenclatures as used by the Village Rabhas and the Rajbansis of the villages studied differ from those of the Rajbansis as mentioned by Sanyal to a considerable extent. This may be due to the fact that Sanyal's work is in Rajganj area which is quite near the Jalpaiguri town but far from Manasi area. The difference may be largely regional.

Second and Third Ascending Generations from Ego

In the second ascending generation, FaFa and FaMo are referred to in the original Rabha terms as *aoabuda* or *aoa* and *ayebudi* or *aye* respectively. Here *aoabuda* means 'old father' *aye* and *ayabudi*, 'old mother' (*buda*, *budi*=old). But MoFa is termed as *achu* and MoMo, as *oai* or *ambudi* the last term also means 'old mother'. The siblings of the two grand-fathers and the two grand-mothers are referred to by the respective derivatives. For the difference of jural ritual relationships of the ego with his father's and mother's parents and one of such parents from another, different terms are used for different grand-parents.

In the case of Rajbansi terms as used by the Village Rabhas, four different terms are used for four different grand parents, *burabapu* (FaFa, meaning 'old' father), *aju* (MoFa), *burima* (FaMo, meaning 'old' mother), and *abo* (MoMo). The classificatory siblings of each of the grand-parents are also referred to by the same term as those referred to the grand parents, i.e., *aju* refers to both MoFo and MoFaBr and *abo* both MoMo and MoMoSi and so on.

Another interesting point is that both the Rabha and the Rajbansi terms used by the Village Rabhas for the members of ego's third ascending generation are also the same for the members of the second ascending generation. This means *acho* (*aju*) includes MoFa, MoFaBr and MoFaFa ; *oai* (*abo*) refers to MoMo, MoMoSi and MoMoMo. Similar is the case with other two terms. It means that the Village Rabha do not have kinship term for the members of the kin group beyond second ascending generation.

First Ascending Generation

In the first ascending generation both classificatory and denotative terms are found. Here *bau/bapo* (Fa) is distinguished from *atei/jyato* (FaElBr) or *dadi/kaka* (FaYoBr) and also from *mama* (MoBr). Similarly *amai/io* (Mo) is distinguished from *akay/jyatai* (MoElSi) or *eiti/masi* (MoYoSi) and also from *mani/mami* (MoBrWi). In the same way *mani* (FaSi) can be distinguished from *akay* (FaElBrWi) and *eiti* (FaYoBrWi). Though derivative denotative terms are used to designate FaYoBr (*dadi*) and FaYoSiHu (*bongtei*), but the common classificatory terms, *etei* referring to FaElBr and MoElSiHu and *mama* to FaElSiHu, FaYoSiHu and MoBr are in vogue. Similarly a common classificatory term, *akay* for MoElSi and FaElBrWi, *eiti* for FaYoBrWi and MoYoSi and *moni* for FaSi and MoBrWi is used. But in case of the Rajbansi terms as used by the Village Rabhas, different denotative terms are used to designate each of the above relatives, except in cases of FaElBr and MoElSiHu where a common classificatory term, *jyato* is used. Similar is the case with their respective spouse. Both FaElBrWi and MoElSi have a common term, *jyatai*. Further, the Rabhas distinguish father from son's wife's father and daughter's husband's father by using two different terms, *bau/bapo* and *biyai* respectively the latter term covers both SoWiFa and DaHuFa. In a similar way Mo is distinguished from SoWiMo or DaHuMo.

It is important to mention here that among the Village Rabhas some colloquial Rajbansi terms like *pachhua*, *sangna* and *dhoka* have been introduced. When a widow lives with a man without performing any marriage ceremony, she is called *pachhua* and the man is known as *sangna*. But when marriage is performed, she is termed as *dhoka* wife of the man. The child of the man's previous marriage calls the woman, *dhokama* or *pachhua-ma* while the child of the woman's previous marriage calls him *dhoka bapo* or *sangna-bapo* (Choudhuri, 1903 : 146).

Ego's Generation

Ego's siblings are the most important members of Ego's generation. In both Rabha terms and the Rajbansi terms as used by the Village Rabhas, the brothers and sisters, elder and younger, have distinct denotative terms. Accordingly, *ada/dada* refers to the ElBr and *ajong bhai* to the YoBr. Similarly, the term *aya/baio/didi* indicates ElSi, *anou/bon* is used for YoSi, though there is also a common Rabha term *jenou* for both. The difference is made by suffixing the words, *gada/boro* (senior) or *pumar/choto* (junior). The Village Rabhas following the neighbouring Rajbansis, sometimes call their step-brother as *dhoka* or *pachchua dada/bha* (son of *dhoka-ma* or *pachhua-ma*) or *dhoka* or *sanga dada bhai* (son of *dhoka* or *sangna* father). Similar terms are used for the step sisters also.

A common Rabha term, *jyog* is used to indicate both husband and wife, though sometimes *michlik* is used for the wife. The Rajbansi terms used by the Village Rabhas for the husband and the wife are *swami* (Hu) and *stree/bou* (Wi). Similarly, distinct denotative terms are used for the siblings of the husband and the wife and also their respective spouse.

In case of the Rajbansi terms used by the Village Rabhas a bit different pattern is met with. Here HuSiHu is *dada* or *baio* but WiDlSiHu is *jyetopoth* and WiYoSiHu is *shalpoth*. Again a common term *bain* or *didi* is used to indicate wife of both HuBr and WiBr.

The Rabha terms for the ego's cousin brothers and sisters are the same. While *ada* indicates FaElBrSo, FaYoBrSo, FaElSiSo, FaYoSiSo, MoElSiSo, MoElBrSo and MoYoBrSo all senior to ego, the term *ajong* is used for all the above cousins junior to ego. Similarly, the Rabhas use two terms *aya* and *jenou* to indicate all the cousin sisters, senior and junior to ego respectively only that they use one more term, *anou* to refer to MoSiDa and MoBrDa. It is important to mention here that the Rabha terms for the own brother and cousin brother and own sister and cousin sister are same, and moreover a different term *anou* also refers to YoSi (ms), MoSiDa and MoBrDa.

In case of the Rajbansi terms used by the Village Rabhas, distinct denotative terms are used to designate different cousin brothers and sisters. For example, FaYoBrSo is *khura-beta-bhai*, FaSiSo is *pishi-beta-bhai*, MoYoSiSo is *masi-beta-bhai* and MoBrSo is *mama-beta-bhai*. The only variation lies with MoElSiSo, FaElSiSo and FaElBrSo in whose cases a common classificatory term *jyeti-beta-bhai* is uscd. Similar is the case with the cousin sisters.

By both the Rabha and the Rajbansi terms the mother of both SoWi and DaHu is indicated by a common word, *biyaini*. Similar, *biyai* refers to the father of both SoWi and DaHu by the Rabha as well as Rajbansi terms.

First Descending Generation

The Rabhas refer to their son by *sa* or *miasa* by their own term. Similarly daughter is indicated by *samichik* or *michiksa*. But by Rajabansi terms the Village Rabhas call their son as *beta* and daughter, *beti*.

While WiBrSO and WiBrDa have a common term *bagnaisa* (which also refers to SiDa), WiSiSo and WiSiDa are referred to by three different terms *eteisa* [also includes YoSiSO (ms) and YoBrDa (ms)], *akaisa* [also includes YoBrSo (ws) and YoSiDa (ws)] and *Eitisa*[(also includes ElSiSo (ws) and ElSiDa (ws) considering the senior or junior position of the persons concerned to ego. Similarly children of HuBr are known as *eteisa* (includes persons stated above), *bangteisa* [also includes children of BlBr (ms)] and HuSiSo as *bagnai* (also includes SiSo (ms) and HuSiDa], *bargnaisa* [also includes SiDa (ms)].

The *bhajya*, which is a Rajbansi term used by the Village Rabhas, includes WiBrSo, WiSiSo and HuBrSo. Similarly, the term *bhatijhi* covers WiBrDa, WiSiDa and HuBrDa. But for HuSiSo and HuSiSo two different terms *bhagna* and *bhagni* respectively are used.

There are two more persons who belong to this generation, and they are SoWi and DaHu. The term for the former is *namsa/bouma*. For the latter it is *kilang/jamai*.

Second Descending Generation

This generation includes children of ego's son and daughter and also of ego's sibling's son and daughter. There are only two terms which include all these persons. The term *achusa/nati* includes all male children of ego's children and ego's sibling's children. Similarly *aoisa/natni* covers female children of the above relatives.

CRITERIA OF DISTINCTION

Rabha Terms

The criterion of sex differentiation is reflected in the kinship terminology of the Rabhas. Though many of the terms are used for relatives of only one sex, there are some which apply to members of both sexes among the Rajbansi (Mukherjee, 1962 : 52), the Garo (Burling, 1963a : 349 ; 1963b : 73-74 ; Mukherjee, 1956 : 47) and the Pnar (Banerjee, 1963 : 166). Both the Forest and the Village Rabhas denote MoBr and FaSiHu by *mama* but MoBrWi and FaSi by *mani*. That means MoBr and MoBrWi are distinguished by two different terms. Similarly, while Fa is termed with *bau*, Mo by *amai*, FaElBr and MoElSiHu by *etei*, their respective spouse by *akay*. In the younger generation also similar sex differentiation is noticeable in certain cases. While *bagnai* indicates SiSo (ms), *bagnaisa* refers to SiDa (ms) and HuSiDa (ws), and so on.

But certain terms are not governed by the rule of sex differentiation. Terms are the same when the same relatives of both sexes are meant. For example, *eteisa* covers both YoBrSo and YoBrDa and *eitisa*, ElSiSO (ws) and ElSiDa (ws). Similarly *anang* includes both ElSiHu (ms), YoSiHu (ws), ElBrWi (ws) etc.

Rajbansi Terms

The Rajbansi kinship terms as used by the Village Rabhas can be distinguished on the basis of sex. None of the terms has ignored this criterion of sex. While FaElBr is termed as *jyato*, FaElBrWi is mentioned as *jyatai*. While FaSi is called *pishi*, FaSiHu is *pisha*. DaHuFa and SoWiFa are termed as *biyai* but DaHuMo and SoWiMo as *biyaini*. HuBrSo is referred to as bhajya, HuBrDa as *bhatijhi* and so on.

GENERATION

Rabha Terms

The Rabha kinship terms in general follow the rule of generation differentiation. The term *aoabuda* means FaFa and FaFaBr, and the term *achu* refers to MoFa and MoFaBr. In the same way, by the term *ayebudi*, FaMo and FaMoSi and by *ambudi*, MoMo and MoMoSi are indicated.

Similarly, in the ego's first ascending generation, FaElBr and FaElSiHu are termed as *etei* and FaElBrWi and MoElSi, as *akay*. In the same generation *eiti* refers to FaYoBrWi and MoYoSi, *hau*, WiFa and HuFa, *nei* WiMo and HuMo and *mama* MoBr and FaSiHu etc.

In the ego's generation, *ada* indicates ElBr, FaBrSo, FaSiSo MoSiSo and MoBrSo while *jenou* refers to ElSi, YoSi, MoBrDa and HuYoBrWi.

In the first descending generation *jenounisa* is used for YoSiSo (ws), *eteisa* for YoBrSo (ws) and YoBrDa (ms), and *eitisa* for ElSiDa (ws) and ElSiSo (ws).

In the ego's second descending generation too, SoSo and SoDa are referred to as *achusa* and *aoisa* respectively.

But only in case of the remote upper and lower generations this rule is ignored. As such MoMo, MoMoSi and MoMoMo are termed with *oai* or *ambudi*, and FaFa, FaFaBr, FaFaFa with *aoabudi* and so on.

Rajbansi Terms

Like the Rabha terms, the Rajbansi terms as used by the Village Rabhas, are found to follow the above rule. In this case too, members of the different generations are clearly distinguished by their terms. And like the Rabha terms the second and the above generations have identical terms i.e., similar terms are used for FaFa and FaFaFa and so on. In connection with the terms used by the Rajbansi, Mukherjee says that the criterion of generation is ignored in the terms *bapoi* (YoBr, FaSiSo, MoSiSo and So), *mai* (YoSi, FaSiDa, MoSiDa and Da), *jato* (FaFaFa and FaElBr) and *jatai* (FaFaMo and FaElBrWi) (1962 ; 49-52). But Sanyal's (1965) list of Rajbansi kinship terms show no such violation. In the case of Garos deviation of the criterion of generation differentiation is noted in some terms,

> "Remote generations up and down, are assimilated to the second ascending and descending generations respectively. Thus MoMoMo, MoMoMoMo and MoFaFaMo are all called *ambi* just as MoMo and FaMo."
>
> (Burling, 1963a : 349 ; 1963b : 74)

RELATIVE AGE

Rabha Terms

The Rabhas give much value to the criterion of relative age differentiation in the kinship terms. They often distinguish the senior relatives from junior ones by using different terms. Sometimes they use some words to indicate senior or junior, elder or younger relatives. The word, *gada* is used to refer to senior or elder relatives, but *pumar* mentions junior or younger ones. These two words are suffixed after the core relative terms. For example, sister elder to ego is termed as *jenougada*, but younger to ego as *jenoupumar*. WiElSiHu is termed as *sodgada*, WiYoSiHu is *sodpumar* and so on. Sometimes, the word *majer* is used to indicate intermediate one, for example father's intermediate brother is termed as *eteimajer* while father's eldest brother is *eteigada* and the youngest brother is *eteipumar*. This is so termed when the father has at least two more elder brothers and one younger brother. Besides using the words *gada*, *majer* or *pumar* the Rabhas are found to use certain terms which themselves indicate whether these relatives are senior or junior to the ego. While FaElBr is termed as *etei*, FaYoBr is *dadi*. MoElSi and FaElBrWi are *akay* but MoYoSi and FaYoBrWi are *etei* and so on. MoElSiHu is *etei*, but MoYoSiHu is *bongtei*. In the same way

ElBr is *ade* but YoBr is *ajong*, HuElBr is *bhasur* but HuYoBr is *doora* and so on. In all cases the relative age is reckoned with respect to the age of an intermediate sibling pair, and that is why FaElBrSo and ElBr have the same term, when they are elder than the ego.

So, the criterion of relative age of the speaker is followed almost everywhere, except in the grand-parents and grand-children's generations. It is seen that the Rabhas use the same term (*achu*) for MoFa, MoFaElBr and MoFaYoBr. Even in these cases words like *gada*, *pumar* etc., to indicate position (senior or junior) of the person are added. Similar is the case with FaFa and his classificatory brothers, FaMo and her classificatory sisters and MoMo and her classificatory sisters and so on. But in some cases (second and third ascending generations) the criterion does not hold good, such as MoMo and MoMoMo have same term.

Rajbansi Terms

In the Rajbansi terms as used by the Village Rabha relative age differentiation is noticed. While FaElBr and MoElSiHu are termed as *jyato*, FaYoBr and MoYoSiHu and mentioned as kaka and *mousa* respectively. Similarly, FaElBrWi and MoElSi are termed as *jyatai*, FaYoBrWi and MoYoSi are called *kaki* and *masi* respectively and so on. In the same way ElBr is referred to as *dada*, YoBr as *bhai*, WiElSi as *jyethani*, but WiYoS as *shali*, WiElSiHu as *jyatopoth*, but WiYoSiHu as *shalpoth* and so on. But unlike Rabha terms here relative age does not reckon with respect to the ages of an intermediate sibling pair, and that is why FaElBrSo and ElBr or FaYoBrSo and YoBr have distinct term for each.

In the Rajbansi terms as used by the Rabhas, distinction in some cases is not always maintained on the basis of relative age. This is ignored in the grand-parents', children's and grand-children's generations.

But Mukherjee observes that the criterion of relative age of the speaker is obeyed everywhere except in the grandparents', children's and grand-children's generations and in the terms of WiBr, HuSi and SiHu (1962 : 52). In case of the Garo terms also siblings, mother's sisters and father's brothers are distinguished according to their relative age. (Burling, 1963a : 51-55 ; 1963b : 77-78).

COLLATERALITY

Rabha Terms

A distinction may clearly be made between the father and his collateral brothers and between mother and her collateral sisters as among the Garos. (Burling, 1963a : 51-56 ; 1963b : 77-78). While Fa is termed as *bau*, his ElBr is *etei* and his YoBr is *dadi*. Similarly the term for Mo is *amai*, the term for MoElSi is *akay* and MoYoSi is *eiti*.

Rajbansi Terms

Among the Rajbansi terms as used by the Rabhas similar distinction can be made between lineal and collateral relatives. One can clearly distinguish mother from her collateral sisters or father from his collateral brothers. Among these people "Criterion of collaterality is recognised throughout with the sole exception with the terms for siblings which are in usage for all categories" (Mukherjee, *op. cit*). Among the Garos too, a distinction can be made between lineal relatives (parents) and collateral relatives (classificatory brothers of the father and classificatory sisters of the mother) in the first ascending generation. No corresponding distinction is made in other generation. (Burling, 1963a : 51-56 ; 1963b : 77-78).

AFFINITY

Rabha Terms

Between the consanguineal and affinial relations, a dichotomy is noticeable in certain kinship terms of the Rabhas. The term *akay* indicates both FaElBrWi and MoElSi. In the same way for FaYoBrWi and MoYoSi one single term, *eiti*, and for FaElBr and MoElSiHu a term *etei* are used. But deviation is also noticed in this regard. In the case of FaYoBr and MoYoSiHu two different terms *dadi* and *bongtei* respectively are used to distinguish the two. Similarly, this criterion is ignored in the terms for parents and parents-in-law.

Rajbansi Terms :

In the Rajbansi terms as used by the Village Rabhas similar dichotomy is marked in some cases. Here also both FaElBrWi and MoElSi are called by the term *jyatai*. Similarly, the term *jyato* refers to both FaElBr and MoElSiHu.

But in case of FaYoBr and MoYoSiHu two different terms are used to distinguish the two relatives. Same is the case with their respective mates too. Similarly, for the parents and parents-in-law different terms are used.

Among the Rajbansis of Jalpaiguri district the criterion of affinity is only ignored in case of the terms used for the parents and parents-in-law. (Mukherjee, 1962 : 52). Same is the condition with the Garos (Burling, 1963a : 350 ; 1963b : 75).

BIFURCATION

Rabha Terms

Among the Rabhas as among the Garos (Burling, 1963a : 350-351 ; 1963b : 15-16) some kinship terms show the violation of the criterion of bifurcation. While FaFa is termed as *aoakuda*, MoFa is called *achu*. Similarly while FaMo refers to as *ayekudi*, MoMoas *amkudi*. In case of MoBr the terms is *mama*, but for FaBr it is *etei* (FaElBr) or *dadi* (FaYoBr) and so on.

In the ego's second descending generation this criterion is obeyed. Here son of both son and daughter i.e. SoSo and DaSO is called *achusa* and daughter of both son and daughter i.e. SoDa and DaDa is *aoisa*.

Rajbansi Terms

The Rajbansi terms used by the Village Rabhas similarly ignore this rule. Terms for the father's parents are different from those of the mother's parents. In the ego's first descending generation, identical difference is also noticed. But in the case of the second descending generation, like the Rabha terms the terms follow this criterion i.e. same term is used for SoSo and DaSo, as also for SoDa and DaDa.

The terms used by the Rajbansi also mark the violation of

this criterion in the terms of the grand parent's and grand-children's generations (Mukherjee, *op. cit.*). Certain Garo terms also show identical deviation (Burling, 1963a : 351-356 ; 1963b ; 77-78).

POLARITY

Rabha Terms

The Rabha terms recognise the criterion of polarity everywhere. Different terms are applied by two brothers, two sisters and others to denote one another.

Rajbansi Terms

The Rajbansi terms as used by the Village Rabhas, also recognise the criterion in a similar way. Mukherjee also states that the criterion of polarity is recognised throughout the Rajbansi kinship terms. (*op. cit*).

SPEAKER'S SEX

Rabha Terms

In the Rabha terms the speakers' sex is mostly ignored. The same terms *ada* is used by a man and a woman for their respective elder brother. Similarly, same terms are used for YoBr, by both a man and a woman. Same is the case with ElSi and YoSi. But this criterion is recognised in certain terms While a man calls his ElSiHu by the term *anang*, a woman by *kabak*, while ElBrWi is termed *jabak* by a man, it is *anang* to a woman.

In the first descending generation too this criterion is well recognised. While ElBrSo and ElBrDa are termed *bangteisa* by a man, they are *adanisa* and *bateisa* respectively by a woman. Similarly, while a man calls his YoBrSo and YoBrDa by the term *eteisa*, a woman by *monis* and and so on.

Rajbansi Terms

In the Rajbansi terms as used by the Village Rabhas, the speakers' sex is mostly ignored, except in case of the terms for YoSiHu, ElSiSo, ElSiDa, YoSiSo and YoSiDa.

But the terms of the Rajbansis as shown by Mukherjee,

the speaker's sex is recognised only in case of YoBrWi, SiSo and SiDa (*op. cit*). The Garos recognised speaker's sex in terms for BrWi, SiHu and some other terms (Burling, 1963a : 35 ; 1963b : 76).

Decadence

The criterion of decadence is altogether ignored in the Rabha terms and also in the Rajbansi terms used by the Rabhas. Mukherjee also reports that this criterion is absolutely ignored in the Rajbansi kinship terms (*op. cit.*).

INTIMACY OF RELATIONSHIP

Rabha Terms

The Rabhas sometimes used the same term to designate a near and a very distant even non-relatives. The terms, *ada* and *ajong* which refer to one's ElBr and YoBr respectively, are sometimes extended to any older and younger man respectively of ones' own generation, whether or not the kinship connection is traceable, though it is fact that the Rabhas make a behavioural distinction between the near and the distant kinsmen. Further, the Rabhas use two terms to indicate two types of relatives. These are *ningosa* and *juku*. The term, *ningosa* which literally means 'we are same' includes the matri-kins i.e., relatives of the mother's lineage, while the term *juku* which means 'outsiders', includes the members of the patrilineage. Here the meaning of the two words indicates the degree of intimacy, and in the Forest Rabha society the difference of these two types of the relatives is clearly visible.

The *ningosa* relatives (i.e. MoBr, MoSi, Si, MoSiSo, MoSiDa etc) are more intimately accepted that the *jukus* (FaSi, FaBr, FaSiSo, FaSiDa etc). But in the Village Rabha society due to the increased intimacy with the *juku* relatives, the degree of difference has been minimised.

Rajbansi Terms

In the Rajbansi terms used by the Rabhas the terms, *dada* ElBr and *bhai* (YoBr) are often extended to some persons older and younger to ego respectively. Moreover the Village Rabhas use two more terms, *nikat* (near) and *dur* (distant), to indicate close and remote relatives respectively. The Garo also have some terms indicating very close and very remote relatives (Burling, 1963a : 350-351 ; 1963b : 75-76).

HEIRSHIP

Rabha Terms

Like the Garos (Burling, 1963a : 350 ; 1963b : 75) the Forest Rabha couple selects one of their daughters as heiress. She is more likely to be the youngest than the elder one, but parents have the liberty to select any daughter as their heiress. The husband of the heiress becomes the heir. As soon as the daughter and her husband are selected as the heiress and the heir respectively, some special duties and obligations are imposed on them. The heiress and her husband must look after the old parents of the heiress so long as they live, and in return they inherit their (parents of the heiress) property. Though there is no special term for the heiress among the Rabhas like the Garos (*noka*), she is always distinguished from the other daughters. Similarly, like the Garos (*op. cit.*) the son-in-law who is selected as the 'heir', is always distinguished from the other sons-in-law, but not by any specific terms.

Rajbansi Terms

In the Village Rabha society the sons are generally the heirs and inherit parental property. No distinction is made from one son and his wife to another son and his wife.

Inter Personal Kinship Relations

The Rabhas, in general like to live with their own people consisting of their relatives, friends and neighbours. With the relatives, near and distant, *ningos* and *juku*, they always maintain a sweet-bitter relation. These channels of communication illuminate authoritative, solidaristive and co-operative relationships.

Husband-Wife

Among the Forest Rabhas the husband usually moves to the

house of the wife after the first issue and starts living with his wife and wife's mother parmanently if his wife is the heiress of her mother ; in case his wife is non-heiress, he usually forms his own household. In case of duolocal residence as the husband visits his wife in frequent nights only, their conjugal relationship becomes complicated because of the system of duolocal residence which does not permit the husband to have a common household with the wife at last for a period of time. Later on when he establishes uxorilocal residence all the complicacies in their conjugal relationship do not disappear due to the presence of several other relatives of his wife's family. But if they establish a new household (in case of the non-heiress only) they can avoid such complicacy till their nuclear household gets embedded into an extended family unit.

Among the Village Rabhas the wife comes to the household of the husband to establish a virilocal residence and the conjugal relationship remains complicated so long they live in an extended family. But as they form a nuclear unit they avoid such complicacies to a great extent.

Authority

In the Forest Rabha society the wife occasionally makes demands on her husband. In his household though the husband usually holds some authority in day to day affair, but he cannot ignore the views of his wife and her matri-kins in case of the major family issues. The authority of the husband is more prominent in the nuclear household than in the matrilineally extended household where the wife and her matri-kins have the major say.

But in the Village Rabha society the authority of the husband cannot be questioned. In his household the husband exerts undeniable authority, though in many familial affairs he consults with his wife. Here his wife's matri-kins have very little authority.

Economic allocation

In the daily life in both the Forest and the Village Rabha society, each spouse produces for the other. The husband earns wages, cultivates the land and looks after his family. The wife prepares food, sometimes helps him in his field of cultivation, and does various household works. In the Forest Rabha society the major portion of what a man earns, goes to his wife or wife's mother. So the husband has to consult his wife or wife's mother, if he wants to dispose what he produces. And in his family as he is the adult male, he is usually consulted by his wife and his mother.

But in the Village Rabha society though the spouse helps each other in their economic pursuits still the husband being the sole owner of his property, sometimes sells the produce of his land without consulting his wife. But the wife has no right to sell any thing without the consent of her husband.

Solidarity

The marital bond in the Forest Rabha society is very fragile. This frail bond in a fair number of cases, does not last till the end of the life of the couple. Serious conflict and the lack of the unity of views often lead to divorce. Barrenness, quarrelsomeness, debauchery etc., are unquestionably vital factors for divorce. It is seen that both husband and wife have divorced and remarried for several times. But of course, there are cases where husband and wife are leading a peaceful life since their marriage.

In the Village Rabha society frequency of divorce is very low. Once married the couple has to lead the married life till death even if they face difficulty or conflict. Here the divorced person is always looked down upon. This attitude may have developed in the Village Rabha society due to the influence of the local Hindus who do not like divorce and in their societies the divorced persons, particularly the divorced females, have a lower position. So the marital bond is more stable here than that present among their forest dwelling brethren.

Mother-Child

In the Rabha society a child always gets his or her mother's *husuk* and keeps a close relation with his or her matri-kins. He or she always lives with his or her mother, the father of course, may not stay with the child due to varied reasons. In the Forest Rabha society a child always belongs to his or her matrilineage. But in the Village Rabha society he or she lives with his or her patrilineages mostly. In the Rabha society of both eco-zones, the mother has the solemn duty to rear up the child, and the child when grows up, feels duty bound to look after the mother in her old age, particularly when the mother is a widow.

Authority

When the children remain immatured, the mother disciplines them; and they also in their turn, obey mother's authority unhesitantly. In the Forest Rabha society when a daughter gets married and remains with her mother (especially in case of the heiress), she has to accept her mother's authority without opposition. Mother's authority is often extended to her married non-heiress daughters who even live in separate households. It is reduced over the sons as they grow up. It diminishes when they get married and settled in their respective wife's house.

In the Village Rabha society on the other hand, the mother trains her children and exerts authority so long they remain under-aged. The daughters avoid mother's authority greatly as they go to their respective husband's house after marriage. Similarly in their boyhood, the sons carry out their mother's authority. But she abstains from exerting authority over the grown-up sons, who even after marriages, live with her.

Economic allocation

In the Rabha society as soon as a girl becomes somewhat grown-up her mother trains her up in the household duties and other day-to-day household works. In the Forest Rabha household the mother also trains her daughter in the art of spinning and weaving. The daughter in both the Forest and Village Rabha societies also learns the various methods of performing religious duties and various rites and rituals of social ceremonies like marriage, etc. when the mother becomes old, in the Forest Rabha society, she becomes dependent economically over her heiress daughter. But in the Village Rabha society the mother on getting old usually depends on her grown-up son but not on her daughter. In both societies the mother does not train her sons in their economic pursuits when they remain under-aged. She only directs them to do their respective works. The grown-up sons maintain their mother so long they remain unmarried (among the Forest Rabhas) or even after marriage (among the Village Rabhas).

Solidarity

The relationship between the mother and her children seems to be both strong and close; both sons and daughters in their turn show their due respect to their mother. The relation is a mixed form of affection and authority, respect and fear. Of course, a few cases are there in the Forest Rabha *bastees* where the conflict has separated the heiress daughter from her mother. Mother's affection on her children, even grown-up, requires no question. She always remains worried of her children's welfare. Similarly, the children also even when grown-up, keep a tender feelings towards their mothers.

FATHER-CHILD

Authority

A child in an extended household of the Forest Rabha society, feels that his or her father is treated like a *juku* or outsider. Still he or she cannot ignore the authority of the father. But in the nuclear household in both the forest *bastees* and villages father is the virtual head of the household. And a child there learns that his clan belongs to his mother but the family is his father's. Father's authority over his son weakens as the son becomes adult and marries. In case of the Forest Rabha the son goes to the house of his wife where the latter, (in case she is the heiress) and her husband continues to live with her parents i.e. within the control of her father, though her mother's authority over them is more. But in the village Rabha society a son brings his wife and lives with his father, while the daughter goes to the house of her husband severing her father's authority.

Economic allocation

In the Rabha society father's labour is the main source of

income for the immatured children. From his boyhood a son learning the method of cultivation and other occupations from his father, helps him in his farm and also in other occupations.

In the forest Rabha society, as the son lives with his father-in-law after marriage or establishes his own household, he keeps little responsibility for his own father. The economic co-operation between them ceases to continue. But the responsibility of the old father is taken by his heiress daughter. It is the duty and obligation on the part of the heiress daughter to look after her parents in their old ages. In the Village Rabha society the son stays with his father till the latter dies. It is the duty of the son to maintain the father in his old age. Here the daughter has little or no economic obligation on her parents after her marriage.

Solidarity

In the Rabha socity the father keeps a close attachment with his children. The affectionate father in his society, also acts as the trainer and disciplinarian. He continues to play this role so long the children remain young. As they grow old, he acts as an adviser.

SISTER-SISTER

Authority

The authority of the older sister over the younger one is not very prominent Of course, the elder sister sometimes does not miss the chance of exerting her authority and power on her younger sister so longer the later remains young. The authoritative attitude of the elder sister often changes as the younger sister becomes adult.

In the Forest Rabha society the elder sister refrains from exerting authority over the grown-up younger sister, who has been selected heiress of her mother. When the widowed elder sister lives with her younger sister, who is the owner of the natal household, the former accepts her sub-ordination under her younger sister.

In the Village Rabha society the elder sister has always

authority over her younger sister so long they remain unmarried and live together.

Economic allocation

In a Rabha household both the sisters help each other in the household duties or in the field of cultivation.

In the Forest Rabha society when one sister is in need of some economic assistance even after her marriage, other sister sometimes comes forward to help her. Similarly, a sister is often found to maintain the widowed elder or younger sister and her children. But in the Village Rabha society the economic-co-operation between the two sisters is usually restricted up to the pre-marital ages. After marriage the two sisters live usually in two different villages and so rarely they can cooperate with each other.

Solidarity

From their childhood a close intimacy develops between two sisters. The elder sister cares for her younger sister. She plays with her younger sister, scolds her when she becomes impertinent and also makes her happy when she becomes angry. When they enter into their adulthood, they are found to confide their feelings about their blooming youth to each other. The close intimacy persists to a great extent between the two sisters even after marriage in the Forest Rabha society. It is not true that they face no conflict between them. But conflict rarely occurs. A friendly and intimate relation usually exists between the two families. But the same amount of intimacy does not exist among the two married Village Rabha sisters.

BROTHER-BROTHER

Authority

Among the two, the elder brother usually exerts authority over the younger brother and compel him to do many works. He rebukes his younger brother and punishes him even for his minor fault. At the same time he plays with him to make him cheerful. When either or both of them grow old and get married the authority of the older in a natural way diminishes.

In the forest *bastees*, the Rabha brothers leave one another after marriage as each of them goes to their respective parents-in-law's house or establishes separate household with the wife and children. So, then the elder brother gets virtually no change to exert authority over the younger brother. In the villages, the Rabha brothers even after marriage, generally live together so long their father remains alive. So, the elder brother sometimes gets scope to exert authority over the younger brother.

Economic allocation

From their boyhood days, the two brothers are working together in the field or in the forest along with their father in order to help their natal family. Sometimes even after marriage the younger brother lives with his married elder brother and helps him in his economic pursuits.

In the Forest *bastees* the brothers go to their respective parent-in-law's house after marriage. As a result the economic co-operation between them gradually discontinues, provided their wives do not belong to one another's matrilineage. Even after marriage if the two brothers live separately in the same village often one brother is found to help the other in the field of agriculture.

Solidarity

In the Forest Rabha society two brothers, like two sisters sometimes live side by side after marriage. But as they live with the members of their wife's matrilineage, an easy transaction between the households of the two brothers is not possible. This is so done only when their wives are sisters. Their wives and wives' relatives with whom they live, prefer to carry out transaction with the households of the wives' relations. Similarly, a brother has less freedom and authority to help his other brothers.

But in the Village Rabha society due to the prevalence of the virilocal residence, the brothers are often found to live together or partition their paternal property and live side by side after the death of their father. Among the brothers close transaction and co-operation in different spheres, viz. economic, social, religious etc. are often found to exist. Even among their family members (i.e. their wives and children) similar relation is present. So long the families of the two brothers live one beside the other in the same village, they ordinarily, remain closely associated and the members help one another in many occasions. When any social or religious ritual takes place in the house of a brother, the other one helps him, at least manually. Between ths wives, a relation of sister grows. The wife of the elder brother considers the wife of the younger brother like her 'younger sister'. The quarrel of these little ones of the two brothers seldom cause conflict between the two brothers and their two wives. Of course before partition a conflict over the property between the two brothers is not uncommon. But peace and happy relation are usually restored after a peaceful settlement.

From their boyhood days the two brothers keep intimate relation. When one brother is in trouble, the other comes forward to help him. In the Forest Rabha society when two brothers live with the members of their wife's matrilineage, an easy transaction between the households of the two brothers is not possible unless their wives are sisters. Their wives and wives' matri-kins with whom they live, prefer to carry out transactions with the households of the wives' other relations.

But in the village Rabha society due to the prevalence of the virilocal residence so long the families of the two brothers live one beside the other in the same village, they ordinarily remain closely associated and help each other on many occasions.

BROTHER-SISTER

Authority

During their childhood the elder of the two has authority over the younger. When the difference of age between them is not much the younger brother often controls his elder sister.

In the Forest Rabha society this situation does not change much even when they are married. The adult brother becomes the adviser of his adult sister in her familial affairs and acts as the disciplinarian over his sisters' household.

The elder brother among the Village Rabha is always authoritative to the younger sister so long they live together. If not absolutely like the Forest Rabhas, the adult brothers in the Village Rabha society exerts some authority exerts some authority over his sister's household.

Economic allocation

In their cultivable land both brother and sister are found to work together for the maintenance of the natal family so long they remain unmarried. So each has claim on the other. But this economic co-operation ceases after marriage when they get separated from each other and live at a great distance.

In both the Forest and the Village Rabha societies, when an adult unmarried brother lives in his sister's house, he must work for his sister and her family. Similarly when an adult sister lives with her brother and his family (very rare among the Forest Rabhas), she works for them. When the brother lives in the same or adjacent village, he sometimes renders his help to his sister in her economic pursuits.

Solidarity

As stated erstwhile due to the practice of the *bastees* endogamy in a larger number of cases, a fair number of the Forest Rabha brothers and sisters lives in a close distance, if not side by side in the same *bastees.* The Forest Rabha woman like the Garos, desires to live in the same *bastee* where at least one of her brothers or mother's brothers lives. A very tender relation exists between a brother and a sister. A brother has usual fondness over his mother's house where his sister (heiress of the mother) lives. He also has the same feelings over his non-heiress sisters. For his residence in his wife's house, his sisters cannot come to him frequently. But he visits his sister's house at a regular interval. In a few cases his help from the personal income, saves his sister's family from the burden of debt. A sister has in the same way, a deep regard for her brothers. In the Forest Rabha society this attachment is more perfectly perceptible than that in the Village Rabha society where the sister leaves her brother after her marriage and usually goes to her husband's house in a different village due to the prevalence of village exogamy and virilocal residence. The frequency of their mutual visits to each other's house of course, gradually decreases as the time passes.

MOTHER'S BROTHER-SISTER'S CHILD

Authority

In the Rabha society the mother's brother plays an important role in the life of the sister's child. Though a cordial relationship prevails between the two, but sometimes the mother's brother exerts his authority and influence over his sister's children particularly when the sister's husband dies.

In the Forest *bastees*, as the brother and sister live side by side, the mother's brother also controls his sister's children.

In the Village Rabha society the mother's brother and sister's children seek advice from their mother's brother in different circumstances.

Economic allocation

Unless a mother's brother lives in his sister's house or close to her house, or a sister's child lives in its mother's brother's house or close to him, the economic co-operation and transactions do not usually take place between them. Their physical closeness develops economic interactions between them. When the sister's son lives in the house of his mother's brother's he definitely works for him. An adult sister's son helps his mother's brother in his cultivable land and also in different other jobs. A mother's brother similarly helps in the construction of a new house of his sister's daughter and in different other pursuit. Similarly at the time of crises, the sister's children often seek economic assistance or loan from their mother's brother. Bharat Moijidong and his four other brothers of Madhya Manasi got landed property from their mother's brothers.

Solidarity

From the birth till death, in all important crises of life of the sister's child, his or her mother's brother plays a very significant role. Among the Forest Rabhas the mother's brother shares the responsibility in moulding the life of his sister's children. 'He is like his mother's brother', often a proud mother expresses her view regarding her son.

In the Village Rabha society, mother brother's role in his sister's son's life usually starts in the *mukhe-bhat* (First feeding of rice) ceremony. It is the *mama* who usually feeds his sister's child with the first morsel of rice ceremonially for the first time. Even in the marriage of the sister's child, the mother's brother takes a leading role. Without the ring given by him, the marriage of his sister's son is not complete. Similarly, the sister's son observes three days' mourning when his mother's brother dies.

MOTHER'S SISTER-SISTER'S CHILD

Authority

Though the mother's sister is much senior to the sister's child in age and status, but her authority over her sister's child is not much perceptible except occasionally.

Economic allocation

The adult children of the sister sometimes give free labour in different economic pursuits on their mother's sister's request. The sister's adult son places his hand in construction of a new building or any other jobs, without any grudge provided they all live in the same or adjacent settlements.

Solidarity

Between the mother's sister and the sister's child, a cordial relation is common. Children go to their mother's sister's house unhesitatingly and move about freely. The mother's sister in her turn, also, does not mind much provided her sister's children create no much chaos in her house. An adult girl helps her mother's sister in her petty household works on her request.

FATHER'S SISTER-BROTHER'S CHILD

Authority

In the Forest Rabha society the father' sister is less authoritative to her brother's child than the mother's sister to her sister's child. The case almost similar in the present-day Village Rabha society too.

Economic Allocation

If the father's sister and brother's children live in the same house or in the neighbourhood in the Village Rabha society, only then economic transaction between these too relatives occurs. The father's sister is usually not refused by her brother's children when she seeks their help in performing some work for her provided her brother's children are not pre-occupied.

But in the forest *bastees*, such intimacy generally does not exist between the father's sister and brother's children even if they live in a close proximity. So economic transactions and co-operation are comparatively less between them.

Solidarity

In general among both sections of the Rabhas a tender but somewhat formal relation is maintained between these two sets of relatives. The father's sister often shows her warm, and intimate attitute towards her brother's child.

FATHER'S BROTHER-BROTHER'S CHILD

Authority

In the Forest Rabha society the father's brother has very little influence on the life of brother's child as the father's brother and his brother's child usually live in different houses. But in the villages these two relatives usually live in the neighbourhood of each other. So the father's brother sometimes, especially in absence of the father, exerts authority over his brother's child as guardian.

Economic Allocation

In the forest *bastees*, the economic co-operation between these two relatives is very weak for the above reasons. But in the villages, among the Rabhas, a co-operative mood is often met with when these two relatives reside close to each other, The brother's child often helps his father's brother in his agricultural operations on the latter's request. Similarly mutual co-operation from both ends are found in different economic pursuits. The economic interaction becomes maximum when they live in the same extended family.

Solidarity

In the forest *bastees* the Rabha father's brother has somewhat formal but cordial relation toward his brother's son. Probably this is due to the difference in their familial environment. But in the villages there lies an affectionate and intimate relation between them for the virilocal residence.

GRAND-PARENTS—GRAND-CHILDREN

Authority

The relation between the grand-parents (FaFa, MoFa, FaMo and MoMo) and grand children (SoSo, DaSo, SoDa and DaDa) is more of affection and joking than of authoritarian in nature. Sometimes of course, the grand-parents discipline the grand-children.

Among the Forest Rabhas the relation between the maternal-grand-parents (MoFa and MoMo) and the daughter's children is more intimate as they live in the same extended household (in case of the heiress) or usually in the same or close homesteads (in case of non-heiress) for the prevalence of the uxorilocal residence. But in the village due to the virilocal residence, the paternal grand-parents live in the same household or in the same village with the son's children.

Economic allocation

Economic relation between the grand-parents and the grand children is not very strong, though sometimes the mother's father and the grown up daughter's son in the Forest Rabha society and father's father and son's grown-up son in the village work together for earning livelihood. Similarly the mother's mother and the daughter's grown-up daughter in the forest *bastees* and the father's mother and the son's grown-up daughter in the villages are found to be engaged together in the same economic pursuit and also in household work.

Solidarity

In both forest *bastees* and villages the respective grand-parents keep a tender and affectionate relation with their respective grand-children who in their turn pay regards to them. The grand-parents are often to carry the little grand-children on their back or on lap, tell them stories or cut jokes with them. The little ones similarly enjoy the company of their grand-pa.

PARENTS-IN-LAW—SON OR DAUGHTER-IN-LAW

Authority

In the Forest Rabha households the parents-in-law are generally found to live with the son-in-law but in the Village Rabha households the parents-in-law reside with the daughter-in-law. However, in both cases the parents-in-law are instructors and disciplinarians in their households, and the son or daughter-in-law as the case may be, is to obey the authority of the parents-in-law. Even when they are in their separate household, the son or the daughter-in-law usually seeks the opinion and advice of the parents-in-law in may of their household affairs. In the same household the authority of the parents-in-law decreases as they grow old.

Economic Allocation

So long they live together, the economic co-operation exists between them. The son-in-law in the forest *bastee*, renders the same labour as his father-in-law does or even more in his father-in-law's field or sometimes substitutes his father-in-law as forest labour. Even before marriage in both societies when he serves his prospective parents-in-law (in case of the marriage by service), he has to give a free service to all economic pursuits in his would-be parents-in-law's house. Similarly a daughter-in-law also works along with her mother-in-law in the latter's house. Sometimes she has to take the whole burden of her parents-in-law's family, when her mother-in-law gets sick or goes to her relatives or becomes very old.

Solidarity

In the Forest Rabha society, unless his wife is his mother-in-law's heiress, the daughter's husband does not live permanently with his wife's parents. After a couple of years or so such son-in-law usually establishes a separate household. But the heiress daughter along with her husband, lives with her parents. The parents-in-law keep a tender and affectionate relation with their sons-in-law though a partial avoidance between the mother-in-law and son-in-law is noticed. The son-in-law in his turn, pays his regards to his parents-in-law. This soft relation turns into a bitter one, when a conflict arises between them.

The parents-in-law and the daughter-in-law usually do not establish a co-residence unit in the Forest Rabha society ; so their formal but tender relation lasts long. A similar partial avoidance is also noticed between the daughter-in-law and father-in-law.

Among the Village Rabhas the parents-in-law and the son-in-law generally do not live together in the same extended household. Here the son brings the wife, and the residence of parents-in-law and daughter-in-law is thus established. The parents-in-law usually keep a tender and warm relation with both the son-in-law and the daughter-in-law. But sometime severs conflict between the parents-in-law and the son or daughter-in-law as the case may be, in the Rabha society, develops a rift in the extended household resulting in the separation between the parents-in-law and son or daughter-in-law and formation of separate households.

KINSHIP USAGES

Avoidance

In the Rabha society, total avoidance between two or more relatives is not present. But partial avoidance is practised by some relatives in regard to some other relatives. Such partial avoidance is noticeable between a man and his wife's elder sister and also between a woman and her husband's elder brother. The son-in-law and father-in-law also observe such avoidance. Again between the Village Rabha mother-in-law and son-in-law and between the Village Rabha father-in-law and daughter-in-law a partial avoidance prevails. Relatives practising such partial avoidance, do not sit together, sleep together and walk together one beside the other. Among the Village Rabha the avoidance is more regidly followed. A newly wed dauther-in-law among them avoids coming before her father-in-law. If at all she comes to him, she covers her head and face with the hem of her *sari*. Any sort of sex relations are strictly forbidden among these relatives.

NAME-TABOO

The name-taboo is present among the Rabha, but it is more rigidly observed by the Village Rabha than by the Forest Rabha. Relatives practicing the rule of avoidance follow the name taboo. Further, a Village Rabha woman refrains from uttering the name of her husband and husband's elder brother and parents. But in the forest *bastees* an old Rabha woman does not hesitate to utter the name of such relatives except that of her husband's father. But the younger woman is ashamed of telling these names. While the young Village Rabha husband hesitates to tell the name of his wife's mother and his wife's elder sister, the Forest Rabha man feels no shame about it.

JOKING RELATIONSHIP

The joking relationship is present among many but those who practise rule of avoidance. The grand-parents often cut jokes with their grand-children. The joking relationship is also present between a man and his elder brother's wife, a man and his wife's younger sister, between two brothers, two sisters, a brother and a sister and various other relatives. Sometimes especially among the Forest Rabha, a husband and a wife cut light jokes among themselves.

TEKNONYMY

Though a common term, *jyeg* refers to both husband and wife, but among the Village Rabha, husband refers his wife as the mother of so and so' (name of his child) i.e. mother of Ram' (where Ram is his own son), mother of Sita' (Where Sita is his daughter). In the same way his wife refers to him as the 'father of Ram' or 'father of Sita'. Due to the prevalence of name taboo, she cannot call him by his name. Her husband similarly cannot call her by her name. This custom is not present among the Forest Rabhas.

CEREMONIAL FRIENDSHIP

Like the Rajbansis (Rabha, 1967 : 136) the ceremonial friendship (*baya haya*) is present among the Village Rabhas. The Forest Rabhas do not have such ritual relationship.

> "Generally they prefer to make ceremonial friendship with their own community people and also with local Hindu people...the friendship is only possible between the persons of the same sex. No one is allowed to make friendship with the member of the opposite sex. Moreover, though there is no restriction regarding the age, but generally friends are selected from more or less of the same age groups". (Das & Raha, 1967 : 86).

Marri ge or sex relationship between the family members of the two persons having this friendly bond, is generally avoided. The ritual of the ceremonial friendship is performed in the same way as that performed by the Rajbansis (Raha *op. cit.*) by exchanging garland of flowers and betel and areca nut by the persons entering into such bond. The *adhikari* (Rajbansis priest) or the Brahmin (Assamese) usually presides over the function. A ceremonial friend (often called as *mitar*) also performs some rites during the marriage of his friend.

CEREMONIAL PARENTHOOD

> "Among the Rabhas (Village dwelling section) a peculiar custom of artificial or ritual parenthood (*Pani-hhithas ma-ban*) is found. In this case during the marriage of a Rabha, an elderly couple of the village is selected as *pani-chhitao ma-ban*..." (Das & Raha, *op. cit.*).

The ritual parents are selected for performing some rites at the time of marriage of the man who is considered as the 'ceremonial child' of the couple. During marriage the ceremonial parent sprinkles sacred water on the head of their ceremonial son and his wife, and sometimes gives some presentation in kind or in cash.

"This ritual son often works for the ritual parents free of charge and at their death, observe mourning. He also performs *praschitte* (ceremonial Liberation) and also gives *pinda* (obsequial offerings) at the *kam* (obsequial) ceremony of his ceremonial parents. On the other hand the ritual parents sometimes give a little share of their property or some money to the ceremonial son" (*op. cit.* : 87).

The Forest Rabhas on the other hand, have no such custom of ceremonial parenthood. Similar type of parenthood is present among the Rajbansi for the similar purpose (Chowdhuri, 1903 : 145).

The Nogou Organisation : The Structure and Process

4

THE NOGOU ORGANISATION : THE STRUCTURE AND PROCESS

Homestead

The Rabha term of the house is *nogou.* The same term is used by both the Forest and Village Rabhas. But the Village Rabhas, following the Rajbansis (Sanyal, 1965 : 22) call the house as *ghar* also. The above term also means the household or family.[1] The homestead is popularly called by the Rabhas as *dar*. But the Village Rabhas have coined another word (*bastu*) for the same from the local Hindus. The Rabha homestead is a compound usually of the *danga* or high land where they build their house and also out-house used as cattleshed, kitchen, store-room, drawing-room etc. Here they prepare kitchen garden too, and keep a clean portion as the courtyard. The homestead consists of one household, sometimes more than one. The Forest Rabha settlements are usually inhabited by the Rabhas (Table 6). The homestead and household belonging to other ethnic groups, are either absent or only a few in number. But almost reverse is the picture

1. The Rabha household may be defined as a group of persons related by blood, marriage or adoption residing together and dining from a common hearth.

found in the villages. At Madhya Manasi the Rabha occupy. 34 (17.44%) of the total of 197 homesteads and 54(15.88%) out of 340 households. The rest of thc homesteads and households are held by other ethnic groups.

TABLE 6

Frequency of Homestead and Households occupied by the Rabhas

	Homestead			Households in those Homesteads		
	Total	No. Inhabited by the Rabhas	%	Total	No. Inhabited by the Rabhas	%
Purodha Forest Basteee	87	87	100.00	108	107	99.07
Nalagarh Forest Bastee	28	28	100.00	35	35	100.00
Kamala Forest Bastee	33	28	84.85	53	40	75.47
All Forest Bastee	148	143	96.62	196	182	92.86
Madhya Manasi Village	197	34	11.26	340	54	15.88
Dakshin Manasi Village	198	32	16.16	290	59	20.34
All villages	395	66	16.71	630	113	17.94
All settlements	543	209	38.49	826	295	35.71

Similarly, at Dakshin Manasi out of the total of 198 homesteads, only 32 (19.70%) and of the total of 290 households 59 (20.35%) are inhabited by the Rabhas. The remaining homesteads and households are resided by different non-Rabha communities, mostly different Hindu castes.

It is found that one homestead-one household formula is

much more favoured by the Forest Rabhas than that by the Village Rabhas. Another striking point is that the Forest Rabhas in general, do not like to live with other community people in the same homestead. But in some cases the Village Rabhas are found to share the same homestead with the people of the other communities.

CHARACTERISTICS OF THE RABHA HOUSE

The typical—house type of the Forest Rabhas is distinguishable from that of the Village Rabhas of Madhya and Dakshin Manasi. The house type is also unlike that of other communities living in the forest *bastees* and also in the villages, for its peculiar elongated shape. The length is much greater than its breadth with three compartments in it separated by partition walls and used for sleeping, cooking and storing purposes respectively. The other peculiarity is that the store portion is constructed on a raised platform, while the sleeping and cooking compartments are on the ground level. The roof is one continuous structure and not of several parts as are found in the houses of different other communities, or of even Rabhas living in the villages. In Jalpaiguri district, about 90 years ago, Sunder found the Rabhas having similar type of houses (1895 : 74).

On the other hand, the Village Rabhas have no marked feature in their house type that distinguishes it from that of the other communities. Structurally and functionally the Village Rabha houses are quite similar to those of other communities in the village especially to that of the Rajbansis. Even the material used for the house is of the same nature. It is difficult to distinguish a Village Rabha house from a house of other communities living in a village at a glance.

House type

The typical Forest Rabha house type is known as *haprang nogou* which is an elongated thatched type of house with rectangular ground plan. These houses are 25 to 30 feet in breadth with a height of 8 to 10 feet on an average. These houses are situated in east west direction. The walls (*nokten*) are made of reed only without being plastered with mud. The roof a continuous framework and made of *shan* grass (*Kusapoa cynosuroidea*, is semi-circular in shape. The houses are situated by the side of the road of the *bastee* perpendicular with it with the breadth side fencing the road. Each house has three compartments partitioned by wall, each partition wall having a small inner door-way. The main entrance of the house known as *nunugdur*, provides entry to the *nu* i.e. bed room. The bed room, has a separate place adjacent to the wall known as *akhnihaga* for sleeping purpose, the kitchen is known as phonkar, In the southern side there is a door (*phonkar mugdur*) to enter into the Kitchen from the bed room. The rear compartments is the store room (*Chasang*) situated on a platform made of bamboo and wood. It is covered on all its sides having only a small opening for entrance. In the northern side of the platfrom is the place (*ching sang gang*) for the household deities (Rungtuk and Bassk). The back portion of the house is called *gadaon* which is used for drinking *chakat*. In the front of the house (*nu*) sometimes a covered courtyard (*har tar kang*) is found. An open space in the southern side of the bed room is used for the sacrifice of pig. This type of thatched house of the Forest Rabhas is devoid of any window. The type of house present among the village Rabhas of Madhya and Dakshin Manasi is quite different from that found among the Forest Rabhas of Purodha, Nalgarh and Kamala *bastees*. These houses (*nogou* or *ghar*) are rectangular or quadrilateral in shape and mostly two sloped; a few four sloped and one or two eight sloped houses are also found among them. The floor (*mejia* or *majar*) is made of beaten earth and plastered with a paste of cow dung, earth and water. The walls (*noaten or bera*) are made of the framework of bamboo splits, reed and jute sticks plastered with a paste of mud, cowdung and water. The roof (*haprang* or *chal*) is made of *shan* grass thatched on a bamboo frame work. Now-a-days a few well-to-do Rabhas are using tin (C.I. Sheets) or country tiles as roofing material. Many of the houses have high plinths made of earth mainly meant to protect the house from rain and flood water. Sometimes a covered varandah (*panchal* hr *chali*), is often used for sleeping, cooking and other purposes. Each house is generally provided with a door (*nogdur* or *duar*) made of wood or bamboo splits but the window (*kharkii*) is usually absent. No decoration is found on the interior or exterior surface of the walls. No carving is also found on the door or window. In most of the cases the facing of the house is away from the main road in order to get rid of the gaze of the passersby. The average length of a typical house varies from 14 to 16 feet, breadth 8 to 10 feet. and height (walls) 10 to 12 feet. The number of room in a house varies according to the economic conditions of the family and the number of family members. It varies from a single room to many.

"A typical Rabhas house (of these two villages) consists of a bed room (*majia, akhni nogou* or *thakna ghar*), one kitchen (*radam nagou* or *paker ghar*), one cattle shed (*mosugul* or *goali ghar*, one goat shed ((*tamum khopro* or *chagal khopra*), a fowlsty (*tou khapra* or *charai khopra*), place of worship (*baidam nogou* or *thakurghar*) etc." (Das and Raha, 1967 : 47). Usually these rooms are arranged on the courtyard (*hetikong* or *agna*) in one corner of which is situated the *tulsi than* or *tulsi mancha* (after of sacred Basil) (Sanyal, 1965 : 26). But the old Village Rabhas admit that in the past they had the similar type of house as that present among the present day Forest Rabhas.

It is important to mention here that at Madhya and Dakshin Manasi houses of all communities are of the same type. No difference is met with even in the houses of the Bangalee refugees who came and settled here after independence. Sanyal describes almost similar type of house among the Rajbansis (1965: 23-27). Similar rectangular two or four sloped thatched house is also common among the Garos of West Bengal (Raha, 1966 : 27).

Long ago the Scheduled Castes and Scheduled Tribes Welfare Department, Government of West Bengal constructed a number of houses for the village Rabhas. These are single roomed, two sloped, rectangular houses, the roof of tin and the walls with bamboo splits. Two or three windows and a door are present in each house. There is a covered verandah in the front. The facings of these houses are in the opposite direction of the main road. But the village Rabhas have not lived in these houses due to some difficulties. They have not used these houses as these are situated far off from their agricultural land they cultivate. They usually like to live nearer to their cultivable land and also around their land owner.

The Forest Department of the Government of West Bengal has also constructed a number of wooden bungalows type wooden houses for the Rabhas, who work as labourers. Each of these houses stands on 8 to 10 wooden piles which are 6 feet in height. These bungalows are provided with two rooms, one is bit bigger (10 × 10 feet) then the other (8 × 8 feet) and each room has a door and two windows. A wooden stair—case connects the room with the ground. But in general the Rabhas do not prefer to use these houses and instead they like their own thatched house. Except in a few cases, the married couples do not use these as their bed room. Some of these are shared by the unmarried boys, and others are used as store room. They do not prefer the houses because of the cracking sound caused by the wooden floor, when one walks inside the house. They believe that this sound disturbs their household deities. They are also not habituated to live in this type of wooden bungalows.

SIZE OF THE HOUSEHOLD

The size of the Rabha households varies in different forests *bastees* and also villages. From the forest *bastee* to village or from one forest *bastee* or village to another forest *bastee* or village the difference in household size is noticeable.

The average size of the households of these people in different forest *bastees* is much higher (6.69) than that in the village (5.29) as seen in Table 7. Among the Rabhas the size of the household varies widely. The size varies from a very small household of single member to a very large one of eighteen members (Table 8). The households with five members are more frequent than any other (18.30%), followed by those with six members (17.97%).

TABLE 7

Average size of Households of different Rabha Settlements

	Name of the Settlements							
	Purodha Bastee	Kamala Bastee	Nalgarh Bastee	All Forest Bastee	Madhya Manasi	Dakshin Manasi	All Villages	All Settlements
Total Population	667	297	253	1217	307	291	598	1815
Total number of Households	107	40	35	182	54	59	113	295
Average Size of the Household.	6.23	7.43	7.23	6.69	5.69	4.93	5.29	6.15

Of the total of 295 households, 182 or 61.70% live in different forest *bastees* studied. Among these households, the size varies from single member to as many as seventeen members. But the households with five members, as usual, have the highest frequency (18.68%). The size of 107 Rabha households of Purodha varies from a very small of one member to as big as with 12 members. But the households with five members found to be the most frequent (21.50%). The size of the 40 Rabha households of Kamala *bastee* varies from two members to seventeen members, households with one, fourteen and fifteen members are absent. The households with five and eight members are most frequent (12.50% each). In Nalgarh bastee, there are 35 Rabha households and the largest size of the households is of fifteen members. Households with one member, three, seven, ten and thirteen members are absent here. The most frequent households are those with six members (22.86%). The entire Rabha households (113) in the two villages constit ute 38.30% of the total households of the five settments. The size varies from one member, to eleven members with the

TABLE 8

Size of the Rabha Households in Different Settlements

No. of persons in a household	Number of households in each settlements							
	Purodha Bastee		Kamala Bastee		Nalgarh Bastee		All Forest Bastees	
	No.	%	No.	%	No.	%	No.	%
1	1	0.93	—	—	—	—	—	0.55
2	4	3,74	1	2.50	1	2.86	6	3,30
3	6	5.61	4	10.00	—	—	10	5.45
4	12	11.22	4	10.00	4	11.43	20	10.99
5	23	21.50	5	12.50	6	17.14	34	18.68
6	14	13.08	4	10.00	8	22.86	26	14.29
7	15	14.02	3	7.50	—	—	18	9.89
8	16	14.95	5	12.50	6	17.14	27	14.84
9	5	4.67	4	10.00	5	14.28	14	7.69
10	8	7.48	3	7.50	—	—	11	6.04
11	1	0.93	1	2.50	1	2.86	3	1.65
12	2	1.87	1	2 50	2	5.71	5	2.74
13	—	—	3	7.50	—	—	3	1.65

14	—	—	—	—	1	2.86	1	0.55
15	—	—	—	—	1	2.86	1	0.55
16	—	—	1	2.50	—	—	1	0.56
17	—	—	1	2.50	—	—	1	0.55
18	—	—	—	—	—	—	—	—
Total	107	100.00	40	100.00	35	100.00	182	100.00

No. of persons in a household	Number of households in each settlements							
	Madhya Manasi		Dakshin Manasi		All Villages		All Settlements	
	No.	%	No.	%	No.	%	No.	%
1	—	—	2	3.39	2	1.77	3	1.02
2	7	12.96	4	6.78	10	8.85	16	5.42
3	2	3.70	9	15.25	12	10.62	22	7.46
4	7	12.96	12	20.34	19	16.82	39	13.22
5	8	14.82	13	22.03	20	17.70	54	18.30
6	17	31.48	9	15.25	27	23.90	53	17.97
7	6	11.11	4	6.78	10	8.85	28	9.49
8	—	—	2	3.39	3	2.65	30	10.17
9	3	5.56	1	—	3	2.65	17	5.76
10	3	5.56	1	1.70	3	2.65	14	4.75
11	—	—	3	5.09	3	2.65	6	2.03
12	—	—	—	—	—	—	5	1.69
13	—	—	—	—	—	—	3	1,02

14	—	—	—	—	—	—	1	0.34
15	—	—	—	—	—	—	1	0.34
16	—	—	—	—	—	—	1	0.34
17	—	—	—	—	—	—	1	0.34
18	1	1.85	—	—	1	0.89	1	0.34
Total	54	100.00	59	100.00	113	100.00	295	100.00

exception of one household having eighteen members. The households with six members have the highest frequency (23.90%). In Madhya Manasi where the total number of Rabha households is 54, the size of the household varies from two members to ten members, except one household with eighteen member. The maximum number of the Rabha households of this village (33.33%) have six members. The strength of the Dakshin Manasi Rabha households is 59. In this village the households are of different sizes varying from the smallest of one member is the largest of eleven members, the household with nine members being non-existent. The highest frequency (22.03%) goes to households with five members. From the distribution of household size, it is evident that the Rabhas prefer medium to large sized household (4 to 8 members) which constitute the major bulk of their households (at Purodha *bastee* 74.77%, Kamala bastee 52.10%, Nalgarh 68.57%, Madhya Manasi 72.21% and at Dakshin Manasi 67.79%). A comparison between the size of the Rabha households with that of some other ethnic groups of Eastern India, shows (Table 9) that the Rabha households with 4 to 6 members have the highest frequency as indicated by an earlier study by Das and Raha (1967: 77-78) The household with same size has also the highest frequency among the Rangdania and Pati (Des, 1955a : 76 : Das, 1960 ; 122) (Das, 1960 : 122) sections of the Rabhas. Garo (B rling, 1963a : 325-328) and the War Khasi (Das Gupta, 1960 : 167) of Assam and the Rajbansi of Madhay Manasi also show an identical trend. Difference is noticed only in case with the next higher frequency. It is also revealed from Table 9 that the Rabhas in general, have larger sized households as compared to other ethnic groups.

Household Types

The Rabhas in general prefer unclear households. The Village Rabhas are particularly more prone to forming this type of household than the Forest Rabhas. Out of a total of 113 village Rabha households, 67 or 59.33% are of this type, while among the Rabhas of the three forest *bastees* 65 household (35.71%) out of a total of 182 are nuclear. Of the three

TABLE 9

Size of the Households of the Rabha and some other Ethnic Groups

Size of the Hosueholds	RABHAS									
	Present study Forest Rabha		Village Rabha		Rangdani Rabhas of Assam (1958)		Rangdani Rabhas of Assam (1960)		Pati Rabhas of Assam (1960)	
	No.	%	No.	%	No.	%	No.	%	No.	%
1	2	3	4	5	6	7	8	9	10	11
1—3	17	9.34	24	21.24	1	3.57	6	5.45	7	14.00
4—6	80	43.96	66	58.41	17	60.71	66	60.00	23	46.00
7—9	59	32.42	16	14.16	5	17.86	24	21.82	13	26.00
10+	26	14.28	7	6.19	5	17.86	14	12.73	7	14.00
Total	182	100.00	113	100.00	28	100.00	110	100.00	50	100.00

Size of the Houscholds	Rabhas of West Bengal (1967)		Garos of Assam (1963)		War Khasi of Assam (1966)		Rajbansis of Madhya Manasi (1967)	
	No.	%	No.	%	No.	%	No.	%
	12	13	14	15	16	17	18	19
1—3	10	22.22	15	25.00	89	44.95	36	32.14
4 –6	19	42.22	33	55.00	81	40.91	48	42.86
7—9	13	28.89	10	16.67	23	11.62	21	18.75
10×	3	6.67	2	3.33	5	2.52	7	6.25
Total	45	100.00	60	100.00	198	100.00	112	100.00

forest *bastees*, Purodha has the highest frequency of nuclear households, while Kamala *bastee* has the lowest. In Purodha *bastee* 43 (40.19%) out of 107 are nuclear type. In Nalgarh *bastee* 12 (34.29%) out of 35 and in Kamala *bastee* 10 (25.00%) out of 40 households are of this type. But much higher freqency of nuclear household is found in both villages. In Madhya and Daksin Manasi 29 (53.70%) and 28 (64.41%) respectivaly belong to this category.

The next type is the extended household. The extended households comprise (i) uxorilccally extended comprising the married couple together with their married daughter with or without daughter's husband, or (ii) virilocally extended where the married couples reside with their married son with or without sons's wife, or (iii) mixed type consisting of the married couple living with both married son and married daughter with or without their respective consort. The other extended types are (iv) where wife's or mother's married brother or sister lives (v) where husband's or father's married brother or sister lives and (vi) combination of the two. The frequency of the uxorilocally extended household is more in the forest *bastees* than in the villages. While there are 37 (20.33%) uxorilocally extended households at different forest *bastees*, only 6 (5.31%) are present in the two villages. On the other hand, the virilocally extended households are comparatively higher in the villeges (11 or 9.73%) than in the forest *bastees* (10 or 5.49%).

Besides the above, a fair number of households found in both the forest bastees and the villages, are either nuclear households with some adhesions or uxorilocally or virilocally extended households with adhesions. The frequency of sororilocally or fraternally or avanculocally extended households is, of course, very low. The other type of households are also fewer owing to the paractice of multiple marriage, polygynous households, though fewer, are sometimes found among both the Forest and the Village Rabhas. So, it may be said that among the Rabhas, in general, nuclear type of family is the societal profile (Das & Raha, 1967 : 75). The dominance of the nuclear households is also observed among the Rabhas of Assam. Das observes 43.6% and 42.8% of the Rangdani

Rabha households of two different areas (1958a : 76, 1960: 122) and 38.0% of the Pati Rabha households belong to this type (1960 : 122). The survey among different communities like the Sahas, the Namasudras, the Rajbansis, the Jugis, the Malos and others, residing at Uttar, Madhya and Dakshin Manasi villages conducted by the author, also shows the higher frequency of nuclear type of households among these communities.

Household Composition

The Rabhas households are composed of different relatives (see Appendix 3). Kins related through blood, marriage or by adoption, are found to share the membership in a household, and different type of relationship bonds are also present among them. Still by judging the composition, the households of the Forest Rabhas can be distinguished from those of the Village Rabhas. Of course, similarity in composition of the households in some cases, is also found. The difference in the composition between the Forest Rabha and the Village Rabha households is apparent. The Forest Rabha households show its characteristic matri-kin orientation in majority of the households, the Village Rabha hhuseholds, on the other hand, differ in this respect by having a patri-kin orientation. The majority of the Forest Rabha households comprise either or both parents, unmarried children, married daughter, with or without daughters' husband and umarried children and with or without any other relative as adhesion. In a number of extended households of the village Rabhas, thc members are either or both parents, unmarried son, son's wife and umarried children with or without any other relative as adhesion. However, in both sections of the Rabhas there are some households which consist of both married son and married daughter with or without their respective spouse and unmarried children besides either or both parents. Further, the relative or relatives present in the Forest Rabha households as adhesion are in most cases typically matri-kins of either the husband or the wife or of the daughter. But in the case of the Village Rabhas such relatives are either the matri-kins or the patri kins of the husband or the son. The early accounts of the

Rabhas give no picture of their household compostion. A somewhat recent study on the Rabhas (Village) of West Bengal shows that the extended or joint families are either matrikin oriented with matrilocal residence or patri kin oriented with patrilocal residence (Das & Raha, 1967 : 75).

> "In the former case the husband lives with the wife with or without children in the wife's parent's house and in the latter case, the housband with his wife with or without children, live in his parents house" (Das & Raha, 1967 : 75).

The households, having parents with married son and married daughter with or without their respective spouse and unmarried children, are also present though the number of such household is quite a few. The Rangdanis and Pati Rabha households of Assam shows that most of the extended households are patrilineal where either married sons live with or without wife and unmarried children in their parents house or married brothers live together with their wives and unmarried children (Das 1960 : 122-125). An identical picture of the household compostion is also available among the Rangdani Rabhas (Das, 1958a : 75-76).

Like the Forest Rabha household,

"the Garo household may include, at most, a married couple and their unmarried children, together with one married daughter (sometimes adopted), her husband and the children (Burling, 1963a : 128). On the composition of households of the matrilineal Garos of Mymanshing, Bose states, "the nucleus of a Garo household consists of two or three generation of women linked by matrilineal Kinship". (1947 : 108, 215, 1941 : 85-87). The Khasi *ing* (household) has the similar composition (Gurdon, 1914 : 63-24 ; Chattopadhyay, 1941 : 19-29). The constituent members of Khasi family being the "Grandmother, her daughters and their children. But the permanent residents are the youngest daughters (*Ka Khadduh*), her husband and daughters. It takes an extended form more often when the children of the deceased sisters of

Ka Khadduh reside there (Mukherjee, 1958 : 209-210). Among the matrilineal War Khasis a typical household includes the husband and wife with or without unmarried children (if any) (Das Gupta, 1966 : 173). But due to their transition from matriliny to patriliny, the Koch households consist of the parents, unmarried children, a married son or married son or married son or married daughter or both with his or her spouse and children (Majumdar, 1967 : 67). The patrilineal Rajbansi society has a typical extended household, composed of the parents, unmarried children, married son, his wife with or without unmarried children (Mukherjee, 1963 : 66 ; Sanyal, 1965 : 124 128). This pattern is similar in different other matrilineal societies. Among the matrilineal chetlat Islanders the households are composed of the mother and her married and unmarried sons and daughters and also sometimes married or unmarried siblings. The married males (brothers or sons) usually visit their respective spouse at night but rarely play the role of husband-father in the same household. (Roy Burman 1967). This is sometimes termed as matrifocal (Kunstadter, 1963 : 64) or female based (Safa, 1965 : 135) household. Among the matrilineal Ashanti too the household consists of an old woman, her daughters, their children and one or two of her sons...... (the spouses of the sons do not form the part of the same household with them...... (Fortes, 1968 : 26). The family consists of a group of brothers and sisters (real or classificator) together with the children and daughter's children of the sisters. (Nakane, 1963 : 23 ; Gough, 1962a : 334). On the other hand, the Tiyyar of North Kerala have both partrilocally extended households consisting of the married couple, their sons, unmarried daughters, sons' wives and sons' children and 'mixed' extended family comprising the married couple, their divorced or widowed daughters and daughters' children or a widow, har daughters and her grand children are found in good number (Gough, 1962a : 408).

Generationwise Gradation of Households

In both the forests and the villages the Rabha households of different settlements are constituted with members of different generations (senior or junior to the self). On the basis of the distribution of members of different generations, the Rabha households of the five settlements have been classified into the following grades :

1. Grade I : Having members belonging to 2nd ascending generation and the generation of self.
2. Grade II : Having members belonging to 1st ascending generation and the generation of self.
3. Grade III : Having members belonging to 1st ascending generation, generation of self and the 1st descending generation.
4. Grade IV : Having members belonging to 1st ascending generation, generation of self and the 2nd descending generation.
5. Grade V : Having members belonging to the generation of self.
6. Grade VI : Having members belonging to the generation of self and first descending generation.
7. Grade VII : Having members belonging to the generation of self and 2nd descending generation.
8. Grade VIII: Having members belonging to generation of self and the 3rd descending generation.

It is apparent (Table 10) that majority of the households of the Forest as well as the Village Rabhas (67.03% and 67.23% respectively) belong to Grade VI. The same holds good for each individual settlement also, though Nalgarh *bastee* has the highest frequency (71.43%) in this regard. Next higher frequencies go to Grade III and Grade VII for the forest settlements (12.64% and 11.34% respectively) and Grade II and Grade III for the villages (10.62% and 9.73% respectively).

So far as the condition of the individual settlement is concerned Kamala Bastee has higher frequency for Grade VII over Grade III (17.50% and 15.00% respectively). At Madhya Manasi Grade III has higher frequency over Grade II (14.81% and 9.26% respectively) and at Dakshin Manasi Grade V and VII (which have an equal frequency 6.78%) are higher in strength than Grade III which is only 5.03%.

TABLE 10

Generationwise Gradation of the Rabha Households of the Five Settlements

Gradation of Generations in a Household	Name of the Settlements					
	Paro Bastee		Kodal Bastee		Andu Bastee	
	No.	%	No.	%	No.	%
1	2	3	4	5	6	7
GRADE—I						
GRADE—II	2	1.87	3	7.50	2	5.71
GRADE—III	13	12.15	6	15.00	4	11.43
GRADE—IV	3	2.80				
GRADE—V	4	3.74	1	2.50	1	2.86
GRADE—VI	74	69.16	23	57.50	25	71.43
GRADE—VII	11	10.28	7	17.50	3	8.57
GRADE—VIII						
ALL GRADES	107	100.00	40	100.00	35	100.00

Gradation of Generation in a Household	All Forest Bastees		Madhya Kamak-hyaguri		Dakshin Kama-Khyaguri		All Villages.	
	No.	%	No.	%	No.	%	No,	%
	8	9	10	11	12	13	14	15
GRADE—I					1	1.70	1	0.89
GRADE—II	7	3.85	5	9.26	7	11.86	12	10.62
GRADE—III	23	12.64	8	14.81	3	5.08	11	9.73
GRADE—IV	3	1.65						
GRADE—V	6	1.29	1	1.85	4	6,78	5	4.42
GRADE—VI	122	67.03	36	66.67	40	67.80	76	67.26
GRADE—VII	21	11.54	3	5.56	4	6.78	7	6.19
GRADE—VIII			1	1.85			1	0.89
	182	100.00	54	100.00	59	100.00	113	100.00

Thus it becomes clear that the majority of the Rabha households of both the forest *bastees* and the villages are composed of the members belonging to the generation of self. It is also observed that the frequency of households with members of one generation only, is much lower than that of the households with members of more than one generation.

Parents in the Rabha Households

In the Rabha households, often the parent/parents live with their married daughter and/or married son with or without spouse. Among the Forest Rabhas the tendency to live with married daughter is more pronounced, while among the Village Rabhas almost opposite is the trend. The Villags Rabha parent/parents are more inclined to live with their married son. Among the Rabhas of the three forest *bastees* (Table 11), out of the total 85 households, where the parent/parents live with their married children with or without their spouse, in 43 (50.50%) cases the parent/parents are found to reside with their married daughtar with or without daughter's husband (11.76% cases without daughter's husband and 38,82% cases with daughter's husband) while in only 20.00% cases they are seen to inhabit with their married son with or without son's wife (in 3.24% cases without son's wife while in 11.76% cases with son's wife). In rest of the cases (29.42%) parent/parents live with both married son and married daughter with or without their respective spouse. The picture is quite opposite among the Village Rabhas. Out of the total 20 households in the two villages having parent/parents living with the married children with/without their spouse, in 12 (60.00%) cases the parents reside with their married son and son's wife. Only in 5 (25.00%) cases both married daughter and husband share the same household with her parent/parents. In 15.00% cases only parent/parents live along with both married son and married daughter with their respective mate.

In the individual settlements also the picture is identical. In Purodha *bastee* out of a total of 46 households of the Rabhas where the parent/parents live with the married children without their spouse, in 26 (56.52%) cases the parent/parents

TABLE 11

Frequency and Distribution of Households Having Surviving Parent/Parents Living with Married Children With/Without their Spouse

Settlements	Total Household having married children with/ without spouse.	No. of Households having surviving parent/parents with							
		Married daughter only.		Married daughter, and daughter's husband		Married daughter, and married son.		Married daughter, daughter's husband and married son.	
		No.	%	No.	%	No.	%	No.	%
1	2	3	4	5	6	7	8	9	10
Purodha	46	7	15.22	19	41.30	—	—	2	4.35
Nalgarh Bastee	19	1	5.26	6	31.58	5	26.32	3	15.79
Kamala Bastee	20	2	10.00	8	40.00	—	—	—	—
All Forest	85	10	11.76	33	38.82	5	5.88	5	5.88

Bastes									
Madhya Manasi	12	—	—	4	33.33	—	—	—	—
Dakshin Manasi	8	—	—	1	12.50	—	—	—	—
All	20	—	—	5	25.00	—	—	—	—
Villages									
All	105	10	9.52	38	36.19	5	4.76	5	4.76

Settlements	Married daughter, daughter's husb- and married son and sons.		Married daughter, married son and son's wife.		Married son only		Married son and son's wife.	
	No.	%	No.	%	No.	%	No.	%
	11	12	13	14	15	16	17	18
Purodha	4	8.70	3	6.52	4	8.70	7	15.22
Nalgarh Bastee	1	5.26	—	—	1	5.26	2	10.53
Kamala Bastee	6	30.00	1	5.00	2	10.00	1	5.00
All Forest Bastee	11	12.94	4	4.71	7	8.24	10	11.76

Madhya Manasi	1	8.33	—	—	—	—	7	58.33
Dakshin Manasi	2	25.00	—	—	—	—	5	62.50
All Villages	3	15.00	—	—	—	—	12	600.00
All Settlements	14	13.33	4	3.81	7	6.67	22	20.95

live with married daughter with or without daughter's husband and in only 11 (23.92%) cases the parent/parents have a common residence with married son with or without son's wife. In Nalgarh and Kamala *bastees* also the frequency of households with parent/parents living with married daughter with or without daughter's husband, is much higher than that of the households with parent/parents living with married son with or without son's wife. In this connection it is to be mentioned that the frequency of the former type of households in Kamala *bastee* (50.00%) is much higher than that of the Nalgarh *bastee* (36.84%), the frequency of the latter type of households is almost similar in both forest *bastees.* But the frequency of the households having parent/parents with married son and daughter with or without their respective spouse, is higher at Nalgarh than that at Kamala *bastee*.

In Madhya Manasi, on the other hand, there are 12 households having the parent/parents residing with the married children with or without spouse. Of these seven (58.33%) households have the parent/parents residing with the married son and his wife, while in 4 cases (33.33%) the married daughter and her husband live together with her parent/parents. Only one household is composed with parent/parents with both married son and daughter and their respective spouse. In Dakshin Manasi too only one household (12.50%) is found to have parents living with their daughter and daughter's husband, while in majority of the cases (62.50%) the parent/parents reside with the married son and his wife.

So, it is seen that while the Forest Rabha parent/parents prefer to live with their married daughter and daughter's husband, the Village Rabha parent/parents have inclined towards son and son's wife.

DEVELOPMENTAL PROCESS IN THE RABHA HOUSEHOLD

As it happens to other communities, the Rabha household has also undergone change in its composition with the change of time. The composition of the Rabha household has never remained constant for a long time. Different crises of life viz. birth, marriage, death, adoption etc., force a household to change its composition. With the occurrence of a death or with matrimony, the household with the change of type and size, also changes its composition. What was once a nuclear household turned into a virilocally or uxorilocally extended household after marriage. The households of the Forest as well as the Village Rabhas are also subject to the change. Two case studies, one from Purodha and the other from Madhya Manasi, showing such developments in the composition of the Rabha households with the change of time, are described here. It is however important to mention that time calculation is approximate ; caution has been taken to make a near approximation of the year and date considering different important incidents of different informant's life, natural phenomena etc. Along with the change of the composition and size, the typological and structural changes in the Rabha household are also noticeable from these analyses.

DEVELOPMENTAL PROCESS IN THE FOREST RABHA HOUSEHOLD

A case-study

Pasang Darboth, father's father of Jastu Uni-Brahmin, of Purodha beates was born in 1840 at Nimti in Kalchini police Station, Jalpaiguri district. He was the only child of his parents when he first saw the light of the earth. Eight years after, in 1848, his sister, Siri Uni-Brahmin, the second living issue of the parents, was born (Fig. Ic). In 1865 when Pasang was about 23 year old, his parents had him married with Mijir Karabojidal who was the fifth issue of her parents (Household-3). Mijir had three brothers and one sister (Fig-Ib) and all of them lived with their parents at Paitkapara in Alipurduar Police-Station, Jalpaiguri. During the time of her marriage her eldest brother went to his wife's house after marriage and started living with his parents-in-law (Household-C). Mijir's elder sister was also married and lived with her parents. Her husband and two sons were also with her. Two years after Mijir's marriage, her eldest sister got separated from her parents and started living independently with her husband

DEVELOPMENTAL PROCESSES OF THE FOREST RABHA HOUSEHOLD

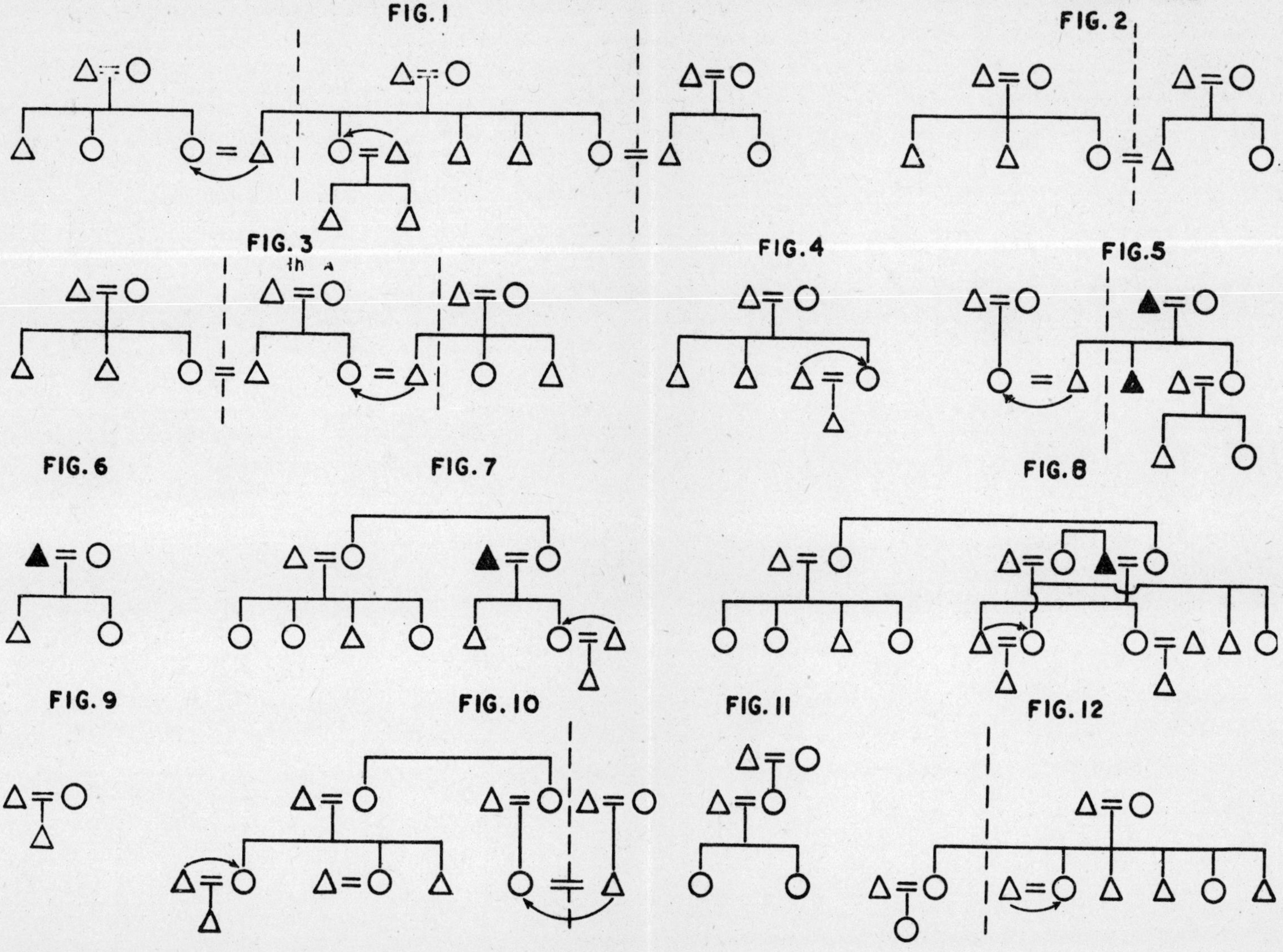

PLATE I.

and two sons. Mijir's parental house was then composed with her parents, herself and her two unmarried brothers (Fig. 2).

Though Pasang was married to Mijir around 1865 they used to live in their respective parental house till the birth of their first child Shamdas in 1869. A few years after Pasang's marriage his sister, Siri was married to some Gade Bandhai of the same sattlement (Fig. 3). When Siri was carrying her first baby, Gadu came to live in his father-in-Law's house permanently (Fig 3). Next year Pasang according to social custom in vogue, went to his wife's parental house at Paitkapara for living permanently leaving his own parental house Within the next three to five years two incidents took place in this household. Pasang and Mijir gave birth to their second child, a daughter named Kim Karabojidal and the father of Mijir died. Two years later the elder brother or Majir got married and went to his parents-in-law's house to live there parmanently. Within a few years Mijir's grown-up younger brother was killed by the wild animal. Both the marriage and the death altered the composition of household which consisted of the widow mother of Mijir herself, her husband and two children, one son and one daughter (Fig 5). This composition was maintained up to 1889-90 when Passing suddenly died. Next year Mijir's mother also died (Fig. 6).

At this time this household consisted of Mijir and two children. A few months later Mijir's elder sister, her husband, one son and three daughters came to her for rendering help and started living with her permanently. In 1893 Mijir arranged marriage of Kim with some Hedim Lengbarai, and the marriage took place in the same year. Since marriage Hedim started living with his wife. Two years later first child of Kim, Tikaram Karabejidal was born (Fig. 7). In 1897 when he was 28 years old, Shamdas married his father's sister's daughter, Bohula Uni-Brahmin of Paitkapara when the latter was in her late teens (Fig. 8). Behuls was the third issue of her parents, and had two elder brothers and one younger sister. Her eldest brother was living with his wife at his parents-in-law's house. Shamdas married Behula arround 1897, but he did not live with his wife at his parent-in-law's house permanently till 1901 when his first issue was one year old (Fig. 9). From 1901 to 1906 some incidents in this household altered the composition. In the same year when Shamdas came to his household to live permanently, his wife's elder brother, Giriraj Uni-Brahmin got married to some Pai Bandadhai. Next year his only son died. In 1905 his second son (the only living son) Ramlal Uni-Brahmin was born, and in the following year Shamdas got separated from his parents-in-law following a conflict. He established as independent household Fig. 9).

In 1908 a group of Rabha from Paitkapara led by their headman, Kusi Chinchat came to the present Purodha *bastee* and founded a new settlement there. But Shamdas preferred his old settlement at Paitkapara. Since Shamdas established his new household (Fig. 10) independently, no incident happened that could change the pattern of his household. This continued till 1932 when his son, Ramlal Uni-Brahmin fell in love with Niru Chinchet of Purodha *bastee.* As Niru was the only child living with her parents, Ramlal had to live with them at Purodha *bastee* soon after his marriage. So, Ramlal left his parents and went to Purodha *bastee* to live with his parents-in-law (Fig. 11). At this time this household (Fig. 12) of Param and Gateng consisted of besides them, their daughter Niru, her husband Ramlal, Gateng's elder sister, Bermi, her husband, one unmarried son, two married daughters, one of the daughter's husband and (Fig. 10). These other children of Param and Gateng, all daughters, left their parental home after marriage and established independent households before Niru got married.

Five years after marrige Ramlal and Niru gave birth to their first child in 1937, a daughter named Riti. Their second daughter Niti, was born three years later. A few years later elder sister Bermi and her husband, Haldhar Lombok with their children and grandson departed and formed separate household unit. Gateng's households consisted of Param, Gaters, Niru, Ramalal and Niru's two daughters, Riti and Niti (Fig.11).

In the following years till 1955 Niru's parents died and Niru gave birth to four more children, three sons and a daughter.

In 1956 and 1957 two more incidents followed. Ramlal and Niru had their eldest daughter married with Barin Bandadhai, son of Balaram Moijidong and Sita Bandadhai, of the same Purodha *bastee*. Two years later when Riti was pregnant, Ramlal brought Barin for help.

In 1957 Shamlal and Niru gave birth to their last issue, a son named Lalbar Chinchet. In 1959 they married their second daughter, Niti with Gopal Chand Uni-Brahmin, a Village Rabha of Madhya Parokata under Alipurduar Police-station (adjacent to Madhya Manasi).

In 1958 Riti gave birth to a dead child. In 1961 she delivered a daughter, Napti Chinchet.

In 1965 Gopal Chand Uni-Brahmin, husband of Niti, joined Ramlal. In 1965 October Barin in the wake of a conflict with Ramlal got separated and established a new household (Fig. 12).

Ramlal Uni-Brahmin lives in a separate household in Purodha *bastee* with his wife, Niru Chinchet, one unmarried daughter, married daughter Niti, and her husband, Gopal. Riti the eldest daughter of Ramlal and Niru lives in a separate household adjacent to her father, with her husband, Barim Bandadhai and only daughter, Nepti Chinchet (Fig. 12).

On the other hand, when Ramlal departed from his parent and came to Purodha to live with his parents-in-law, Shamdas and Behula continued living in the same household. After a year Shamdas died and Behula went to her youngest sister, Surti Uni-Brahmin who was then living at Paitkapara with her husband, Maira Lombok and three daughtres of them the eldest one was only married. Two years later Behula died. Latter on Moira also came to Purodha for permanent settlement.

DEVELOPMENTAL PROCESS IN THE VILLAGE RABHA HOUSEHOLDS

A Case-Study :

Jogendra Bandadhai, father's father of Gablu Chinchat and

Bandaram Chinchat of this village, was born in 1866 at Ambari-Khalta in Alipurduar Police-Station, Jalpaiguri. He had one brother and one sister, both younger to (Fig. I). In 1890 when he was 24 years old, he married Pasni Moijibhobra who was the only child of her parents (Fig. II). After marriage, Jogendra started living with his wife and wife's parents and helped his wife's father in cultivation and other economic pursuits and helped his wife's father in cultivation and other economic pursuits (Fig. II A). In 1892 the first child of Jogendra and Pasni, a son named Sahin (Sajo) Moijibhobra was born. In 1894 and 1898 Pasni gave birth to two more sons, Rohin and Tohin Moijibhobra. Two years later, Pasni's father died. A year after her last son, Kalachand Moijibhobra was born, but she died. Kalachand was brought up by his mother's mother (Fig. III).

In 1908 Jogendra got his first son, Sohin married to some Rajesari Kantran. Sohin and his wife started living with him. In 1911 Jogendra's third son, Tohin died. A few years later Pasni's mother also died. In 1920 Rahin went to Madhya Manasi and served in the house of Thanswar Moiyinakal and Rantesari Lavong for two years as *gharjai* (prospective son-in-law). In 1922 he married Sindisari Lavong, daughter of Thansewar and Rantesari and lived with them for a year (Fig. IV). Later he had his separate household near that of his wife's father.

In the meantime, Jogendra died. A year or two later Sohin desired to keep a separate household. In this situation Kalachand being unable to stay there, went to his elder brother, Rohin in Madhya Manasi in 1924. After a few months, he went to the house of Bisalu Pomrai and Dhubri Chinchat to serve as *gharjai* for their daughter, Annasari Chinchat (Fig. V).

Kalachand served there for nearly two years. In 1926 he married Annesari and lived there. At that time Annesari had a younger brother, her elder brother having died earlier. Three years later she gave birth to a daughter, Kami Chinchet. In 1931 Bhajan Chinjan Chinchet, the second son of Kalachand and Annesari was born (Fig-XI). Within a few years Bisalu died and Annesari's younger brother, Sohin

DEVELOPMENTAL PROCESSES OF THE FOREST RABHA HOUSEHOLD

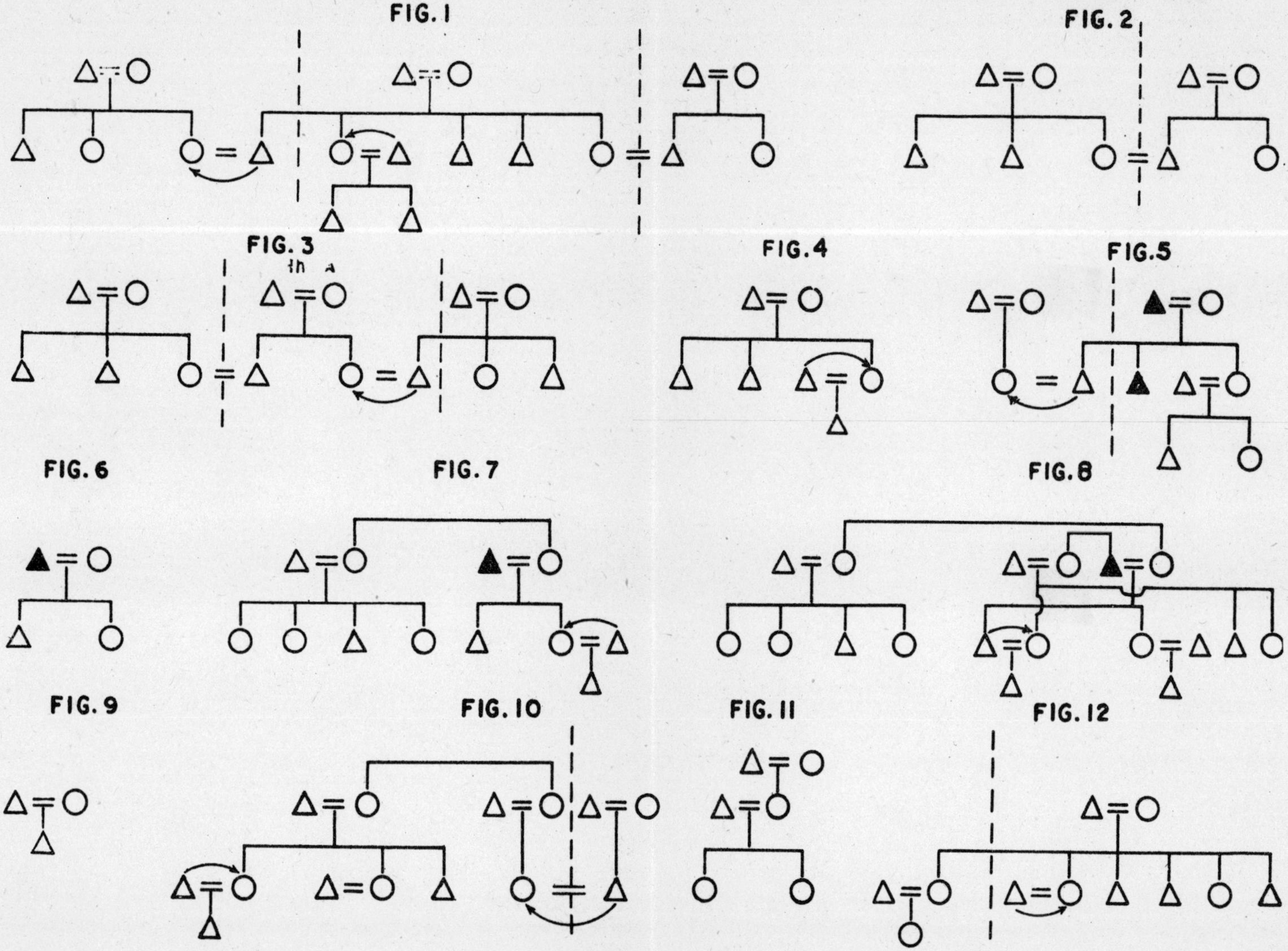

PLATE 1.

DEVELOPMENTAL PROCESSES IN A VILLAGE RABHA HOUSEHOLD

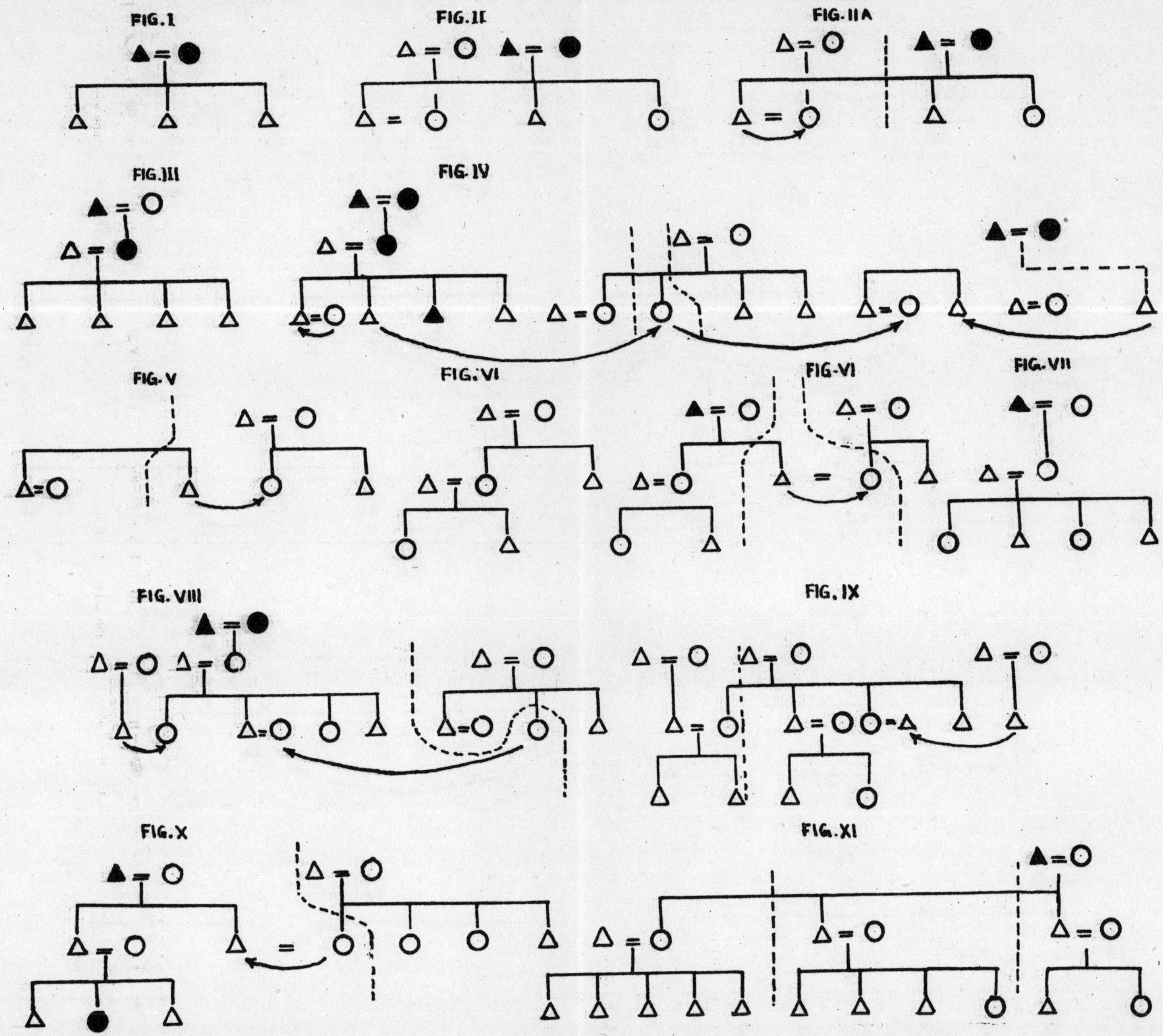

married Somesari Panchibak, younger daughter of Maila Moijipran and Patanesawi Panchibak of Dakshin Manasi (Patanesawi's younger brother, Rataneswar at present, a resident of the Madhya Manasi, later married Annesari's younger daughter, Bhagi) (Fig. VI). A few months later Sohin having disposed of his paternal property, went to Uttar Parokata under Alipurduar Police-Station, Jalpaiguri district, with his wife. He died there soon and Somesari remarried one Goribcharan Dedoi of Daldali under Kumaragram Police Station, Jalpaiguri district. When Sohin left his paternal household it consisted of his mother, his sister, her husband and her two children, one son and the other daughter.

In 1935 third child of Kalachand and Annesari, a daughter, Bhagi Chinchet, and two years later their last issue, a son, Bandaram Chinchat were born (Fig. VIII). When Bandaram three year' old his mother's mother, Dhubri died. After Dhubri's death, the family of Kalachand included his wife two daughters and two sons. There was no change up to 1949. In 1949 one Sakalu Moijibhobra from Goalpara, Assam, came to the house of Kalachand and served for one year as *gharjai* for Kalachand's eldest daughter, Kami. In 1950 their marriage took place, and both started living with Kalachand who in 1953 married his son Bhajan to Sunderbala Pomrei, daughter of Nobin Mositak and Hima Pomrei of Bochamari under Tufanganj Police Station, Cooch Bahar. After marriage Bhajan started living with his father.

After staying with his wife's father for 5 years, Sakulu separated. But before he did separate from his father-in-law, his wife gave birth to two sons Mohindra and Surendra Chinchet.

Bhajan's first child, Abinesh Pomrei, a son, was born after the departure of Sakalu. Two years later in 1957 Bhagi married Ratneswar Panchibak, son of Fakir Tangoi and Phula Panchibak of Madkya Manasi. In the same year, after a few months, Bhajan's wife, Sunderbale gave birth to a daughter, Faguni Pomrei (Fig. IX). Next year in 1958 Ratneswar and Bhagi, after staying with later's father for a year, separated. A year after in 1960 Bandaram married Aloka Mositak, daughter of Biren Kantran and Salu Mesitak of Madhya

Manasi. A few months later, after Bandaram's marriage, his father, Kalachand died, and a month after Kalachand's death Bhajan's third child, a son Tukaram Pomrai was worn. A few months later in the beginning of 1961 Bhajan's daughter, Faguni died (Fig. X). In the same year, after this incident, a conflict arose between the two brothers, Bhajan and Banderam as a result of which the property was partitioned. Annesari who is still alive, took Bandaram's side. In 1961 Bandaram's first male child was born, but died after seven days. In 1963 and 1966 Aloka gave birth to two children, a son and a daughter. Three years after Bandaram's sister, Bhagi witn her husband and children came to her parental house and afterwards settled in a separate household. At present there are three households, that of Bandaram Chinchat and his sister's husband, Ratneswar Panchibak. (Fig. XI). The present eompositions of these three households are given below :

Household No. 1 (Fig-XI)

Bandaram Chinchet, his wife, Aloka Mositak, son, Dipak Mositak and a daughter, Sabita Mositak, and Bandaram's mother, Anesari Chinchet.

Household No. 2 (Fig. XI)

Bhajan Chinchet, his wife Sunderabala Pomrai and two son, Abinesh and Tukaram Powrei.

Household Ho. 3. (Fig-XI)

Ratneswar Panchibak, his wife, Bhagi Chinchet and five sons, Rajesh, Nobin, Jogen and Jiban Chinchet.

Thus from the description of the two households one each of Purodha *bastee* and Madhya Manasi village, the development and change in the household pattern in different generations, is noticeable. It is clearly visible that while the household in Purodha *bastee* retained the matrilineal or uxorilocal character almost all through the generations even after recruitment of members due to marriage or some other reasons, or reduction in number of members due to partition or death, or some other reasons, in the villages, the matrilineal or uxorilocal character of the Rabha households perpetuated up to certain generations, but thereafter the households started adopting patrilineal or virilocal character. Post-marital residence also in case of the Forest Rabha was uxorilocal but the same character in case of the Village Rabhas was replaced after a certain period by the patrilocal or virilocal type. Of course neolocal residence in case of both Forest and Village Rabhas and duolocal residence in case of Forest Rabhas were also in existence.

RULES OF INHERITANCE AND SUCCESSION

Rules of Inheritance

Both movable and immovable belongings of an individual, which he or she earns or acquires by his or her own efforts or receives from his or her ancestor or ancestress or gets as donations are considered by the Forest as well as the Village Rabhas as their property. The Forest Rabhas have only the movable property (which includes utensils, furniture, ornaments, domestic animals and poultry birds etc.), but they do not have any immovable property (land, house etc.) of their own in true sense. The land, house and other constructions in their possession are all actually owned by the Forest Department of the State Government. As stated earlier, the Forest Department gives them (only the official forest labourers) a plot of land for cultivation and house and a house-building and repairing materials, free of cost in exchange of their labour for forest works. A Rabha forest labourer can enjoy the land and the house (even if he builds the same on the site given by the Forest Department) so long he remains as forest labourer. The land, house-site, house etc. are never given to him permanently, and as a result he has no right on the land, house, house site etc., nor can he sell, mortgage or lease out or in any way dispose of it. On the other hand, these forest labourers have absolute right on their movable properties such as cash, ornaments, utensils, clothings, cereals and such other belongings. They can sell these, distribute these, consume these or in any other way dispose of these. These are heritable property, and when the owner dies, his/her heir/heiress (traditionally fixed) receives these.

Among the Village Rabha the movable and immovable property are owned by a person. A Village Rabha may have land, house and other personal belongings such as utensils, furniture, ornaments, clothings, cash etc., of his own. And on these he has every right like other people. He can sell the same, mortgage. lease out or give on rent or in any way dispose of these as permissible under the existing law. In a similar way when one dies, one's property (both movable and immovable) are inherited by one's inheritor(s). Here unlike that of the Forest Rabhas, movable and immovable property do not follow different courses.

The Forest and the Village Rabhas follow different rules of inheritance and of the ownership of the property. Among the Forest Rabhas the rules of inheritance and the ownership are different for movable and immovable property. This is true in case of both ancestral (excepting a very few cases) and acquired property. According to the Forest Rabha rule of inheritance, right on ancestral property flows from the deceased mother to the surviving daughter. In the case of the acquired property whatever a man earns, goes to mother (if he is unmarried and lives with his parents), mother and wife or wife's mother (if he is married and lives with his parents), wife' mother (if he lives with his mother-in-law) or his wife (if he lives separately with his wife or if he has no mother-in-law).

Though the land and the house are officially allotted to a man who is only an occupier and not an owner but customarily (in symbolic sense) these are owned by his mother, wife's mother or wife as the case may be. And when that man dies or is incapable of performing his duty, the name of the husband of that of his daughter who would become the heiress, is forwarded to the Forest authority as his successor. The Forest authority usually accepts this after examining whether he is deformed, culprit or sufferring from any contagious disease as scheduled in the Service Rules. Accordingly the daughter's husband officially becomes the holder (customarily the daughter) of the land and the house.

Among the present-day Village Rabhas on the other hand, "the males are the owner of the property both ancestral and acquired" (Das & Raha, 1967: 91). Only in a very few cases, the females are found to hold some ancestral property which they have received from their mother. The property is inherited by the males, usually the sons. Unlike that of the Forest Rabhas, both movable and immovable property among the Village Rabhas follow the same course as that of the rule of inheritance.

RULES OF INHERITANCE OF THE MOVABLE PROPERTIES AMONG THE FOREST RABHAS

Among the Forest Rabhas the property is owned by the females, and the rule of inheritance like the descent of *husuk*, follows the female line. The rule of inheritance of the movable property is governed by some general principles : (1) that the property should remain within the same *husuk* and should not pass on to a different *husuk*; (2) it should be owned by the females ; (3) the individual inheriting the property will look after the person in old age and his/her family from whom he/she has inherited the property and ; (4) that she should perform the household religious practices and propitiate the household deities (the Rungtuk and the Basek which are also received by the heiress from the owner). The general rules of inheritance and nature of succession have been described below :

(a) As stated earlier the mother is the sole owner of the property of the family. Usually her youngest daughter lives with her till her death and maintains her and her husband (the father or the step father of the daughter) in their old age along with other dependants. So at the death of the mother, this youngest daughter inherits the property. The other daughters generally leave the parental house shortly after marriage and establish separate households. The sons also after their marriage leave the house of their parents and live with their parents-in-law or in separate house-holds with thier wives and children.

At the time of the selection of the heiress, the mother consults with her husband and her brothers and also other kinsmen of her own lineage.

So it is customary among the Forest Rabhas that the youngest daughter inherits the movable property of her mother who was so long the owner of the property.

Though the youngest-daughter-inheritance is the general rule, yet there are some cases found among the Forest Rabhas of different forest *bastees* where deviation from this general rule can be found. Some such cases are cited below:

(b) The youngest daughter is generally selected by the mother as her heiress for her movable property. In case the youngest daughter is very young and unmarried at the time of death of the mother, the latter may select some other elder daughter as her heiress.

(c) It is also seen that if the youngest daughter does not want to stay with her mother after marriage and departs from her and starts separate establishment, or lives with her parents-in- law, then she is not selected as the heiress of her mother, and instead some of her elder sisters, who assures to live with her parents and to maintain them, gets the property. In this case the youngest daughter has no right to demand any part of the ancestral property.

(d) If the youngest daughter becomes deformed or feeble-minded or mad, and thereby unsuitable for marriage, the property in that case, is handed over to some other daughter for the sake of proper maintenance.

(e) If a woman has no daughter but daughter's daughter, or if the heiress (daughter) dies in the life time of the mother leaving a daughter, the daughter's daughter becomes the sole owner of her ancestral property.

(f) When a woman dies without having any daughter or

daughter's daughter, her movable property goes to her elder or younger sister.

(g) If the only daughter leaves her mother during her life time due to certain reasons (such as quarrel), the mother's property goes to her younger or elder sister.

(h) When a woman has no daughter (and thus no daughter's daughter) and also no surviving sister then all her movable property is inherited by her sister's surviving daughter who becomes her heiress.

(i) If a woman has no daughter (and thereby daughter's daughter) or if the daughter leaves her during her life time, her property is usually received by her sister. Some times the co-wife inherits the property instead of sister. Usually the co-wives happen to be sisters here.

(j) In spite of the general rule of female inheritance a few cases can be traced where this general principle has been violated. In these cases instead of daughter or any other female relative, sons have got the property of their mother. In these cases the absence of the matri-kin (female) is the main factor. In one case the only daughter left the mother and went to the village. The mother had no female matri-kin but a son.

(k) In only one case in the three Forest *bastees* the movable property passed from mother to son instead of daughter as the daughters left the mother after their marriage and did not want to stay with her even on request.

(l) The rules of inheritance prevalent among those relatives of the Forest Rabhas, who live in the villages, are based on their own custom as present among the Village Rabhas. In their cases the property (both movable and immovable) are owned by the malefolk and inherited by the sons instead of the daughters.

RULES OF INHERITANCE OF IMMOVABLE PROPERTY AMONG THE FOREST RABHAS

These customary rules of the transmission of the property

rights (immovable) from one to another, follow the following principles ;

(i) Usually at the death or retirement of the father (who is officially a labourer), husband of the daughter (heiress) is selected as the next labourer. After his selection is approved by the Forest Department, he becomes the official custodian of the land and the house of his father-in-law. This is so done because the husband of the daughter (heiress) maintains his parents-in-law in their old age.

(ii) Though the general rule conforms with the succession of daughter's husband, exceptions to this rule are also found. In certain cases other relatives have come in after the death of official labourer and have become the custodian of the land and the house which the deceased enjoyed during his life time. In these cases, too, the labourer and his wife in their old ages, and their dependents were served by the successor. Here the rule has been violated because either the man had no daughter or the daughter had left him and his wife in their old age.

(iii) In another case it is found that a man became the custodian of his wife's mother's elder sister's husband's land and house i.e., the man was declared as the official forest labourer in place of his wife's mother's elder sister's husband.

(iv) There is a case where a man became the official labourer after his sister's husband died without daughter.

(v) There is a case at Purodha *bastee* where a man became the Official labourer in place of his younger sister's husband.

(vi) Besides the above, there are certain cases where sons have been allowed to take possession of their father's land and house. At Purodha six such cases are in records in four of which the sons were the heirs while in the other two cases non-heir sons have become the official labourers in place of their father or step father.

(vii) There is only one case at Nalgarh *bastee* where at his death an official forest labourer was succeeded by his co-husband.

Rule of Inheritance among the Village Rabhas :

(1) Among the Village Rabhas the property is owned by the males and the inheritance follows the male line. While father is the owner of the family property, the same is shared by his son or sons after his death.

> "The rule is inheritance in most of the cases, among the present day Rabha (village dwelling) follow the male line in general.... At present in the (Village) Rabha society the males are the owners of the family property...both ancestral and acquired, and the inheritance follows the male line, i.e., sons are the heirs after the death of the father" (*op. cit.*)

When there is only one son, he becomes the sole owner of his father's property. But when there are more than one son, the property is usually equally shared by all the sons only that the son or sons who maintain the widowed mother and unmarried sisters, get some extra for their maintenance.

(2) On the death of the father, sons get equal share of their paternal property. If any son leaves his father and does not look after him in his old age, he is not entitled to any property from his father in life time nor can he claim any right after the death of the father.

(3) If all the sons leave him in his life time for service or other works, then they have equal right after the death of the father.

(4) If any son is feeble minded, mad or suffering from serious and incurable disease, he is generally deprived of the ancestral property.

(5) If the son is predeceased, his surviving son in that case becomes the heir of the man.

(6) If a man has no son but daughters the property goes to his brother, elder and or younger.

(7) If a man has no son and also no surviving brother, then brother's son inherits the property after his death.

(8) Though the rule of inheritance in most of the cases among the present day Rabha (Village dwelling) follows the male line in general (*op. cit.*) there are yet some cases where the females (daughter or sister) got shares of ancestral property along with the males.

(9) When a man has no son but a daughter and no brother or brother's son, his property or his wife's property is inherited by his daughter.

(10) A woman's property is usually inherited by the daughters.

(11) In one case it was seen that a man had only a daughter. She became the heiress and inherited all the father's property. But in the next generation the property went to the sons.

(12) In certain cases among the Village Rabhas also the property was found to have been owned by the female. The rule of inheritance followed the female line. But in the later period this trend did not continue. This male line of inheritance started operating. This rule still persists.

(13) In a few cases the wife received her husband's property, when she had no son or had a minor son.

(14) In certain cases, some wealthy Rabhas have been found to have given some property to their sisters or sister's sons to help them to maintain themselves.

The Crises of Life-I : Birth and Infancy

5

THE CRISES OF LIFE–I : BIRTH & INFANCY

It is an old Rabha belief that the marriage leads to pregnancy and childbirth. To a Rabha the birth of a child is an important event of life. While the Forest Rabhas like the Garos (Burling, 1963 : 77-78) pray for a female child, the present day Village Rabhas like the Rajbansis, desire more for a male child. But none of them show apathy to the child of opposite sex. Infanticide is not dreamt of. The Forest Rabhas seek for a female child because their daughter (and her husband) would live with them and look after them in their old age. The son, on the contrary, would go to his parents-in-law, soon after marriage and deprive them (parents) of his earnings.

The Village Rabhas, on the other hand, hold the opposite view and say that the female child will go to her husband's house after marriage and will not look after her parents in their old age. But a son will stay with them even after his marriage and feed them when they will be old and maintain their property.

Among both the Forest and the Village Rabhas childlessness is considered as disgraceful. A married woman without child is always looked down in comtempt. "A barren woman is called 'Panmadwa'. She is looked down by the community" (Sunder, 1895 : 74). The husband of a barren wife is often goes for divorce and subsequently remarries.

The birth of a child is not only necessary for the salvation of the parents after their death (a Village Rabha belief), and maintaining the continuity of the family-line but also for the economic stability of the family and maintenance of the parents in their old age. One of the most important factors connected with the birth, is the inheritance of the property. All parents expect that their property should be inherited and enjoyed by their child/children and not by others. Social prestige is also connected with the birth. A childless couple has much less prestige.

The first pregnancy and the birth of the first child, are significant and joyous events to a Rabha couple and their family. Among the Forest Rabhas in the first pregnancy, a chicken is offered to the deities, *pertani*, the child catcher, the *maitani* and the *michik-bai* the two deities for the welfare, on 5th, 7th or 9th month of pregnancy. No offering is made in the successive pregnancies. The Village Rabhas celebrate no particular ritual in connection with the first or successive pregnancies and childbirth but sometimes make vow to Goddess Sasthi (goddess of child welfare) for a safe delivery. But in Assam, among the Rabhas a sacrifice has to be made to *bai-ma-bai*, the creator, if the wife becomes pregnant (Friend-Pereira, 1912 : 143).

Among the Rabhas of West Bengal the couple goes by certain restrictions when the wife is pregnant. The restrictions and rigidities thereof are imposed more on the wife than on the husband. The latter refrains from killing certain living creatures and is prohibited from taking active part in a funeral ceremony.

> The wife, on the other hand, abstains from "going to any burial or cremation ground, or the house where any pollution (death or birth) has taken place, or crossing a leveller or ladder or a rope with which is tied a cattle or a goat." (Das & Raha, 1967 :96).

She is also not allowed to go alone to

> "any jungle or lonely pond or some unearthly place, riverside etc., nor can she take active part in some socio-religious ceremony (birth or funeral), or allowed to bring water with

pitcher taking in her waist. She is also not allowed to stay outside the house after dusk in dishevelled hair, nor can she take food from a stranger or give anything to any outsider (*op. cit.*).

Sex-life during pregnancy is also restricted and as such the husband does not indulge in sex-relation with the wife when the pregnancy is sufficiently matured (usually 7th month and onwards).

When a pregnant woman in the Forest Rabhas society, gets sick, the *huji* (medicine man) is called in to treat her with some magical means or by offering something to the deities and spirits.

In case of the Village Rabhas, the *kabiraj* (medical man) or the local quack treats the patient by magical means or by prescribing the decoction of certain herbs and roots etc. In recent years with the advantage of the easy availability of the doctors and modern medicine, both allopathic and homeopathic, some enlightened and well-to-do Rabhas take help of these for the treatment of their pregnant women if her condition is severe and not cured by the local quacks.

It is also seen that a Village Rabha woman wears *jap* (a kind of sanctified black thread) or amulet given by the *kabiraj* or *ojha* for protection from the evil spirits. The pregnant woman also keeps a piece of iron as a prophylactic charm.

In the Forest Rabha society the pregnant woman does not wear *jap* or *dhop* but keeps a piece of iron to get rid of the evil. In case of any evil action, the *dhami* or *huji* wards off the evil spirit or appeases it so that the woman gets cured soon.

For child-birth no extra lying-in-room is constructed and the birth takes place in the main room (*nu*).

When the labour pain starts the expectant mother takes shelter in the main room. She usually remains there till the end of the pollution period. From the day the labour pain starts till the end of the pollution period (*subodu*), her companions are some experienced elderly women (relatives or non-relatives) who do the nursing and take care of her during the period of her confinement. One of them acts as the midwife. These women must be married. No unmarried woman is allowed to do these (Sunder, 1895: 74). Any stranger or non-Rabha is forborne from attending or seeing the child-birth because of the fear of the evil action.

No midwife from other community is employed by the Forest Rabhas nor any medical practitioner (allopathic or homeopathic) nor the trained nurse is called in. Similarly hospital delivery is also not heard of. Some professional mid-wives (untrained but experienced), who, in some cases, work for the Village Rabhas and the Rajbansis (Sanyal, 1965: 62-67), never go to the Forest Rabhas for midwifery. The Forest Rabhas, in their turn, rest content with their own community women. A few enlightened Village Rabhas have started sending their women for delivery to the Health Centres or hospitals.

When the labour pain starts, the attending women take care of the parturient woman. If the pain becomes acute, the attending women gently massage the belly and the abdomen of the pregnant woman with some lukewarm oil to reduce the pain. The *huji*, or the *dhami* or the *roja* also tries to relieve the woman of acute pain by magical means. Worship of several deities and spirits, especially, the *michik-bai-perthani* and *mai-tani* for the relief from pain and safe delivery is also done by the Forest Rabhas.

Sometimes, for quick and safe delivery the *dhaini* (midwife) performs some magical rites, known as *jalkasa* when she sancti-fies some water by some magical means and gives it to the expectant mother to drink.

After the start of the labour pain but before the child birth in case of the Village Rabha woman, the *dhaini* performs the *solamatrika puja* for the safe, and quick delivery and also for the welfare of the child.

> "After the *puja*, the *dhaini* gives her patient a little sacred water to drink and also keeps some flowers of the *puja* on her bed. After child-birth all the article used in the *puja* even the flowers in the patient's bed, are thrown away." (Das & Raha, 1967 : 98-99).

Just at the time of birth the pregnant woman remains in the kneeling or squatting position till the delivery. As soon as the child is borne, one of the attending women cuts the umbilical cord with small dirk or bamboo knife as is done by the Assam Rabhas (Friend-Pereira, 1912 : 143). Among the Village Rabhas, the child is allowed to touch the ground first in order to get the blessings of the Mother Earth as among the Rajbanssis (Sanyal, 1265).

After cutting of the umbilical cord, the attending woman wash both the mother and the new-born baby with lukewarm water. The midwife who cuts the umbilical cord, takes the placenta (*parr*) in a *kalar donga* (plantain-bark container) and buries it outside close to the wall of the same room. The area is fenced with some reed stick to prevent the malevolent spirits and animals from doing harm. Sunder, on the other hand, reported that the Rabhas used to keep the *parr* (placenta) in an earthern pot (*matak*) and to bury it in the ground at some distance and to fence the place. (1895:74).

When the fragment of the navel (*atpai*) dries up and falls down after a few days, it is buried either within the main-room (i.e. at at present lying-in-room) or in thc kitchen (*phonkar*).

After birth, the attending women take bath.

Among the Forest Rabhas the birth pollution (*subodu*) is observed for five or seven days. Sunder also marked the seven days pollution for the Rabhas and seven to nine days for the Rajbansis when the woman becomes 'outcaste' (1895:53-74). But among the present day Village Rabhas this period lasts for 30 days as among the Rajbansis (Choudhuri, 1903:142 ; Sanyal 1965:64-67). According to Friend-Pereira the Rabhas observe birth pollution till the naval string is dropped (Friend-Pereira, 1912:143). But Choudhuri is of the opinion that the Rabhas do not observe any unclean period after birth (Choudhury, 1903:500).

During *subodu* period both the Forest and the Village Rabha mothers observe almost similar restrictions as mentioned earlier.

On 5th or 7th day of the pollution period, the *subodu*

pareni or Final Purifiication among the Forest Rabhas is done. On this day the brother or any male relative of the woman belonging to her *husuk*, cuts a lock of hair from the head of the new-born and buries it within the lying-in-room. Then all male relatives and also the mother and the new born purify themselves by paring their nails and shaving (only by the male relatives) and then by taking bath. But no barber (*napit*) is employed by them for this purpose.

Among the Village Rabhas like the Rajbansis the pollution period ends with the *chhua kaman* (final purification) ceremony. A former 'first shaving' ceremony (*ek-kaman*) of course, is done on the 7th day of pollution when a barber (*napit*) cuts a lock of hair from the head of the new-born baby which the mother buries under some tree (plantain or jack fruit). The male members of the family inclusive of the father of the new-born baby, pass through some purifiicatory rites. No other rite takes place on that day. While the mother goes on observing the prohibitions of the unclean period till the day of the final consecration (*chhua-kaman* or *do-kaman*) ceremony, other members of the family including the father of the new-born, are exempted from observing the *chhuo* from the day of *ek-kaman* ceremony. They are then allowed to do their normal duties excepting the celebration of any social or religious ceremony in the house or attending such festivities.

On the day of 'Final Purification' ceremony (*chhua-kaman* or *do-kaman*) a barber performs the shaving ceremony. The Rajbansis also perform both *ek-kaman* and *do-kaman* or final purification in a similar way (Sanyal, 1965:67).

Sunder also mentions the *sudaparani* (*subodu pareni*) ceremony among the Rabhas. It is observed after the 7th day pollution when "a cock is killed by the *huzi* or priest inside the house in which child may be born and he repeats various *mantras* there to satisfy Rishi". (Sunder, 1895:74).

Among the Forest Rabhas, the *dhami* after taking *chakat* accompanies the family members and some other neighbours and goes to the *husuk-jampiri* (clan-altar) situated in the near-by forest to worship several deities and spirits such as, Jaga, Thakur, Metri, Pertani, Maitani, Kaltani, Birsali, Michikbai and others, with offerings and sacrifices.

When the worship is over, the mother with her new-born, comes to this place of worship where she is permitted to come only when the worship is over. The mother then takes a little of the food (*maye*) prepared with rice, vegetable and meat of sacrificed bird there and touches a little of it in the mouth of the new-born and then takes herself. The priest then blesses the child.

The *maye* and *chakat* are then distributed to all. This ends the *lengju* ceremony.

When the purification ceremony is over, the Village Rabhas call the *adhikari* for performing the *balaram pnja.* The *adhikari* after celebrating rhis *puja* near *tulsi mancha* by offering several articles to the deities, puts a mark of the mud of the Basil altar (*tulsi mancha*) on the forehead of the child (if the child is a male) or mark of the vermilion of the *puja* (in case of a female child) and blesses the child.

The *puja* ends with the distribution of *prasad* to the assembled persons.

NAME GIVING CEREMONY

The "Name -giving" or *mung tanniga* ceremony takes place the same day with *lengju* ceremony or one or two days after in case of the Forest Rabha section, while among the Village Rabhas, it takes place on the day of *chhua kaman* (i.e. 30th day of pollution) or a little later but in no case after three months. Sunder on the other hand, states that the name-giving ceremony among the Rabhas takes place one week after the birth along with the *sudaparni* ceremony (1895:74) while Friend-Pereira reports that among the Assam Rabhas it is held a fortnight or a month after the birth (1912:143).

In the afternoon, the *deosi*, after worshipping the Rungtuk and Basek with offerings, asks the assembled persons to select the name. The mother of the child finally selected one name from among those suggested. The *deosi* then holds a cock and ascribes the left leg of the cock in the name of the new-born and attributes the right leg to the name of the Rishi. He then cuts its head and holds the cock horizontally. If the right leg of the cock attributed to Rishi, gets up on the left leg symboliszed in the name of the new-born, then the name selected is very good and auspicious. If it is reverse, the name is considered to be ominous. It is rejected and a new name is selected, though in this case generally the result is not determined by such sacrifice.

When this name is thus given, the *deosi* under the *zerphak*, propitiates Rishi by some offerings and sometimes with the sacrifice of a fowl for Rishi's blessings to the new born child.

Among the Village Rabhas the burden of selecting a suitable name for the new born rests on the shoulder of the priest (Brahmin or *adhikari* as the case may be) who selects a name after consulting the *panji* (almanac) or some mythological book. There is yet another means of selecting a name. This was once prevalent among the Village Rabhas. Now only a few families observe it. This ritual is performed on a suitable day selected by the Brahmin or *adhikari* after consulting the *panji*, when the child's mother's father or mother's brother drops some rice within water contained in a pot while uttering the name to be selected.

> "If the rice floats, then this name is considered to be selected for the child. If it sinks down, another grain is taken, another name is selected and the same procedure is repeated. This process continues until a rice floats and a name for the child is selected (Das & Raha, 1967:102).

This method is surprisingly alike to what is found among the Oraons of Sunderban (southern part of West Bengal) (Das & Raha, 1963 : 164-165).

> "The name-giving ceremony does not take place in the month of *jaistha* (May-June), *vadra* (August-September), *pous* (December-January) and *chaitra* (March-April) and on the days like Friday and Saturday as these are considered inauspicious months and days (Das and Raha, 1967 : 103).

Likewise new-moon and full-moon days are also avoided. If this ceremony takes place during the above-mentioned days or months, the priest performs an expiatory rite before the ceremony.

When the ceremony is over in case of both the Forest and the Village Rabhas the assembled relatives and others are given a feast.

Sunder in connection with the name-giving ceremony of the Rabhas of Jalpaiguri district stated that the *huji* ascertained the name of the child by killing a cock and declared the name of the child he had selected (1895 : 74).

Sometimes the mother of the child selects the name and very curiously, she is often influenced in her choice of name by some incident in her own life (Friend-Pereira, 1912 : 143). McSwiney in the Census Report of Assam has described a peculiar way of giving the name of the Totla Rabhas of Assam.

> "On the fifth day, after performing the necessary purificat-ion ceremonies, a number of relations and kinsmen are called and a fowl is given to the kinsmen or *dewri*, who with the stem of a plantain leaf goes on striking the fowl uttering names in each stroke. The name which uttered with the stroke that kills the fowl, is given to the child" (1912 : 76).

FIRST FEEDING OF RICE CEREMONY

Among the Forest Rabhas the 'First feeding of rice' cere-mony is celebrated along with *lengju* or *maye noaya* ceremony on the fifth or seventh day of the pollution period.

The *mukhe-bhat* or *bhat-chhoa* (the first feeding of rice) ceremony among the Village Rabha, is not observed by all but by some comparatively well-to-do families. In their cases this ritual is observed when the child is 9 months old (for the male child) or 7 months old (for the female child). Among these people, this ritual is observed in the same way as among the Rajbansis (Sanyal, 1963 : 73). The significance of this cere-mony is to give cooked rice ceremonially to the new-born child for the first time. The father of the child arrange this ritual and some Brahmin or *adhikari* performs the *balaram puja* in the same way as is done in connection with the child birth. At the end of the *puja* the mother's brother of the child taking him (the child) on his lap, feeds him a little of the *payes* (rice boiled with sweet in milk). Throughout the feeding ceremony musical instruments are played. Lastly, a feast is given to the assembled relatives and villagers.

Some Village Rabhas think that the rice, being the staple food of the people, cannot be given to a new-born child unless it is first touched by the deity or deities. Once this *prasad*, which was offered to the deity, is taken by the child, it acquires the right of taking every kind of food (Das & Raha, 1967 : 104).

DORMITORY SYSTEM

The dormitory system is not universal among all the tribal people of the world. But it is found to exist among many of them. According to Peal (1893) this system was in existence from Bhutan to New Zealand and from the Marqesas to the Niger. Many tribes and other ethnic groups of India have dormitory for both sexes even in these days. In Eastern and north-eastern India, the Abors call their dormitory as the *mollsup*, the Garos, the *nokpants*, the Mikirs, the *terung* or *deka*, the Adis, the *moshup* or *rasheng*, the Kukis, the *zwalbak* and the Magas, the *morung*, etc. In Behar the Oraons have the *dhumkuria* or *jonkhorpa*, and the Birhors, the *gitiera*. Among the Juang of Orissa, there is the *darbar* or *majang* (Ghose & Basu, 1964). The Gonds of the Central India also have dormitory called *ghotul*. Among the Bhotias of Northern India the dormitory is known as the *rangbang*. Similarly the Uralis or Bette Kurumbas of South India have the dormitory known as the *chitalpere* or *chitalmane* for the bachelors and *bangiri* for the spinsters (Fürer-Haimendorf, 1950).

Like all these ethnic groups the bachelors' dormitory, known as *naksa* is found to exist among the Forest Rabhas of the district of Jalpaiguri only where the unmarried young boys pass their nights. But it is non-existent among their village dwelling brethren. Like the Andamanese, the Adis, the Birhors or the Uralis, the Forest Rabhas do not have any separate dormitory for the spinsters nor they have a mixed dormitory for both sexes like the *ghotul* of the Gonds. The early accounts on the Rabhas also fail to give any evidence of the existence of association for the unmarried girls. The aged informants too could not recollect the existence of the same from their memory. It is difficult to say why such institution for the spinsters is not present.

An early account of the district of Jalpaiguri gives the evidence that in the past the unmarried young Rabhas (males) used to remain in a covered platform called *tarao naksa* which was built on posts alongside the house (Sunders : 1895).

In the Forest Rabha society, when a boy is 10 or 12 years old, he receives the permission from his parents and the elders of the *bastee* to enter into the bachelors' dormitory, known as the *naksa*. He stays in this *naksa* so long he remains bachelor (*tarao*). After marriage, as he becomes the married person (*janang deda*) he loses his right as a member of the dormitory. Usually after marriage, a Rabha does not sleep in the *naksa* at night. At present the *naksa* is found in different forest *bastees* where a considerable number of the Rabhas live.

The *naksa* is a rectangular thatched one-roomed hut placed on a number of long wooden posts, a few feet above the ground. Three side of this room are covered. A ladder connects the room with the ground. The hut is mainly built by the members of the dormitory.

As stated previously, the Forest Rabha boys, at the age of 10 or 12 start living in the *naksa*. They assemble in the *naksa* after their night meal and spend the whole of the night in the dormitory. The married persons do not allow their unmarried young boys to sleep with them in their own family huts. The main reason for such a prohibition is that the bachelors are not allowed to see the sexual acts of the married family members. The Rabhas consider it a great sin on the part of an unmarried young boy to see the sexual activities of his parents or any close relatives. The same thing is present among the Murias also who consider it 'sinful for parents to sleep in the presence of their children'. 'As soon as a child understands what it (the sexual intercourse) is, we send it to the '*ghotul*', is the view of the Muria parents. (Elwin, 1968). Elwin believes that the fundamental reason for the *ghotul* is to prevent children from watching what Freud called 'the primal scene' (*op. cit.*). Mills noted the same feelings among the Rengma Nagas too (Mills, 1937). Shakespear suggests that the object of the dormitory is to prevent incest (Hodson, 1911). The other probable reason as present among the Rabhas is to keep them apart from the young unmarried girls at night. Though the last one has been stated as a reason by Sunders (1895), but often the bachelors can find out suitable opportunities to establish intimacy with the unmarried girls. This intimacy sometimes, lead to the premarital pregnancy, though it is true that the girls are not allowed to stay at night in the *naksa*. It is felt necessary that a girl should learn about the sex life as she attains her puberty. This is the reason why she is not debarred from staying with her parents or other married couple of the house at night.

Like the Garos (Burling, 1963) the bachelorhood is an exciting period in a Forest Rabha boy's life as from the day he sleeps in the *naksa* he becomes somewhat free from the discipline of his parents and other elders of the family.

No ceremony marks the transition when a boy enters into the dormitory for the first time and becomes a member. As he first enlists his name he becomes the junior member (*tarao-pumar*) while the members of the senior category are called *tarao-gada*. One of the elders of the village becomes the supervisor of the dormitory (*tarao-pare*) though he may be married. His duty is to keep watch over the members of the *naksa* so that they can lead a disciplined life and avoid doing any sinful act. But occasionally some daring boys slip the watchful eyes of the *tarao-pare* and meet their lady-love in the darkness of the night or in the shadows of the forests. Their colleagues keep an eye in every direction so that they are not caught. The girls similarly, if they like to, can escape from the eyes of their guardians. At the *naksa*, the senior boys' discussions revolve round the girls for quite a time. They do such misdeed daringly, though they know that they will be rebuked or fined if they are caught.

In the dormitory the boys keep a few of their personal belongings like beddings, musical instruments, weapons for hunting small games, etc. It is the training school for the boys wherefrom they learn the norms, values, etc. prescribed by the society.

When a community festival is celebrated in the village, they extend their helping hands under the guidance of the *tarao-pare*. When their co-operation is sought by individual family in connection with certain social or religious ceremonies held in the house, they render their co-operation in exchange of food and especially of *chakat* (rice-bear).

The *naksa* of the Forest Rabhas may be considered a seat of learning for social, economic and religious activities and co-operation. Likewise the aim of the Oraon dormitory (*dhumkuria* or *jonkherpa*) as summarized by Roy as having been in its time

> 'an effective economic organisation for purposes of food quest, a useful seminary for training youngmen in their social and their other duties, and an institution for magico-religious observances calculated to secure success in hunting and to augment the procreative power of the youngmen' (Roy, 1915).

Similarly, among the Konyak Nagas the *morung* is the 'centre of village's life and pillar of their social and political organisation'. (Fürer-Haimendorf, 1938).

The Rabha *naksa* is not a lineage-based one as found in the Garo society among whom the *nakpante* (bachelor's dormitory) is built for each dominant lineage of the village (Nakane, 1961).

But among the Forest Rabhas, one forest *bastee* consists of one *naksa* usually. Boys from different lineages stay there. Though the *naksa* played once a very important and significant role in the Rabha society, at present it is fast losing its hold as evidenced from the disappearance of this community dormitory and the formation of the same at the household level among the Forest Rabhas of some forest *bastees*, and the absolute non-existence of the same among the present-day Village Rabhas among whom this institution was once in existence.

The Crises of Life—II : Marriage

6

THE CRISES OF LIFE–II : MARRIAGE

Marital Conditions

Census of 1971 returns that out of total of 2,426 Rabhas of West Bengal majority (56.93%) have not been married. The Rabhas with married status held 36.50% of the total, The number of divorced or separated Rabhas in this State is only 6.20%. Somewhat same picture has been depicted by the Rabhas of the district of Jalpaiguri. Among them 54.52% are never married and 40.23% are married. The rest of 5.25% are either divorced or separated persons.

The present survey among 1,815 Rabhas of five settlements gives almost same idea about the marital status of the Rabhas (Table 12) of this total population surveyed the number of unmarried populace is larger (53.00 %) than that of the married persons (41.09%). The frequencies of widowed and divorced or deserted persons are very low. The frequency of both unmarried males and females is equally high. But the frequency of widows (7.39%) is much higher than that of widowers (0.53%).

The higher frequency of unmarried persons over the married is also met with in 'All Forest Bastees', 'All Villages' and all individual settlements except at Nalgarh *bastees* where the

TABLE 12

Marital Conditions of the Rabhas of Different Settlements

Settlements		Unmarried			Married		
		M	F	T	M	F	T
Purodha	No.	180	162	342	146	149	295
Bastee	%	54.38	48.21	51.27	44.11	44.35	44.23
Nalgarh	No.	71	54	125	59	63	122
Bastee	%	54.62	43.90	49.41	45.39	51.22	48.52
Kamala	No.	101	65	166	59	56	115
Bastee	%	61.58	48.87	55.89	35.98	42.11	38.73
All	No-	352	281	633	269	268	532
Forest	%	56.32	47.47	52.01	42.24	45.27	43.71
Bastees							
Madhya	No.	100	75	175	56	56	112
Manasi	%	62.89	50.69	57.00	35.22	37.84	36.48
Dakshin	No.	90	64	154	60	60	120
Manasi	%	59.60	47.71	52.92	39,74	42.86	41.24
All	No.	190	139	329	116	116	232
Villages	%	61.29	48.26	55.02	37.42	40.28	38.80
All	No.	542	429	962	380	384	764
Settlements	%	57.97	42.72	53.00	40.64	43.64	42.09

Settlements		Widowed M	Widowed F	Widowed T	Divorced Deserted M	Divorced Deserted F	Divorced Deserted T	Population M	Population F	Population T
Purodha	No	—	19	19	5	6	11	331	336	667
Bastee	%		5.65	2.85	1.51	1.79	1.65	100.00	100.00	100.00
Nalgarh	No.	—	5	5	—	1	1	130	123	253
Bastee	%		4.07	1.98		0.81	0.39	100.00	100.00	100,00
Kamala	No.	2	9	11	2	3	3	164	133	297
Bastee	%	1.22	6.77	3.70	1,22	2.26	1.68	100.00	100.00	99.99
All	No.	2	33	35	7	10	17	625	592	1217
Forest	%	0.32	5.57	2.87	1,12	1.69	1.40	100.00	100.00	99.99
Bastees										
Madhya	No.	2	16	18	1	1	2	159	148	307
Manasi	%	1.26	10.81	5.86	0.63	0.67	0.65	100.00	100.00	100.00
Dakshin	No.	1	16	17	—	—	—	151	140	291
Manasi	%	0.66	11.43	5.84	—	—	—	100.00	100.00	100.00
All	No.	3	32	35	1	1	2	310	288	598
Villages	%	0.97	11.11	5.85	0.32	0.35	0.33	100.00	100.00	100.00
All	No.	5	65	70	8	11	19	935	880	1815
Settlements	%	0.53	7.39	386	0.86	1.25	1.05	100.00	100.00	100.0 0

number of married females (51.22%) is higher over that of the unmarried females (43.90%).

Another point to be noted here is that in all the settlements the frequency of unmarried males is comparatively higher than that of the unmarried females. As regards to the proportion of married males and females, it is seen from Table 12 that except in Kamala *bastee*, the married females are proportionately higher in number than the married males at Purodha and Nalgarh *bastee*. At the two villages, the proportion is equal.

Regarding the frequency of the widowed persons, it may be said that at Purodha and Nalgarh *bastees* there is not a single widower. But in all other settlements the widows dominate over the widowers by higher number. Further, in comparison with the Forest *bastee*, the number of widowed persons particularly the widows, is much higher in the villages.

It is also important to mention here that though in general, the frequency of the divorced or deserted persons is very low in all settlements, still the said frequency is much higher in the forest *bastees* than in the villages. That is to say that the case of divorce or desertion is much less among the Village Rabhas.

Among the Rabhas in general, seldom a grown-up boy or a girl is found to remain unmarried throughout his/her life. Like the Garos (Burling, 1963 : 75) no boy and certainly no girl, has any desire to remain single throughout life. Particularly among the Forest Rabhas even most of the widowed people are anxious to remarry. Only mentally and physically handicapped, and those who show definite signs of evil in their body and behaviour, cannot marry. The same was true in the past (Sunder, 1895 : 74).

Endogamy

The rule of endogamy was rigidly followed by the Rabhas in the past. They were not allowed to marry the non-Rabhas. This rule is still strictly followed by the Forest Rabhas. In all the three forest *bastees* there were two cases of marriage with the non-Rabhas ; at Purodha a Rabha married a Mech woman and at Kamala some Gajo Kantran married a Rajbansi boy, Haren Kaswap. But in the case of the Village Rabhas this rule has much been relaxed these days. Several eases of marriage with the non-Rabhas, particularly with the Rajbansis, can be noticed among them. The Rabhas consider such marriages as prestigious. Marriage between a Rajbansi boy and a Rabha girl is quite frequent, but the reverse i.e., marriage of a Rajbansi girl with a Rabha boy, is not so common. Only a single case was found in Dakshin Manasi where some Paran Uni-Brahman, a Rabha married a Rajbansi girl, Sumati Kaswap. Cases of marriage with different other Hindu castes, the Nepali, and the Mech are also found in the villages.

In a good number of cases Rajbansi boys have been found to have married Rabha girls. At Madhya Manasi a Saha from Bihar has married a Rabha girl. Rabha girl, at Dakshin Manasi was married to a Goala (milkmen). Similarly, in a few cases Rabha girls were found to have married to the Mech boys. While in the forest *bastees* there is only one case of the breach of tribal endogamy in the villages there is at least 10 cases (8.62%) where the same rule has been violated (Table 13). In all these cases the non-Rabha brides or grooms, as the case may be, live in the Rabha society. The marriage with the Assam Rabhas is not very frequent, and in most of the cases these are with the Koch Rabhas.

In West Bengal no bar is found in the marriage between the two ecological groups, the Forest Rabhas and the Village Rabhas. Some such marriages have indeed, taken place. But they prefer marrying in their respective ecological group. This is probably because of cultural difference between these two ecological groups. In connection with the Rabha-non-Rabha marriages Friend-Pereira found the Rabha of Assam marrying the Garos, the Kacharis and the Rajbansis also; but in these cases, the 'woman sinking to the level of her husband and a man rising to the position of his wife' (Friend-Pereira, 1912 : 142). But the other view is that a Rabha can marry a Kachari girl, but a Kachari boy usually does not like to marry a Rabha girl (Gait, 1872 : 232 ; Baines, 1912 : 129). But Endle opines that a Rabha can marry a Kachari (1911 : 84).

TABLE 13

Distribution of the Endogamous and Exogamous Marriages Among the Rabhas of Different Settlements

Bastee Village	Total Marr-iages	Marriage within Same Husuk		Marriage within Different Husuk Group		Same ethnic Group		Different Ethnic Group		Identity of the Ethnic Groups*
		No.	%	No.	%	No.	%	No.	+	
1	2	3	4	5	6	7	8	9	10	11
Purodha Bastee	147	—	—	147	100.00	147	100.00			
Nalgarh Bastee	63	—	—	63	100.00	63	100.00			
Kamala Bastee	59	—	—	59	100.00	58	98.30	1	1.70	Rajbansi—1
All Forest Bastees	269	—	—	269	100.00	268	99.63	1	0.37	Rajbansi—1
Madhya Manasi	56	1	1.79	55	98.21	50	89.29	6	10.71	Rajbansi—5 Saha—1
Dakshin	60	1	1.67	59	98.33	56	93.33	4	6.67	Rajbansi—3

Manasi									Goala—1
All	116	2	1.72	114	98.28	106	91.38	10	8.62	Rajbansi—8
Villages									Saha—1
									Goala—1
All	385	2	0.52	383	99.48	374	97.14	11	2.86	Rajbansi—9
Settlements									Saha—1
									Goala—1

*Inclusive of the marriages with different gotra (for marriages with different communities).

Exogamy

The Rabhas in general follow the rule of *husuk* exogamy in utmost rigidity which has been discussed in details in the chapter on 'Husuk Organisation'. A Rabha cannot marry within his own *husuk*, within *saru husuk* or *neoya husuk*, the breach of which specially that of *husuk* exogamy, is considered as a very scornful act. Early authors also marked the clan exogamy among them (Friend-Pereira, 1912 : 142 ; Sunder, 1895 : 72.7 ; Costa : 1054 : 1050 ; Burling : 1963 : 22-23).

As among the Garos (Costa, 1954:1050; Burling,1967:22-33) the Khasis (Playfair, 109:66-67; Gurdon, 1914:65; Nakane, 1961:119), and the Koches (Majumdar, 1967:66-67) among the Rabhas also, such a marriage 'is considered as worst kind of sin...... worse than homicide.' But no such restriction was noticed among the Rajbansis as they have only one *gotra*, Kaswap (Sanyal, 1966:89-90).

A survey of 386 Rabha marriages in five settlements (three forest *bastees* and two villages) show (Table 13) that while the Rabhas of the three forest *bastees* have not broken the rule of *husuk* exogamy their compatriots of the two villages have broken the same at least in two cases (1.72%), one for each village. In only one case among the Forest Rabhas (at Ramala *bastee*) a Rabha woman has married a Rajbansi. Among the Rabhas of the two villages in as many as 10 cases (8.62%) marriages have taken place with the people of other ethnic groups (e. g. the Rajbansi, the Saha and the Goals). That means while the Forest Rabhas still favour marriage within the community and outside own *husuk*, the Village Rabhas have a tendency to amend these rules.

The village Rabhas are in many cases found to prevent marriage with any members of the three ascending generations from both father's and mother's side. But they do not entirely go by the rules of *sapinda* exogamy i.e., prohibiting marriage with a woman who is a *sapinda* (literary, connected by having in common particles of the body) (Mayne, 1953:47). This rule excludes marriage between ego and his (or her) own agnate (i.e. father's) of six ascending generations, and his (or her) mother's agnates of four ascending generations." (Madan, 1965:105; Kapadia, 1947; Chap-II & VIII, Karandikar, 1929 -

Chap-IX and X). They do not follow this rule not because they cannot remember the names and exact relation of the members of all these ascending generations, but because they do not fully understand the concept of *sapinea* and other Hindu marriage rules. The Forest Rabhas often show their reluctance in this regard.

MONOGAMY AND POLYGYNY

Among these people of Purodha, Nalgarh and Kamala *bastees* there are 295, 122 and 115 married persons respectively (Table 12). Except a few cases, all have gone through monogamous marriage. Similarly, among the Rabhas of Madhya and Dakshin Manasi out of the total of 112 and 120 married Rabhas respectively all have gone through singular marriage. Though the Rabhas in general prefer monogamy, still there is no bar in this society of Jalpaiguri for polygyny, i.e. 'marriage of one man to two or more wives at a time' (Murdock, 1949 : 24 ; Rivers, 1932 : 42). But the cases of the plural marriage are extremely rare. "Polygyny is not most people's means and therefore is infrequent in practice" (Ameer Ali, 1935:229). Among the Rabhas both sororal and non-sororal polygyny are found to exist. Though in the two villages studied, there is no case of sororal polygyny, but a few of such cases are found in the neighbouring villages.

At both Purodha and Kamala *bastees* the *mondols* (Headman) have polygynous marriage, and in general, the *mondols* of the forest *bastees* are comparatively well off and can afford to go in for plural marriage. Usually the wealthy and or person with high status, are found to practise polygyny among the Rabhas.

Quoting Buchanon-Hamilton, Martin states, "A Rabha can marry as far as seven wives; it is rare, however that a Rabha ventures upon more than one wife at a time" (1838: 549). Sunder also observes that a Rabha of the district of Jalpaiguri can have more than one wife, but very few have more thon one. He says that the plural marriage has complication as different wives have different deities (1195 :73). (The youngest daughter usually inherits the family deity after the death of the mother). According to Friend-Pareira, the Rabhas of Assam rarely indulge in polygyny. It is allowed only when the first wife is childless or incapable of attending to household duties (1812:143). Endle also holds similar view (1911:85).

It is difficult to say how far the 'strong stability of women and the fluid nature of men in terms of residence' which explains the existence of polygyny among the Garos (Nakane, 1961:137), holds good in the Rabha society as well. Among the Village Rabhas the stability of women is not strong and in terms of residence the male folk are quite stable. Yet polygyny is in vogue.

Regarding the existence of polygyny among the matrilineal societies, various opinions are found. Ehrenfels classified the Garo and the Lyngngam polygyny as the East Asain type, with its characteristic of alloting different legal position, status and function to the first and second, or subsequent wives of the same husband (1955 : 312-313), yet he echoes Gurdon's view that polygyny 'would naturally not be in vogue amongst the people who observe the matriarchate as the Khasis do not have polygyny' (Gurdon, 1914 : 77). His view is that the Garo and the Lyngngam polygyny 'is a residue of the patrilineal past of these two communities' (Ehrenfels, 1955 : 319). He, however, remarks in connection with the Lyngngam polygyny that 'a condition of polygyny among the Lyngam makes it appear more integrated into the Lyngngam matrilineal, and frequently uxorilocal marriage system' (*op. cit.* 313). Gough holds the view that both sororal and non-sororal polygyny are rarely practised by the matrilocally resident husbands in matrilineal societies. (1962 : 622-623).

It is difficult to say when, how and from whom the Rabhas adopted polygyny and what was their social system at that time. But it may be said that 'at some remote period of time the matriarchate was in full vigour' among them (Friend-Pereira, 1912 : 142), and polygyny was also practised since long as would appear from a few genealogies. It is likely that the Rabhas might have borrowed this cultural trait from the Rajbansis who are practising polygyny since time immemorial (Sanyal, 1965 : 69).

Position of the First wife

Among both the Forest and the Village Rabhas if the first wife is barren or suffering from an incurable disease, he (the husband) can marry for the second time. As among the Garo and the Lyngngam, among the the Rabhas too, "before taking a second wife, it is customary for a man to obtain the permission from the first and a breach of this rule entitles her to compensation" (Playfair, 1909 : 69 ; Ehrenfels, 1955 : 313). Whenever a Rabha wants to marry for the second time during the life time of his first wife, he takes consent of the first wife, and also of her relatives formally. The wife usually gives consent. After marriage the position and status of the first wife remains unaltered. She still holds the position of the female head of the family and maintains her seniority. But it is also not true in case of the Rabhas, that "a man will not have sexual relations with the *jiugite* (the younger wife) *until* the older wife specifically permits him to do so..." as among the Garos (Burling, 1963 : 149).

Sororate and Levirate

Both the Forest and the Village Rabhas do not disregard the marriage with the wife's younger sister, though the frequency of this type is very low. But marriage with wife's elder sister receives no social approval in both groups. Unlike the Garos (Burling, 1963a : 141 ; Playfair; 1909 : 68, 69 ; Costa, 1954 : 1050), the parents of the wife or her lineage groups among the Rabhas do not take responsibility of supplying a second consort if the first wife dies. As a result the number of sororate type of marriages is very rare among them. In the event of either of the couple dying, the perpetuation of the two contracting households or lineages (the husband belongs to one lineage while the wife and the children to another like the Garos) (Burling, 1963a : 141 ; Costa, 1954 : 1050), is not maintained. At the time of remarriage a Rabha (except husband of the heiress) enjoys more freedom than a Garo (Playfair, 1909 : 68-69 ; Costa, 1954 : 1050) as he or she does not require to take permission from the members of the deceased consort's family or the lineage' in case of the death of the heiress, her husband (i.e. heir) seeks the permission for remarriage, as it is connected with the property and rule of inheritance and succession.

Like sororate, levirate is also extremely rare among the Rabhas. They approve the marriage with deceased elder brother's widow only. But marriage with deceased younger brother's wife is strictly prohibited. Among the Forest Rabhas very few cases of the levirate marriage are found, while among the Village Rabhas, no such case is met with. Though there is no bar, still they do not favour this type of marriage. Among the Rabhas of Assam, too, though 'a widow may marry her husband's younger brother (she cannot marry her husband's elder brother), but she is not expected to do it' (Friend-Pereira 1912 : 143). Endle also reports the ban on the marriage with deceased husband's elder brother in the Rabha society of Assam (1911 : 85). The extreme paucity of the levirate type of marriage among the Rabhas reminds Kunstadter's view. If put in a reverse way, it states 'Levirate would not exist in a society in which the matrifocal family was strongly enforced ; (Kunstader, 1963 : 58). Levirate is also not found among the matrilineal tribes like Khasi (Gurdon, 1914 : 78; Nakane, 1961 : 119 ; Chattopadhyay, 1941 : 21-24, 33-39). The reasons behind the practice of levirate may be that 'the widow is a valuable property for whom bride-price has been paid and she should not be allowed to go out of the family' (O'Malley, 1912 : 322 ; O'Malley : 1934 : 150).

Cousin Marriage

Like other types, the cousin marriage is also not common among the Rabhas. Of the two types of cousin marriages, cross-cousin marriage is present among the Forest Rabhas, but it is rare. Cross-cousin is not a preferential mate unlike the Garos (Playfair, 1909 : 68 ; Bose, 1941 : 87, Burling, 1958a : 746-747; Burling, 1958b : 115-116, Nakane, 1958 : 8; Raha, 1966:30-31. The other type, the parallel cousin marriage is altogether absent. Among the Village Rabhas, like the Rajbansis (Sanyal, 1965:99) both cross-cousin and parallel cousin marriages are forbidden. That cousin marriage was present among the Rabhas of the district of Jalpaiguri in old days, is evidenced from an early account which states that a man could marry his mother's brother's daughter, but could not marry his father's brother's daughter, (Sunder, 1895 : 73). Friend-Pereira also observes that among the Rabhas of Assam a man may marry his father's sister's daughter or mother's brother's daughter (1912 : 142). When a man has no son but only a daughter, he adopts his sister's son to whom he gives his daughter in marriage (*op. cit.*)

Marriage by Service :

Marriage by service is somewhat common among the poorer section of the Rabhas as among the Rabhas of Assam (Friend-Pereira, 1912 : 112).

> "Sometimes a poor Rabha who cannot afford to pay the bride-price, (and also marriage expenses), serves a rich Rabha in his field and also does various household works for a period varying from six months to two years. At the end of this period of service (sometimes even before the completion of the period of service), he marries the daughter of his master. In this case the master remains responsible for giving his daughter to this man in exchange of his service. This man thereafter stays with his father-in-law, and in rare cases, returns to his parents. He sometimes, builds a new house for his own family and shifts there" (Das & Raha, 1967 : 104-105).

Among the Village Rabhas this marriage is known as *gharjai* marriage (*ghar*=household, *jai*=son-in-law) as among the Rajbans is (Mukherjee, 1963 : 68-69).

Marriage by Exchange

Marriage by exchange is not very common, nor it is altogether unknown to the Village and the Forest Rabhas. In some cases it is seen that when two men have a son and a daughter each, they exchange them for marriage. One takes the son of the other for his daughter, and gives his son to other's daughter. This is mutual exchange. No bride or bride-groom price is involved in such cases. Besides, it is also seen two brothers marrying two females who are sisters. This is also found among the Garos (Mukherjee, 1956 : 49 ; Raha, 1966 : 31) and the local Rajbansis.

Marriage by Force

Among tne Forest Rabhas marriage by force or *jeksangi* type takes place when a girl falls in love with a boy to whom she cannot express hcr feelings or if he does not pay any interest in this matter. She tells every thing to her mother and expresses her desire to marry the boy. The mother of the girl consults her husband and some other relatives secretly. One day they bring the boy at their house from the *nasksa* (bachelors' dormitory) whcn he goes there at night or from any other place either by force or by tempting him. When the boy comes to the house of the girl, parents and other relatives of the girl tell him the whole story keeping the girl before him and give him a new napkin gamchha and *pan—gua* (betel and arecanut). The boy then understands everything, and if he selects the girl and agrees to their proposal, he accepts the napkin containing *pan—gua*. Then he confides this to his friends and hides the napkin and *nap—gua* somewhere in house. Next morning when his parents find these, they understand the whole thing and enquire about everything from the boy. If they agree to the proposal, they negotiate the matter with the parents of the girl. The ceremony in case of the *jekesangi* marriage, is done in a similar way as is done in the marriage by negotiation. But if they (parents of girl) fail to convince the boy, they further proceed with the negotiation with the boy's parents. It is sometimes seen that due to marriage with an unwilling boy, the marriage ends in a bitter situation, or the married life ends with a divorce or the boy deserts the girl sometimes after matriage.

This type of marriage is not in vogue among the Village Rabhas nor amog the Rajbansis, though love affairs take place among the youth. Among the Garos somewhat similar type of marriage is present (Playfair, 1909 : 67-68 ; Burling, 1963a : 83-93).

Age At First Marriage

The Rabhas do not prefer child marriage. Rather adult marriage is the rule. Usually the malefolk marry at the age between 25 to 34 while the females, between 15 to 24. It is further seen that the Village Rabhas marry earlier than the Forest Rabhas do. At the end of the last century, Sunder found the Rabhas in Jalpaiguri district marrying at the time of puberty (Sunder, 1895 : 73). While even earlier, they used to marry at the age of twelve or thirteen (Buchanon-Hamilton, 1810 ; Martin, 1838 : 348).

From an account of the three Forest *bastees* surveyed it is seen that 85.43% of the males with married status (married, widowed or divorced) are found to get married within the age-group of 25 to 34. None of the males is found to have married beyond the age of 34 or below the age of 15. In case of females in these forest-clad habitats 91.30% have married in the age group of 15 to 24 but none of the fair sex has married at the age below 10 or above 24.

But among the village dwelling Rabhas of the three villages majority (84.21%) of the males with married status (married, widowed or divorced) have preferred 20 to 29 age group for their marriage. But no male has married at the age below 15 or above 34. Females with married status in these villages on the other hand, have chosen comparatively lower ages for marriage. 73.24% of them have considered the age-group of 10 to 19 as the most suitable one. No female is found to have married at an age below 10 or above 29.

It is interesting to point out here that among the Forest Rabhas older generations are found to have married in a comparatively higher age groups than the younger generations who have married at a comparatively tender ages. Identical is the situation in case of the village Rabhas.

Further a comparison of the age at first marriage between the Forest and the Village Rabhas proves that the Village Rabhas have married at a comparatively early age than their congeners living in the forest *bastees*.

The tendency of early marriage among many village Rabhas was probably due to the influence of local Hindu castes particularly the Rajbansis, the marriageable age among whom is between 13 to 28 for the boys and between 7 to 10 for the girls (Mukherjee, 1963:69). They did not have infant marriage in the past. Later on, probably due to the impact of the caste Hindus, marriage in the tender ages was introduced (Risley, 1891 ; I:497—498 ; Sanyal, 1965:90). Friend—Pereira also observes that among the Rabhas of Assam, a tendency of adopting the infant marriage is probably an imitation of the Hindu customs (1912 : 143). Others have advocated adult marriage among them (Allen, 1903 : 50; Endle, 1911 : 85; Das, 1958 : 78) .

Besides their long and close contact with the Rajbansis, the Rabhas have come in contact with many other Hindu castes, such as the Namasundra, the Jugi, the Malo, the Saha and others. Among them marriage at a lower age is the prevailing custom.

Time of Marriage

The Forest Rabhas prefer to give their children in marriage after harvest in the months of *pous* (Dec—Jan), *magh* (Jan—Feb) and *palgun* (Feb—March). There is however, no restriction in any month. Marriage may take place at any time in any day except the day of new moon. Usually the rainy season is avoided. They favour post—harvest period because their economic condition remains comparatively better in these months.

Among the Village Rabhas, like the Garos (Playfair, 1909 : 69) there is no system of bride—price or bride—groom price. This system also did not exist in the past. Among the Village Rabhas there are some cases where bride—price was paid. Buchanon—Hamilton (1810) and Martin (1838:549) observed the absence of bride—price among the Rabhas of their time. But both Endle (1911) and Friend-Pereira (1912:142) found this to be prevalent among the Assam Rabhas. Among the Village Rabhas at present widower in some cases has to give some marriage payment when he marries for the second time. "When a widower or a divorced person marries a widow or a divorced woman, he may pay a bride—price varying from Rs. 20/—to Rs. 60/—" (Das & Raha, 1967:105). But if he marries an unmarried girl, the amount of bride-price becomes higher. The go—between usually settles the actual amount of *gao—dhan* (bride—price) to be paid by the bride-groom after consulting both parties.

In Madhya Manasi out of a total of 56 surviving married couples in 19 cases (33.93%) bride—price had been given and the amount paid as bride—price varied from Rs. 40.00 to Rs. 200.00.

In Dakshin Manasi only in 14 cases (23.33%) out of 60, bride—price had been given, the amount of which varied from Rs.30/— to Rs.150/—. No one paid more than Rs 150/—as *gao—dhan.*

Though many Village Rabhas do not favour taking bride-price yet the practice exists. It is important to mention here that among the Rabhas villages, this system of taking bride-price is of recent introduction. There is not enough evidence to suggest that this practice existed in the past. It was possibly introduced in their society in the wake of influence of the Rajbansis among whom bride-price is still prevalent, and the amount of this price varies from Rs. 50/-to Rs. 1,000/- in different areas. (Sanyal, 1965:90). Even in the bygone days this was present among the Rajbansis. Sunder mentions the amount varying from Rs. 40/- to Rs. 120/- in his time (1895:51) and Sanyal points out that it was from Rs. 40/- to Rs. 50/- in Cooch Behar in 1911 (Sanyal : *op. cit.*).

> The idea that transaction of bride price is considered as "a means of stabilizing the marriage, as the hall-mark which testifies that the union has been consummated under condition approved by society and as the criterion of the legitimacy of the children of the marriage" (Mandelbaum, 1948:98)

has not been widely shared, by the members of this community.

In recent years some enlightened young Village Rabhas have started thinking of accepting dowry or bride-groom price from the father of the bride. This idea of taking dowry has possibly infiltrated in the Village Rabha society from the high caste Hindu (Bengalee) people living around them who have such system (Gangopadhaya, 1964:88-100). Now-a-days instead of giving bride-price, the young Village Rabha boys are demanding from their would be father-in-law, the object of their choice, some fancy or useful goods such as cycle, radio, wrist watch etc. The same tendency is also found among the Rajbansis (Sanyal, 1965 : 91).

Place of Premarital Residence

It is the usual practice of the Forest Rabhas to marry in the same Forest *bastee.* In Purodha as seen from the Table 14 61.90% couple had pre-marital residence in the same *bastee* i.e. husband and wife are inhabitants of the Purodha *bastee.* Similar condition prevails in the other forest *bastees* also. In Nalgarh 49.78% and in Kamala *bastee* 53.72% of the married persons preferred their spouse from their respective *bastee.* But even in forest *bastees* cases where either of the married couple came from different forest *bastees*/villages, are quite high. At Purodha the strength of such cases is 41.48%.

Something different is noticed among the Village Rabhas. Here though a good number of couples (23.21%) have pre-marital residence in the same village but in the majority of the cases, either member of the couples had different villages as their residence prior to marriage. The last condition is found in 60.72% of the couples of Madhya Manasi (Table 14) and 61.25% of Dakshin Manasi.

It is interesting to notice that among the Forest Rabhas of Purodha, a considerable number of couples (9.52%) has either of the partners from some village, and in a few cases both partners had pre-marital residence in village, and later on they settled at Purodha *bastee.* Similar interesting feature is found in a village (Madhya Manasi) too, where in 7.14% of the cases either of the surviving members of the couple is a Forest Rabha i. e. either of the partners had pre-marital residence in the forest *bastee.*

Place of Marriage

It was usual among the Rabhas to hold the marriage ceremony in the house of the wife's parents. The same was the condition as early as 1895 (Sunder, 1895 : 73). But in Assam the Rabha girl was usually brought to the house of the groom and the wedding took place there (Friend-Pereira, 1912 : 143). The same condition also prevails among the Rabhas of West Bengal of the present day.

TABLE 14

Places of Pre-marital Residence of the Rabha Husband and Wife

Sl. No.	PURODHA BASTEE Places of Pre-marital Residence	No.	%	MADHYA MANASI Places of Pre-marital Residence	No.	%
1	2	3	4	5	6	7
1.	Husband and wife-both of the same Forest *bastees*.*	91	61.90	Husband and wife-both of the same village.**	13	23.21
2.	Husband of the same Forest *bastee* and wife of different Forest *bastee*.	14	9.52	Husband of the village and wife of the different village	24	42.86
3.	Husband of the same Forest *bastee* and wife from village	7	13.60	Husband of the same village and wife of Forest *bastee*	2	3.75
4.	Wife of the same Forest *bastee* and husband of different Forest *bastee*.	20	13.60	Wife of the same village and husband of different village	10	17.86
5.	Wife of the same Forest *bastee* and husband from village	7	4.76	Wife of the same village and husband of Forest *bastee*	2	3.57
6.	Husband and wife-both from Forest *bastee*	3	2.04	Husband and wife-both of different village	5	8.93
7.	Husband and wife-both from villages	5	3.40			
	TOTAL	147	100.00		56	100.00

* Same Forest *bastee* means Purodha Forest *bastee*.

** Same village means Madhya Manasi.

Among the present day Forest Rabhas marriage takes place usually in the house of the bride as is the case with the Garos (Burling, 1963a : 213). Similar is the case with the Village Rabhas. In olden days wealthy Village Rabhas used to bring the girl in their own house and marriage used to take place there. This was connected with higher social prestige.

Some comparatively well-to-do Rabhas of the village still prefer to have their son's marriage in their house by bringing the bride in their respective house. O'Malley also advocates for the said custom among the Rajbansis (1912 : 327). Recent studies among the Rajbansis of Jalpaiguri district shows that the marriage takes place either in the boy's or girl's father's (Sanyal, 1965 : 101, 107 & 108 ; Mukherjee, 1963 : 68) house.

However frequency of different places where Rabha marriages have taken place in Rabha settlements studied, is given below :

TABLE 15

Distribution of the Places of Marriage

Sl. No.	Place of Marriage (in the house of)	Purodha Bastee No.	Purodha Bastee %	Madhya Manasi No.	Madhya Manasi %
1	2	3	4	5	6
1.	Husband	2	2.02	1	1.70
2.	Husband's elder brother	—	—	2	3.57
3.	Husband's parents	7	7.07	10	17.86
4.	Husband's mother's Brother	2	2.02	6	10.71
5.	Wife's elder sister	7	7.07	1	1.79
6.	Wife's brother	—	—	7	12.49
7.	Wife's Parents	60	60.61	27	48.21
8.	Wife's mother's brother	10	10.10	1	1.79
9.	Wife's Mother's sister	5	5.05	—	—
10.	Wife's mother's mother	2	2.02	—	—
11.	Wife's other maternal relations	4	4.04	1	1.79
	Total	99	100.00	56	100.00

From Table 15 it is evident that in Purodha *bastee* the maximum numbcr of marriages (60.61%) have taken place in the house of the wife's parents. The next higher frequency (10.10%) goes to the house of the wife's mother's brother. In the majority of the cases, marriages have taken place in the house of the wife's relatives (88.89%).

Among the Rabhas of Madhya Manasi the most frequent place of marriage is the house of the wife's parents (48.21%). Unlike the Rabhas of Purodha, the next most frequent place (17.88%) is the house of husband's parents. The house of relatives is preferred to by the majority (66.07%), still the house of the husband's relatives is no less important.

Residence

Varied types of post marital residence are found among the Rabhas of West Bengal. Among them, like Garos (Burling, 1963: 212) there is a clear difference between the viilage residence and household residence. If

> "a boy moves to his wife's village at his marriage but sets up a new household with hcr there, such a residence is uxorilocal with respect to the village but neolocal with respect to the household" (*op. cit.*).

In regard to the village residence, the married couple may be grouped into four categories (i) 'Foreign' (The word 'Foreign' indicates here that person, man or woman, comes from other forest *bastees* or villages and not a local people) man marries 'Local' women (The 'Local' indicates that the person concerned, man or woman, is the inhabitant of the same forest *bastee* or village i.e. Purodha *bastee* or Madhya Manasi village), (ii) 'Foreign man marries 'Foreign' woman (iii) 'Local' man marries 'Foreign' woman, (iv) 'Local man marries 'Local' woman. All of them settled locally i.e. in the same forest *bastee* or village as the case may be.

In Table 16 the residence of the married Rabha couples of both Purodha *bastee* and Madhya Manasi village in respect of the above categories, has been discussed.

TABLE 16

Residence of the Rabha Married Couples

Sl. No.	Nature of Village Residence	Purodha No.	bastee %	Madhya No.	Manasi %
1	2	3	4	5	6
1.	'Foreign' man married Local woman	27	18.37	12	21.43
2.	'Foreign' man marries 'Foreign' woman	8	5.44	5	8.93
3.	Local man marries 'Foreign' woman	21	14.29	26	46.43
4.	Local man marries local woman	91	61.90	13	23.21
	TOTAL	147	100.00	56	100.00

From Table 16 it is apparent that in the majority of the cases among the Forest Rabhas of Purodha (61.90%) *bastee* endogamy has been preferred by the couples as both husband and the wife are of tne same *bastee* (Purodha). In this case the residence is unilocal (Murdock, 1949 : 74-75). This clearly shows that the Forest Rabhas like to give in marriage their children in their own settlement instead of sending them outside. The next higher frequency goes to the category where the 'Foreign' marries the 'Local' girl and settled in the same settlement with the girl (18.37%). The Rabhas from different settlements have married girls of Purodha *bastee* and settled in Purodha. In this case the village residence is uxorilocal (Adam, 1947 : 678). The village residence is virilocal (*op. cit.*) in 14.29% cases, and in these cases the 'Local' marries the 'Foreign' girl (i.e. girl of the other settlement) and lives in his own settlement with his wife. The neolocal village residence i.e. where both husband and wife are 'Foreign' and living in Purodh *bastee*, is fewer in number.

Among the Rabhas of Madhya Manasi (Table 16) the village residence pattern is quite different. Here the frequency of the virilocal village residence is the highest (46.43%). Then of course, comes the cases where both husband and wife are of the same village i.e. village Madhya Manasi. The uxorilocal village rresidence however, has a significant (21.43%). The number of the neolocal village residence is not high.

The Forest Rabha girls make their first choice from among their own *bastee* males as also found by Majumdar (1967 : 68). Among the Garos, though Burling's (1963a : 113-116) findings among the latter goes to the 'Foreign' males married by the 'Local' girls which gets next preference among the Forest Rabhas. That is, while unilocal and uxorilocal village residences are given first and second preferences respectively, the Forest Rabhas, the Village Rabhas have virilocal and unilocal village residences as their first and second choices.

The household residence among the Rabhas have some peculiarities. In this regard the Forest Rabhas differ from the Village Rabhas. Among the Forest Rabhas it is a general custom that after marriage the husband goes to the house of the wife and lives with her family members. But exactly the husband does not live in his wife's house immediately after marriage. After marriage the husband lives for a certain period in the house of his mother while his wife is with her mother (duolocal residence). Gough describes duolocal residence when spouses live separately in their natal units with the husband visiting the wife (1962a : 335; 1962b : 548, 556, 561). This period of separation among the Forest Rabha extends up to the birth of at least one child, when the husband moves to his wife's house and lives with the wife, children and members of his wife's matrilineage permanently or temporarily. During the period of separation the husband visits his wife frequently at nights.

In case of the heiress the husband lives permanently with his wife and her matri-kins (uxorilocal residence) while in case of the non-heiress, he may live for a period (usually a year or two) with his wife's matri-kins after the birth of the first or second child (uxorilocal residence), and then establishes a separate household (neolocal residence). Sometimes of course, instead of having an intermediate uxorilocal residence, they directly set up their neolocal residence after the issue.

When the husband (when the marriage within the same vlllage takes place) lives at a short distance from the wif'es house, he usually visits his wife's house in almost every night and returns to his own house the next morning, i.e. he keeps close touch with his own and his wife's matri-kins. But if the distance is far as in case of two distant forest *bastees*, the husband devotes his time even in the day time for some consecutive days to work for his wife's matri-kins. This is to ensure his labour to be rendered for his wife's family. In this case the residence pattern suddenly changes into uxorilocal type for a short period within the length of duolocal one. So, it is interesting to have such a changing system of duo-uxorilocal residence in the uxorilocal family type. On the other hand, when the husband lives uxorilocally, he sometimes visits his own natal house and stays there for a few days if the distance between the houses is great or returns in the day if his natal house is nearby.

> "In societies with either matrilocal grand families or matrilocal extended families, the residential habits of men tend to approach something akin to duolocal residence if the population density permits this. Where husband's and wife's natal units are far apart, as sometime among the Bemba and Navaho, the matrilocally resident husband necessarily has to make his major commitment to his wife's units when, however, husband's and wife's units are within easy walking distance as is usual among the Hopi, many Trukese, some Mappilas, and many Yao husbands are likely to drift home often on visits their matrilineal kin." (Gough, 1962a : 559)

Sometime it is also seen that when the wife's matri-kins, mainly her parents among the Forest Rabhas, are old and have no son or any male member, they request the parents of their daughter's husband to relieve latter and permit him to stay with them (wife's parents) or sometime make condition for the same at the time of marriage. In this case the man soon after marriage, starts living with his wife and her parents and other matri-kins thus forming an immediate uxorilocal household residence as among the Khasis (Nakane, 1961 : 122-123), without having an intermediate residence. Of course, now-a-days the type of visiting husband, which once existed, is not usually found in the Khasi society (op. cit. 1967:83-88). The males among both the Pnar (Gurdon, 1914:79 ; Banerjee, 1963:165; 1964 : 107-110) and the Chetlat islanders (Roy Burman, 1967:1) stay in the places of their mother, but visit wives in the night time. But in their case the husbands permanently live in their mother's house, and as such, both parents and children are rarely found to live in the same household. Among the Nayars also "a husband visitcd his wife after supper and left before breakfast next morning" (Gough, 1959:26). The difference between the residence pattern of the Chatlat islanders and the Syntengs or the Pnars is that among the Chatlat islanders or the Pnars or the Syntengs the husband in rare cases, forms a co-residence units with his wife and a household in the true sense is never constituted with the husband and the wife. The husband is simply a nocturnal visitor. But among the Forest Rabhas the duration of this duolocal residence is short-lived. It usually ends with the birth of one or two issues, and thereafter, the household residence becomes uxorilocal permanently (mainly in case of the heiress) or temporarily (in case of the non-heiress) which ultimately settles into a neolocal residence. And with the formation of the letter types of residence, the nocturnal visits of the husband cease to continue.

In some cases the Forest Rabha society of Purodha, Nalgarh and Kamala *bastees* also bears the avanculocal residence. Besides duolocal, uxorilocal and neolocal residences. there are a few cases where the residence is virilocal. In this case the man may be the only issue of the parents or his sisters are very young having no other male member in his parent's family, or the sisters have left the natal home after marriage.

The minor practice of the virilocal residence in this society whose arrangement is basically uxorilocal, is not the personal attachment only but mainly for the management of the family and its property. In such cases if the son goes to the house of his parents-in-law, his parents have none to cultivate their land or work for them. So for the maintenance in their old ages, they persuade their son and his wife to live with them after marriage. Among the Garos too, the minority people practise virilocal residence and the reasons behind this is their personal attachment (Nakane, 1961:56). 'A man', in their society 'brings his wife to live in his village because the woman of his lineage need to have a male relative present (Burling, 1962a : 213; Burling, 1958a : 744-745; 1958b : 116). Among the matrilineal Truk 'if the residence with the wife's kin would have taken the husband too far away from where his own lineage house is located, it may appear advisable for him to bring his wife to live at the latter place' (Goodenough, 1956:32).

Among the Village Rabhas, though the uxorilocal, virilocal and neolocal types of household residences are prevalent, the virilocal type overwhelmingly dominantes over the uxorilocal one. The neolocal type has of course, a good frequency. The duolocal type in the true sense is altogether absent. But in case of a pre-pubertal marriage, as among the Rajbansis (Mukherjee, 1963:69) the Rabhas stay in their paternal house until the girl attains puberty. She is then sent to her husband at her father-in-law's house. But during their stay in their respective father's house, the husband does not visit his father-in-law's house and spend night with his wife frequently, except occasionally.

As stated earlier, the Village Rabhas form the uxorilocal household residence only in some cases, especially in case of the marriage by service or *gharjai* marriage when the bridegroom lives in the house of his father-in-law either permanently or temporarily. In the latter case he builds a new household of his own after sometimes.

Besides the above type of uxorilocal household residence among the Village Rabhas, sometimes some Village Rabha parents, who have only daughter or daughters but no son, keep at least one daughter, and her husband to support them in their old age. He later becomes the head of the household when his father-in-law dies. Further, some cases of avunculocal residence where the man with his wife lives in his mother's brother's house, are also found among them.

Divorce And Remarriage

Divorce occurs more frequently in the Forest Rabha society than in the Village Rabha society. Among the Forest Rabhas divorce is easy. It requires no particular ceremoney. Both the husband and the wife have equal right to divorce in the event of a severe conflict. For this purpose an appeal is made to the *bastee* council. The usual fee for such appeal is a certain quality of *chakat* for the members of the council. A hearing is made and the members of the council try to persuade for mutual compromise. If it fails then separation is granted.

If the husband is willing to divorce his wife against her will, the man has to pay some quantity of paddy or some cash in the form of compensation to his wife. If the wife divorces the husband she needs not give any compensation.

Among the Village Rabhas divorce is also prevalent, but the frequency is very low. In their cases too, the consent of both parties and also of the council of elders is required. But always an endeavour is made to make compromise between the two conflicting parties. If it fails, divorce is allowed. But usually pressure is brought on the parties for not to proceed with divorce suit. If the husband divorces the wife against her will he has to suitably compensate the wife. In the event of the wife proceeding with divorce suit against the consent of the husband, she has to return the bride-price, if any, or pay a compensation.

Among both the Forest and the Village Rabhas a husband or a wife sometime forsakes the spouse instead of divorce, and in this case he or she cares for no advice. This case is also more frequent among the Forest Rabhas than among the Village Rabhas.

Among the Rabhas, remarriage of the widowed and divorced person is not very difficult though now-a-days the Village Rabhas do not favour this. Usually no ceremony is attached with this marriage. Simply the man comes to the house of the woman and a feast is given to some relatives of both parties and some villagers, and this completes the marriage. If a widower or a divorced man marries an unmarried girl, an elaborate marital procedure is followed. Again sometimes a widow or a divorced woman lives with a man (married, widowed or divorced) as his concubine. Over a century ago divorce among the Rabhas was not allowed, but the "widows are permitted to live with the widowers as a superior kind af concubines; and even a man who has a virgin spouse, may share his affections with a widow" (Martin, 1938:548-549). Later on both divorce and remarriage were found to be practised by the Rabhas of Assam and West Bengal. This can be traced also from the writings of some early account writers (Sunder, 1895:73; Friend-Pereira, 1912:143; Endle, 1911:85). Divorce is also found to be prevalent among both the Rajbansis (Sanyal, 1965 : 98-99; Mukherjee, 1963 : 68-69) and the Garos (Playfair, 1949:68-71; Burling 1963a : 145-152, 258-262).

MARRIAGE CEREMONY-FOREST RABHA STYLE

Selection Of Spouse

In the Forest Rabha society the parents start finding out a suitable mate for their child by themselves or through their relatives and friends. Sometimes they employ their community match-maker (*badeth*) for this purpose. Usually they look for an active and bold man with good health for their daughter and a girl expert in househould duties for their son. Even in the present days, unlike the more advanced Village Rabha parents, the Forest Rabha parents do not show any interest for an educated, handsome son-in-law or a beautiful learned daughter-in-law.

Negotiation And Selection Of The Bride And The Groom

Being informed of a suitable mate for their daughter, the girl's father, mother's brothers, some other relatives, the *mondal* and the *dhami* or the *deosi* on a selected day, go to the house of the boy's father in the morning where the priest of the girl's party watches the boy carefully with a view to finding out evil signs (if any) in his body and gesture. If the evil signs are prominent, the girl's party stops the negotiation. However, if the result is satisfactory the party selects the boy. They request the boy's party to visit the girl's *bastee* for the same purpose. On the selected day the boy's party in a similar way, select the girl.

Counting Of Omen

Sometimes even for getting a suitable boy for their daughter the parents further test the suitability of the union by some magical means. This is done by examining the position of the legs of a sacrificed chicken. If one of the legs of the chicken considered as *Rishi*, the supreme deity, goes up over the other leg, the marriage is considered to be very favourable, and the couple will be very happy. But if the condition is reverse, it is thought that this union will bring a great misfortune in the life of the couple, and the negotiation is usually abandoned.

Among the Garos also with a pair of fowls the priest counts the omens 'to ascertain whether the couple will be happy and prosperous or the reverse' (Playfair, 1909:101-102; Bose, 1947:243).

Final Selection Of The Bride And The Bridegroom

The final selection of the boy and the girl starts after counting the omens. The mother's brother of the boy presents the girl a cloth (*shokok*) or a small amount of money.

Similarly, after a few days the boy is finally selected and blessed by the mother's brother of the girl.

The day of marriage and other preliminaries are finalised as per advice of the priests and the headmen of both parties.

Among the Rabhas of Assam the selection of the bride takes place by offering her the *dhupchaul* and besmearing her hair with mustard oil and vermilion. Thereafter a date for marriage is fixed (Friend-Pereira, 1912 : 143).

Arrangement For The Wedding

On the day of marriage the members of the boy's and the girl's families remain busy from the dawn for the arrangement of the marriage. The marriage generally takes place in the evening (*mesugatang ta* or at early night (*gasam*).

The *deosi* worships Rishi and Rungtuk and Bosak, and prays for a peaceful marriage before the boy's party starts for the girl's *bastee* for the marriage. After worship, the boy bows to the deities and gets blessings from the priests, headmen, relatives and other elderly persons of the *bastee*.

Wedding Procession

Then the boy's party's consisting of the boy, his father, some male relatives of his mother's and father's sides, friends, the *dhami*, the *deosi*, the *mondal* of the *bastee* and same co-villagers, proceeds for the girl's *bastee*. The boy usually travels by a bullock cart. As they reach the outskirts of the girl's house, they are warmly received.

Marriage Proper

On the side of the courtyard the boy and the girl sit side by side. The *dhami* then starts worshipping various deities and spirits of the Forest Rabha pantheon. After worship, the *dhami* places the left hand of girl on the right hand of the boy and prays, "May the life of the bride and the groom becomes like that of the doves (the dove and its mate are always seen to move together). May they love each other widely and never forsake each other. May no danger befall on them". The boy and the girl pay their reverence to the deities, then salute the *dhami* first, then all the elderly persons assembled there. Then the boy and the girl exchange *pan-gua* (betel and nut) as per direction of the *dhami* who at that time utters the mystical hymn.

The exchange of *gua-pan* was a part of the marriage ceremony of the Rabhas of the district of Jalpaiguri in early days also (Sunder, 1895:73).

When the worship by the *dhami* is over, the *deosi* proceeds with the worship of Rungtuk and Basok within the room and then Rishi and Mahakal at the *kcrphak*. After the worship all persons including the guests, and the boy and the girl are served with chakat which is followed by a feast of rice and pork or chicken curry.

Next day usually after meal, the boy's party departs with the newly wedded couple with them. The bride stays in her parents-in-law's house for a few days or a few weeks. Usually she stays for a few days after marriage and then on a selected day her relatives come and take her to her parents' house.

After marriage when the boy with his wife first returns to his parental house, the *deosi* of the *bastee* worships Rungtuk and Basek with the sacrifice of a fowl. The parents of the boy arrange a feast.

In connection with the essential rites of the marriage ceremony of the Rabhas, the early account writers are of opinion that the sacrifice of the fowl, the offering of the liquor to Rishi and the exchange of the betel leaf and nuts are the essential traits (Martin, 1838 : 549).

Marriage Ceremony-Village Rabha Style

In the Village Rabha society the parents start searching for the suitable mate by themselves or by their friends and relatives or sometimes employ a match-maker (*badeth* or *karea*) who is either a Rabha or a Rajbansi by caste.

Selection of Spouse

Like the Forest Rabhas, the Village Rabhas of these two villages consider similar qualities, i.e., efficiency and activeness in the work, during the selection of a mate for their child. A local proverb clearly indicates the quality a man and a woman should have.

Kame Katone Tri Bare Sase Giri.

(A good cultivator is one who grows many crops. A good woman is one who always works and is busy).

Formal Negotiation

On getting information the girl's father or her mother's brother and some other relatives or both paternal and/or maternal side, some neighbours and friends visit the village of the boy for formal negotiation and also to see the boy. They are warmly received by the boy's father and others. Discussion relating to the economic condition of the two families, nature, education, efficiency and qualification of the boy and the girl is made. At this time the omen which the guests have marked during the course or their journey is also given importance. The Rabhas believe that there are some auspicious and inauspicious objects and actions which are helpful or detrimental to a person and the work he is going to do.

When the discussion is over and if the girl's party is satisfied, they request the boy's party to visit the girl's house.

On the appointed day the boy's party visits the girl's father's house to see the prospective bride. If the boy's party selects her, both parties then sit together to discuss about the related matters concerning the marriage. When these are all settled the day for the 'blessing ceremony' (*dara-gua*) by the girl's party is finalised.

Dara-gua Ceremony

On the day fixed for the *dara-gua* (the blessing and the final negotiation) ceremony, the girl's party consisting of the same members as before, comes to the house of the boy's father when the boy is brought before them. "He carries a brass plate consisting of a lighted lamp, some paddy, *durba* grass and *kajal* (black-paint) (Das & Raha, 1967 : 108)." The assembled guests and the other persons bless him, and he salutes the assembled persons. The father (in absence, mother's brother) of the girl, blessed him with the same article such as a *dhuti* or a shirt and some cash money varying from Rs. 2.00 to Rs. 10.00. On another fixed day similar ceremony is observed in the girl's house for the above purpose and the boy's father blesses the girl with "exactly double the amount as given by the girl's father during his visit to bless the boy" (ibid : 109). He also gives same other articles such as a *sari* or ornament etc. if he likes.

When the *dara-gua* ceremony is over, a date is fixed for marriage after consulting the almanac by the Brahmin.

The marriage ceremony of the Village Rabhas is a combination of several rites and rituals which may be grouped into three major heads ; and these are

(1) Rites observed on the day before marriage.
(2) Rites observed on the day of marriage.
(3) Rites observed after marriage.

A schematic distribution of rites under the above heads, is stated below.

Marriage Ceremony of the Village Rabhas

1. Rites observed on the day before marriage.	*2. Rites observed on the day of marriage.*	*3. Rites observed after marriage.*
(a) Thansiri and Balaram Puja	(a) Solomatrika and Basatdhara Puja	(a) Basi-Biya or Stri-Achar.
(b) Neoya-Kamani	(b) Nannimukh or Briddhi-sradha	(b) Baubhat or Andhan

(c) Gaye-Halud
(d) Adhibas

(c) Sarak-jal
(d) Satpak and Subha-dristi
(e) Hukur-bhanga
(f) Barbaran
(g) Biya, Sampradan and Gotradan
(h) Mitar and Panichhitas Ma-Bap
(i) Hom Joutuk and Khai-chhitani
(j) Santidan
(k) Stri-achar
(l) Wedding feast

(c) Athar-Bhanga

The above rites and rituals connected with the marriage ceremony are described below in brief. It may be mentioned in this connection that the marriage ceremony of the Village Rabhas is absolutely identical with that of the Rajbansis living in Alipurduar sub-division or Jalpaiguri district and Tufangunj Sub-division of Cooch Behar district as the same Brahmans preside over the function and the marriage rituals are performed as prescribed in the Hindu scripture.

1. THE RITES OBSERVED ON THE DAY BEFORE MARRIAGE

Thansiri and Balaram Puja

In the morning of the day before marriage, the housewives of the two Rabha families coming into union, perform *thansiri*, and *balaram puja*. The *thansiri* (i.e. *Rungtuk*) *puja* is only done by these families who have Thansiri or Rungtuk. Thereafter the senior male member of the family goes to the *tulsi-mancha* (Basil altar) for *balaram puja* which is done by offering several articles to Lord Balaram with a prayer for the well-being or the persons entering into the union.

Neoya-Kamani

This ceremony is only done in the house of the groom before the *balaram puja* when shaving of the beard and moustache of the groom and his relatives is done by the barber.

Adhibas

The *adhibas* ceremony is usually observed on the day before marriage or sometimes in the morning of the day of marriage also by both parties.

When the above worships (*thansiri and balaram puja*) are over, the Brahmin starts the *adhibas* rite and worships five different gods (*pancha devata* i.e. Ganesh, Dinesh, Shiva, Brahma and Narayan) with the offerings of several articles. Then three *bairatis* (married girls) anoint the head of the groom with scented oil thrice and give him a small looking-glass and a comb, and garland him with a necklace of shell beads. They also mark the forehead of the boy with collyrium (*kajal*) and vermilion (*Sindur*). The groom keeps all the article with him till the end of the marriage ceremony.

Solo-Matrika Puja

In the morning of the day of marriage after the *adhibas* ceremony in both bride's and bride-groom's house, the priest starts the *solo-matrika puja* (worship of Sixteen Mother Goddesses*) by offerings of various articles for the well-being of the couple and the smooth running and the peaceful performance of the ceremony.

Basatdhara or Haragouri Puja

The Brahmin performs this *puja* at the northern wall of the main room (*basat*=living room or the main room, *dhara*= wall, actually means wall of the main living room). Just at the junction of the wall and the floor, he keeps five small cowries (*kari*) representing the deities of the house (*basat-deota*) and Hara-Gouri (Lord Shiva and His consort, Durga), to whom he makes offerings.

Nanni-Mukh or Briddhi-Sradh

The *nanni-mukh* or *briddhi-sradh* is the ritual in which water, *pinda* (obsequial cakes) and many other articles are offered to the departed ancesters and the ancestresses by the members of bride's and groom's families to get the blessings.

*The sixteen mother goddesses are Gouri, Padma, Sachi, Medha, Sabitri, Bijeya, Jeya, Debsena, Swaha, Swadha, Santi, Pusti, Dhriti, Atma Devata, Kule Devata and Jara.

(*Nanni* or *Nandi*=Prosperity ; *Mukh*=for whom the prosperity is sought) (Ghosh Choudhury, 1932 : 205).

Sarak-Jal

In this ritual water from the nearby river or stream is ceremonially brought for the ceremonial bath of the bride and the bride-groom in their respective house by the *bairatis* after touching the water with an iron scythe to get rid of spirits and launching two earthen lamps (*dewari*) at the same time in the river. If these two lamps are drifted away by the flowing water while one touching the other, it is thought that the union will be full of happiness and everlasting.

The bride and bride groom take bath in this *sarak-jal*.

Gaye-Halud

The *gaye-halud* or 'turmeric smearing ceremony' takes place in both bride's and the groom's house independently.

The elder or the younger married sister of the bride/bride-groom (in absence, one of the relatives of the mother's side who has the same *husuk* with the bride/groom) bedaub the bride/groom three times with the turmeric paste mixed with oil.

The Wedding Procession

When everything is ready, the groom's party consisting of the groom, his father, brothers, mother's brother, sister's husband, some other relatives, neighbours and some friends, starts at a suitable time for the bride's house carrying different articles such as some cosmetics, some garments for the bride, bride's mother, mother's brother's wife, father's brother's wife a *dhuti* for wife's younger brother, some sweets, sometimes a few jars of *chakat* (rice-beer) and some *gua-pan* (betel and nut). Groom's *mama* (mother's brother) usually carries the bride-price (if any).

Bar Baran

As the party reaches the house, the *bairatis* at the girl's side, heartily welcome the party and take them in a clean and somewhat decorated room.

Installation of Marital Canopy

On the courtyard of the girl's house a marital booth (*maroa* or *mandop*) is erected where marriage takes place.

Hukur-Bhanga

As both parties give their consent for the marriage, the priest starts the *hukur-bhanga* (breaking of earthen plate ; *hukur*=earthen plate ; *bhanga*=to) eeremony when the groom and the father of the bride sit near the *tulsi-than* and utter *mantras* as per instruction of the priest while offering articles to the deities, Balaram and Narayan.

Afterwards, the father of the girl breaks an earthen plate with the pressure of his palms keeping his hands cross-wise (*hukur bhanga*).

Yajneswar Puja and Gao-Dhan

The priest performs the *yajneswar puja* inside the marital booth. At the end the father of the bride offers the groom the dowry, if any.

At the same time the father of the boy hands over to the father of the girl, the bride-price, if any. Both bride price and bridegroom price are called *gao-dhan.*

Satpak and Mukh-Chandrika

When the offering of the *gao-dhan* is over, the bride is brought by her relatives.

"The bride's elder sister's husband then moves anti-clockwise round the boy for seven times taking the bride in his lap. As soon as one round of rotation is complete, the bride throws a handful of *khai* (parched paddy) on the groom over the curtain. In this fashion the bride moves round the groom seven times and throws seven handsful or *khai* on the groom" (Das & Raha, 1967 : 113).

The bride and the groom then stand up in east-west direction facing at each other.

"A veil is then placed over the heads of both the bride and the groom, and the covering cloth is removed from the groom's face. This is done for the first looking ceremony so that the bride and the groom can look at each other ceremonially for the first time" (ibid, 114).

Gotra-Dan

One of the main events of the marriage proper is the *gotra-dan* (giving of *gotra*). As the Rabhas do not have any *gotra* like the Hindus (though they have their own clans which the Hindu Brahmin does not count as being tribal in nature and non-Hindu), so at the time of marriage they are given the Hindu *gotra*. This is so done as the marriage ceremony of the present day Village Rabhas takes place in the Hindu method. The only *gotra* that is given to the Rabhas is *Kaswapa**.

In connection with the *gotra-dan* ceremony, Ghose--Choudhuri states that in Assam and North Bengal as many communities do not have any *gotra* the Brahmins, in order to carry on their *jajmani* over these communities, have given each of them a *gotra* (1932 : 6). Risley in connection with the Rajbansis remarks that these people who had no *gotra*, have borrowed one *gotra*, the Kaswapa (1891, 1 : 494). The same view has been expressed by Sanyal (1965 : 89).

Acceptance of Matul-Angti

Before the actual *sampradan* (handing over the bride) starts, the mother's brother of the boy gives two finger rings made of gold, silver or brass (*matul-angti*) to the boy, one for his bride and the other for himself. This is considered as very important on the part of the boy and his mother's brother. The mother's brother must give these rings to his sister's son and his wife during the marriage ceremony. If he cannot give the ring at the time of marriage, he must manage to give the same in the nearest opportunity. So long he cannot give these, he must not accept food and drinks or any other articles or any presentation from his sister's son. The marriage is also considered

---

*Shri T. Chakravarty, a Brahmin from Assam but residing in Madhya Manasi mentioned about a rule that prescribes that 'those who have no *gotra* can get only *Kaswap* gotra.

as incomplete. If the mother's brother presents these to his sister's son and his wife, sometimes after the marriage he has to perform a *nobut* ceremony by the Brahmin or the Adhikari making some offerings to Balaram and Narayan.

Kanyadan-Sampradan

The father of the bride then as per direction of the Brahmin, symbolically hands over his daughter to the boy who in the same way, accepts her uttering the *mantras of sampradan* (offering of the bride).

Then the priest uttering *mantras*, ties one end of the *anchal* (hem) of the bride with one end of the *chaddar* (wrapper) worn by the groom. This tie is known as *lagan-githu.*

Mala Chandan

The *sampradan* is followed by the *mala chandan* ceremony i.e. exchange of garlands of flower made by the *bairatis* of girl's side. In this ritual the boy and girl stand facing at each other and garland each other.

Pani-Chhitao Ma-Bap and Mitar Dhara

In the marriage rituals of the Village Rabhas the *pani-chhitao ma bap* (ceremonial parents) and the *mitar* (ceremonial friend) play important roles. A few days before the marriage, a married couple of the village belonging to the Rabha community, is selected for this purpose. Similarly, a friend of the groom becomes the ceremonial friend (*mitar*) of the groom.

Firstly, the ceremonial parents after presenting some cash or kind to the boy and the girl, sprinkles water from the sacred *ghat* (earthen pitcher) kept in the *maroa* by means of a mango twig three times each of the newly wedded couple. The couple then salutes the ceremonial parents. In a similar way the *mitar* (ceremonial friend) gives some presentation (usually a few pice) and sprinkles water from the *mitar Ghat* (i.e. pitcher) for the ceremonial friend on them.

Hom-Yajna

When all the above typical rites are over, the priest performs *hom-yajna* by preparing a small fire-place and offering various articles the name of the various deities, ancestors and the ancestresses uttering *mantras* (Das & Raha, 1967 : 115-116).

Sindur Dan

Though in general the married Village Rabha women do not paint the parting of their fore-head with vermilion excepting a few, but the *sindur dan* (painting the forehead of the bride with vermilion by the groom) is an essential part of the marriage ceremony. As directed by the priest, the groom paints the forehead and the partings of the head of the bride with the sacred vermilion of the ceremony three times. Thereafter the bride in her turn, gives three dot marks on the forehead of her husband with sacred *kajal* (collyrium). In case of the Rabhas of Assam, the vermilion and bangles made of conch shell are essential in marriage (Barua, 1951 : 36).

Ayena-Dekhana

When the *sindur dan* ceremony is over the *ayena-dekhana* or 'looking in the mirror' rite starts. The bride takes a looking glass and holds it before the face of the groom who looks his face in the mirror. Similarly in his turn, the groom now holds the looking glass and the bride looks in it.

Santi-Dan

With the end of the above two rites (*sindur dan* and *ayena-dekhana*), the priest concludes the marriage ceremony proper with blessings and tranquillization (*santidan*). The couple pays homage to the gods and goddesses and salutes the priest and other elderly persons who also bless them.

Wedding Feast

At the end of the marriage ceremony, the father of the bride arranges an elaborate feast for all who have assembled.

Next morning the couple takes bath with the *Sarakjal* and pay homage at *Tulsi-Than* and offer some food there. Then after a light refreshment with curd and chapped rice (*chida*) the groom's party starts for their own village where the relatives, friends and the neighbours of the groom cordially receive the newly wedded couple.

Andhan or Boubhat

In the next day the *andhan* (rice by the new bride) or

wedding feast is given by the groom or groom's father in which the main function is

> "the distribution of food by the newly wed bride to all the relatives and guests, who assemble during the occasion. The bride distributes it to all in order to get accepted by the society. If the society does not accept the bride none would take the food from the hand of the bride ; it indicates that they (the members of the society) have not accepted her as one of their society" (Das & Raha, 1967 : 117). The guests and relatives who come

and attend this ceremony sometimes, give some presentations. But instead of kind, usually some cash is given as presentation.

Athar-Bhanga :

On the eighth day after marriage a number of relatives of the bride comes to the house of the groom to take the bride back. At this time the boy does not accompany the girl. The girl is brought back to her husband's house after a month or so by her husband and some of his relatives.

With the end of the *athar-bhanga* ceremony the wedding ceremony of the Village Rabhas ends.

It is important to mention here that the marriage ceremony of the Rajbansis of Alipurduar Subdivision, Jalpaigiri district, is absolutely identical with that of the Village Rabhas described in the foregoing pages. The same priests (Brahmin or *Adhikari*) conduct the marriage ceremony of both the Rabhas and the Rajbansis of these villages. The most of the rituals described in connection with the marriage ceremony of the Rajbansis by Sunder (1895 : 51-52) and Sanyal (1965 : 100, 113) are similar with those of the Village Rabhas. Both Ghose-Choudhuri (1932 : 204-205) and Bishi (1956 : 15-16) found some identical marital rites and rituals among many Hindu castes of North Bengal and Assam.

The Crises of Life—III : Death

7

THE CRISES OF LIFE–III : DEATH

Death Ceremony

A death in a Rabha house is indicated by loud wailing of the women and children. Hearing them wailing or hearing the news of the death, relatives of the dead and others assemble in the room and one after another according to the seniority, offer *chakat* (rice-beer), *chaika* (water) and *mai gungi* (rice flour) to the departed soul, the offerings of the matri-kin remaining closer to the dead body.

Soon after, male members of the family of the deceased (usually the husband of the heiress of the dead, if any, or the nephews or the brothers) in the Forest Rabha society plant four bamboo poles with a piece of white cloth tied to the upper ends to form a canopy. The relatives, mainly the matri-kins, friends and neighbours arrange for the funeral. The Village Rabhas do not pitch any such canopy.

Nature of Disposal

Among the Forest Rabhas cremation is customary. In the case of death of a very young child whose permanent teeth have not yet grown and the death results from animal bite or from a contagious disease or an epidemic, burial within dense forest is the rule.

Among the Village Rabhas cremation is the general rule, but bnrial is also done as a supplementary method. As the cremation is a costly process, the poorer Village Rabhas often remain satisfied with the inhuming of the dead body. During rainy season, due to heavy rain, they sometime prefer burial to cremation. It is also seen that during agricultural season, especially at the time of transplantation and harvest, the Village Rabhas often resort to burial because of lack of sufficient time and man-power as the adult malefolk remain busy with the agricultural pursuits. In case of the death of the children before teething or whose milk teeth (*nanasani fatong*) have not yet erupted, burial is the custom. Like the Forest Rabhas the Village Rabhas also practise burial when deaths occur following contagious diseases such as Cholera, Small Pox or snake-bite, tiger molestation, suicide etc. Burial is practised in case of unnatural deaths.

On the Rabha method of disposal of the dead in the district of Jalpaiguri in the past, Sunder writes, "If the person died of leprosy or sores he is buried. If he is poor and has no relative or friend, he is also buried. If he has left a widow and children and has property, the body is burnt" (1895 : 79). Choudhuri is also of the same opinion that the Rabhas of this area used to cremate their dead bodies. Burial was practised only during epidemic (1903 : 600). But in Assam the Rabhas used to cremate those killed by the tiger. When a person died of some epidemic or contagious disease or met with violent death the corpse was buried and not burnt (Friend-Pereira, 1912 : 143). Allen (1903 : 51) and Endle (1911 : 85) also hold the view that the Assam Rabhas used to burn their dead body, except during epidemic.

Place for the Disposal of the Dead

Among the Forest Rabhas, the cremation is done in a specific place which is situated in the neighbourhood of the *bastee* and is usually in the north. For burial there is no fixed place. Any place within the Reserve Forest is chosen for burial. Conversely, among the Village Rabhas there is no fixed place for the disposal of the dead (*samshan*). Usually, the banks of any river, stream and canal (*jampoi*) are considered suitable for this purpose. This cremation site on the bank of any water source is called *chika hasami.* Where once a dead body is cremated or buried, it is not chosen again.

Generally, among the Rabhas the dead body is disposed during the day time. At least the body is taken to the *samshan* in the day. If the death takes place at night, or in the evening, the disposal is postponed till the next morning.

Preparation of Bier

Male relatives and neighbours prepare the funeral bier (*moirsangrang*). Among the Forest Rabhbs a long bamboo pole is used as a bier, while among the Village Rabhas the bier is prepared by means of two bamboo poles and some bamboo-splits in the form of a ladder.

Preparation for the Disposal

The death-canopy is pitched among the Forest Rabhas. Hereafter, the *dhami* selects four able-bodied and healthy persons of the settlement to carry the dead body to the *morgandi* (place of disposal of the dead) and do all that is necessary in connection with the disposal of the dead. The *dhami* sprinkles sanctified water on them so that no spirit can harm them. These men are thus protected from the spirit action. The dead body brought out of the room is placed on a new or old white cloth which was previously spread on the courtyard. One of them brings the belongings of the dead such as clothings, beddings, etc., from the room of the deceased and keeps these near the head of the dead body. Then they wrap up the dead-body with the white cloth and tie it with the bamboo-pole.

Among the Village Rabhas the bier-carriers are not so treated. Two or three persons who may be relatives, friends or mere neighbours bring the dead body outside the room and place it on the bier with a piece of cloth placed underneath. They carry the bier to the place of the disposal of the dead.

Before proceeding to *morgandi*, the bier-carriers move round the courtyard with bier. In case of the death of a male they move round nine times but in case of female, for seven times.

Funeral Procession

The funeral procession starts for the *morgandi.* Someone takes the belongings of the dead. They are followed by relatives, friends, and neighbours. In the funeral procession are included the deceased's elder sister, mother, mother's sister (if alive) and other persons of the deceased's mother's line. Some persons take with them digging and cutting implements and other objects necessary for the funeral. Throughout the journey the Rabhas remain silent while the highly Hinduised Village Rabhas loudly utter the name of *Lord Hari* (*hari, hari, balo*) like the Rajbansis (Sanyal, 1965 : 118-119). On the way to *morgandi* they play their own musical instruments, like *dansi* (a type of drum), *ham* (flute) etc. The male members always try to touch the bier. One male relative also follows the funeral procession taking a big scythe (*dioai*).

On reaching the *morgandi* every one salutes the earth, and bier-carriers put the bier down in the north-south direction. Then four men prepare the funeral pyre with wood or bamboo or dig grave for the disposal.

Cremation : Forest Rabha Style Preliminaries

When the pyre is complete, those two men, taking the dead move round the pyre twice in the anti-clockwise direction, and then place the same on the pyre keeping the head in the northern direction and the face upwards. Before placing the corpse on the pyre, the belongings of the dead are spread over the pyre and on these the dead-body is laid.

Obsequial Offerings

The near female relatives such as the sister, mother, mother's sister and such others having the same *husuk* with the dead, offer obsequial food on the northern side of the pyre. Sitting on the southern side of the pyre, they utter mystical hymn, and offer different articles and a little *chakat* and also water.

These two persons as per direction of *dhami*, ignite the pyre after circling round it with the burning jute sticks twice along with the prayer of the *dhami* to the departed soul not to disturb the inhabitants of the *bastee*. Before they lit the pyre, they wash the dead body. On both sides of the pyre they keep two pipes (*turu*) horizontally and hang a chicken. They have a belief that the deceased person cannot leave the world alone; so he wants one companion and for this reason they offer a chicken to the dead.

Among the Garos also same type of belief is found. Sinha in connection with the Garo mortuary rite states, "A chicken is also tied by means of a thin rope with toe of the dead person. This chicken is killed and its blood smeared on the *ganchi* pyre. Then the dead body is placed on it (19 : 37).

When the dead body is completely burnt, these two persons pour water on the pyre from a pitcher (*Kambai*) and erect that awning over the pyre.

Collection of Bones

Before the cremation is over one of the four men collects some charred bones and charcoal, and keeps these within a small earthen pot or bamboo container which is then kept hanging in a nearby tree with the idea that the soul (*chirpak*) of the decased would reside there. The collection of bones is also done by the Rabhas of Assam. (Friend-Pereira, 1912 : 143-144)

Burial: Forest Rabha Style

For burial Forest Rabhas at first find out a suitable place where they dig a pit. The first three clods of the earth are kept separately when they dig the pit.

When the pit is thus complete, the body is laid down within the pit with its head northward and face upward after it is circumambulated twice round the grave in the anti-clockwise direction. The obsequial offerings and prayer are done in the same way as in case of the cremation. The belongings of the dead are also kept within the pit.

Then the nearest male relative (son, father or husband of the heiress), followed by the other attending persons, pour some earth within the pit from the first three clods of the earth kept aside. Lastly they cover the pit and ram the place. After the burial they erect the awning.

Purificatory Bath :

Afterwards all the attending persons take purificatory bath in the river or stream, and then come back to the house of the deceased silently. Before entering the house, all the persons purify their body by sprinkling water in which they keep piece of gold or silver. After reaching the house of the deceased all the attending persons sit in the room when the deceased breathed his last. Then they offer wine and water to the departed soul. On a banana leaf they also offer rice and chicken, which is known as *mai judag*. By the side of the *mai judag* they keep rice, meat and vegetables on three separate leaves. A piece of new cloth, one plate and one pitcher are also offered in the name of the deceased person. The *deosi* sprinkles water and *chakat* to all members for purification. This ceremony is known as *mair rasan*.

Invoking the Spirits

When the funeral procession reaches the house of the dead, the *dhami*, as also present among the Rabhas of Assam, (Friend-Pereira, 1912 : 144) invokes the departed soul to be satisfied with the offered articles. Thereafter he sacrifices a chicken in the name of the soul of the deceased and then moves round the house of the deceased uttering spells in order to seal the house from the spirit-intrusion.

Mourning Period

The forest-dwelling Rabhas observe pollution period for cremation only but not in case of burial.

The mourning period (*chhutna*) lasts for 5, 7 or 9 days. Usually this period is required to make sufficient quantity of *chakat*. No rigid restriction is, however, observed during the mourning period. Only fishing and hunting are generally forbidden by the members of the family. No ceremony (social, religious or any other type) is observed during this period. For the married couple of this family who are close relatives of the deceased and have the same *husuk* with him, it is customary to abstain from any sex-relation during the *chhutna* period. They believe that the child born from the cohabitation during this period, should be harmed by the spirits, and that it would be deformed physically or mentally.

Obsequies and the Final Purification

On the day after the mourning period is over, the *deosi* is called in for performing the obsequial rites and final purification. That day in the morning sons and daughters of the deceased along with other family members go to the nearby river or spring for purificatory bath. After bath they come back to the house. The *deosi* plants the *zerphak* in front of the house where he starts invoking Rishi (Mahakal) with offerings, sacrifice and prayer for the safety and security of the house. He worships Rungtuk and Basok situated in the house of the deceased in a similar way. With rice, some vegetables and the meat of the sacrificed chicken, he prepares some food (*maya*) which he offers at the *zerphak* first and then distributes to all the family members who observe the mourning period. The completion of death pollution is called *shanchinbakeya*.

Lastly all are entertained with sufficient quantity of *chakat*.

Tauleng Chaei

This ceremony is observed on the fourth day after cremation. This ceremony is done exclusively by the females. On southern side (*nakjumai*) of the deceased person they fix two bamboo poles one parallel to the other and tie one bamboo cross-wise. Then the wife of the deceased person keeps rice powder on a piece of new cloth and covers the rice with banana leaf. Thereafter the females keep a piece of cloth on the bamboo poles. The women present there cry loudly. They believe that the soul of the deceased person goes away keeping impression on the rice powder.

Mai Lesen

They observed *sardh* ceremony (*mai lesen*) just a year after death. This ceremony is held in the same room where the deceased person died. On this occasion they sacrifice one pig (*bag*) which is a compulsory one. As the sacrifice is over they keep the tail of the pig (*bag jumei*) on the *mai judag* for the departed soul because they have a belief that the soul of deceased person crosses 'sungi' river with the help of this tail. They also cut the lung of the pig into pieces and keep these on the three sides of the *mai judag*. Then one after another according to age, they offer rice, water and wine to the departed soul. All the relatives gathered there take their food and drink. This ceremony is to be performed on the day a year after the death is completed. If a Rabha does not observe the *mai lesen* just the day a year after death is complete then the society punishes that man. As punishment he has to offer wine (*chakat*), chicken (*toi*) or meat of the pig to all his relatives and neighbours.

In case of the accidental death nature of disposal is the cremation. In this case they cannot follow all rules and regulations. But on the second day of cremation they observe *lam jaraya*. On this occasion either the wife or some relatives of deceased person gives rice, wine, water, meat etc. on a banana leaf at the crossing of the road. They prepare the food in the standing position and give fuel to the oven with the leg instead of hand.

If a woman with a child in her womb dies, then they cut open the abdomen and take out the child. After the *mukhe-agun* (touching the mouth of the deceased with fire) of the mother they bury the mother and the child together. In this case also they observe *lam-jaraya*.

When these are over the family members are allowed to lead normal life.

But they do not observe any obsequial rite and ritual in case of the burial. The purificatory bath after the burial marks the end of the function.

CREMATION : VILLAGE RABHA STYLE

Placing the Dead-Body on the Pyre

When the pyre is complete, the body is placed on the pyre keeping the head of the dead in the north and the face upwards. "More Hinduised Rabhas revolve the dead body in anti-clockwise direction round the pyre for seven times," before placing the same on the pyre (Das & Raha, 1967:124).

Offering of the obsequial food and water

Then a female relative of the dead having the same *husuk* i.e. the matri-kin (usually the sister, mother's sister, mother's sister's daughter or such other relatives of deceased's mother's side) performs the ritc of *jalpinda* by offering a little water, some food and a little *chakat* in the mouth of the dead uttering some mystical hymn. Now-a-days 'this burden is taken by the males in many (Village) Rabha houses' (*op. cit.*). In this case this male is usually the dead man's brother or mother's sister's son, or such other male relative who has the same *husuk* with the dead.

At present some more Hinduised Rabhas of Madhya and Dakshin Manasi do not pour *chakat* during the performance of the said rite ; instead, they drop *tulsi jal* (water or sacred Basil leaves) for the salvation of the dead.

Then one after another the *chita-ghora* i.e., 'circumambulating the pyre and *mukhe-agun* 'touching the mouth of the dead with fire, rites are performed. These are observed by the chief mourner who is usually the eldest son. In his absence, the next son, in absence of the son, the nearest male relative bearing his (deceased) clan, becomes the chief-mourner. In case of the dead unmarried son and daughter, their living brother, in absence of brother, the mother's brother or mother's sister's son, performs these rites. In case of a childless wife, her husband, her brother or her sister's son, and in case of a childless husband, his brother or his mother's brother or his sister's son, does these.

Chita ! Ghora Rite

In this rite one of the bier-carriers becomes the *deori* or *gahesthi*. He directs the chief mourner as to the method to be followed by the latter in performing this rite. The *deori* lights a bunch of jute-sticks with the fire of the *bhuti*. The chief mourner takes bath and in wet clothes he takes this lighted bunch of jute-sticks, circumambulates the pyre three times in anti-clockwise direction. He is followed by the *deori* who takes a small earthen pot filled with water. As the chief-mourner crosses a bamboo pole after touching the same with the glowing bunch, the *deori* pours a little water at the bottom of the pole.

Mukhe-Agun Ceremony

When this is complete, the *deori* lights a cotton wick. The chief-mourner then touches the mouth of the dead three times with this. During touching the mouth of the dead with the fire, the performer must not see the face of the dead but keeps his face in the opposite direction. During *mukhe-agun* ceremony the assembled persons utter "*hari hari balo*."

Firing the Pyre

At the end of the *mukhe-agun* ceremony, the chief-mourner ignites the pyre from the bottom and the assembled persons "utter, "*hari hari balo*." Then those who carried the bier and prepared the pyre, inflame the pyre thoroughly so as to burn the body into ashes.

Burial : Village Rabha Style

Among the Village Rabhas, if the dead is to be buried instead of being cremated, it is done in the same way as is done by the Forest Rabhas. But the *jalpinda* rite in case of burial is performed before placing the body within the grave.

In burial also, the *chita-ghora* and the *mukhe-agun rites* are performed. The *chita-ghora* ceremony is done in a similar way but instead of touching the pyre poles with the burning bunch of jute-sticks, four corners of the pit are touched thrice by the chief-mourner. The *deori* pours water in the four corner of the pit while moving round the pit, keeping himself behind the chief-mourner. The *mnkhe-agun* rite is performed by touching the burning bunch of jute-sticks instead of burning wick as in the cremation.

Collection of Bone

Before the body is completely burnt out, the chief mourner collects a piece of bone of the dead (a little earth of the grave in case of the burial) and keeps the same in a bamboo-container, as is the practice among the Rajbansis (Sanyal, 1965 : 120). Later on he keeps this container near the *tulsi-mancha*. The Rajbansis, similarly, collects the bones and buries these under a Basil plant and after a few days throw these down in the river (Sanyal, 1965 : 120).

Hoisting of the Funeral Awning and Flag

At the end of the disposal, the bier-carriers plant an awning of a small white piece of cloth by means of four bamboo poles over the place. This is meant for giving the shade (peace) to the departed soul. Some flags are also hoisted. Sometimes a miniature thatched hut is also constructed there.

Formal Purification

After the funeral rites, the assembled persons take purificatory bath and return to the house of the deceased. Water in which pieces of gold and silver have been dipped, is sprinkled on them for future purification before they enter the house. Sometimes, the more Hinduiscd ones utter the name of *Lord-Hari* '(*hari hari balo*)'. The chief-mourner and other mourners, change their old clothings and put on new unwashed (*kora*) *dhuti* after bath. A long piece of cotton thread (*paita*) having a piece of iron (usually an iron key) tied with it, is worn by the mourners round their neck.

Restriction during mourning Period

During the mourning period a number of prohibitions and regulations are observed. For example, the mourners "do not take fish, meat, egg, onion, *musuri* pulse etc. They do not wear any clothing except what they wear after cremation, nor do they use shoe, sandal, oil, cosmetics etc." (Das & Raha, 1967 : 125). Besides, they are forbidden to attend religious or social ceremonies. Nor any social or religious ceremony takes place in the mourners' house. They are also not permitted to take food or water from any other house nor they would serve food or water to any person etc.

"If the father dies children should not take banana (ripened or green) and in case of the mother milk" (*op. cit.*) the banana symbolises the genital organ of the father which has procreated them, and the mother has nourished them with her breast milk. So out of regards the Village Rabha children refrain from taking these things, when their parents die.

Observation during mourning Period

Among the Village Rabhas of the two villages, the mourners perform *habishya* i.e. to take vegetarian diet, for the first ten days after death. Cooking of *habishya* is done once a day in an earthen tumbler, not to be used second time. If the tumbler breaks down at the time of cooking the cooking is abandoned for that day. After the cooking is over the chief-mourner offers a little of this with a pan-gua (betel and areca nut) and a little water to the departed soul. A lamp is kept burning every evening for the whole mourning period.

Post Funeral Rites

The post-funeral rites consist of four main ceremonies: (A) *tauling chaei* or *chaturthi.* This ceremony is observed on the fourth day after cremation. (B) *Dasa*, observed on the tenth day. (C) *Kaman* on the 29th day and (D) *Kam* on the 30th day of the mourning period.

A. TAULENG CHAEI

If the death occurs in the day time the dead is disposed of in the day, it is customary for the chief-mourner to offer a *pinda*[1] (obsequial food) on that day and three more *pindas* on the fourth day of mourning period, the rest six on the day of *dasa* ceremony. If the death occurs in the night and the disposal is done next mourning a small altar is made near the place of disposal of the dead where the chief-mourner offers two *pindas.* Two more *pindas* are offered on the fourth day of the mourning period, and the remaining six, on the day of the *dasa* ceremony.

This custom is not very widely followed. Instead, all ten *pindas*, are offered at a time during the *dasa* ceremony for saving additional expenditure.

B. DASA CEREMONY

The *dasa* (*dasa-ten*) ceremony takes place on the tenth day after cremation or burial.

The *dasa* ceremony has several rites such as *kharu*, *praschitta*, *pancha debatar puja*, *chita-kuran*, *pinda-dan*, *vairab puja*, *dahan*, *labri-bhasan*, *nabut* etc.

---

1. The *pindas* are made of several articles such as par-boiled rice (*atap chal*), ripened banana, curda, milk clarified butter (*ghee*), honey, sweet etc., which are mixed together to form balls.

In *dasa* ceremony the attending relatives, friends and neighbouring villagers bring curd and chapped rice for the mourners. These are generally used for entertaining the guests present.

Inside a palisade a small *than* (altar) is constructed on which the *pinda-dan* (offering of obsequial food) ceremony takes place. On the other side of the fencing, a miniature thatched hut is built where *vairab-puja* i.e. worship of Vairab is held.

Kheru-Karma

Before the priest (Assamese Brahmin) starts the *dasa* ceremony, the relatives, friends, and villagers of the deceased who joined the funeral procession, have their beard and moustache shaved and their nails pared off. The barber (Assamese Napit) does this work. This is known as *kheru-karma* (shaving of hair ceremony).

Pryaschitta

In the meantime the priest starts the ceremony known as *prayaschitta* (expiatory rite) with the chief-mourner who offers several things along with *mantras* (incantations) uttered by the priest. Thereafter, he cleans the place and takes bath in the river for purification.

Pancha-Debatar Puja

After bath, he again sits, with a napkin round his neck and worships five deities (*pancha-devatar puja*)[1] with offerings. Throughout the ritual the priest utters *mantras.*

Chita-karan

Chita-karan (cremation of bone) rite starts after the previous rite, when the chief-mourner makes a small symbolic pyre where he places the *asthi* (bone of the dead) to cremate the same symbolically. When this pyre is extinguished, the *asthi* is kept on the altar.

1. These five Gods and Goddesses are *Ganesh*, *Shiva*, *Saraswati*, *Parbati*, and *Brahma*, all are of the Hindu pantheon, as informed by Shri Dhanesar Chakravorty of Madhya Ranasi.

Pinda Dan

After the above rite the *Pinda-dan* ceremony beings with the offerings of several articles by the chief-mourner. He pours a little curd, milk, *ghee*, honey, dew, urine of the cow in a container in which he drops the *asthi* for purification. The chief-mourner then puts the *asthi* within a pit having wrapped it up with a lotus-leaf. The pit is then rammed with the *padmamati* (*padma*=lotus, *mati*=mud, i.e., the mud which remains attached at the base of a lotus plant) and on it, he spreads a bunch of *kush* (*khanda kush*) i.e. a kind of grass, over which he offers *pindas* and water one after another. The first *pinda* is offered in the name of the departed soul, while the others are given in the name of the ancestral souls belonging to the ascending generations.[1] Lastly after a course of offerings, he pays his regards to the departed soul and other ancestors and salutes the sun.

After paying his regards to the sncestral souls, he throws away the *pindas* in the river or in the canal and digs out the *asthi* which he keeps in a bamboo-container.

Vairab-Puja

After the *pinda-dan* ceremony, the chief-mourner starts the *vairab-puja* ceramony. This ceremony is performed by only the well-off Rabha families, with offerings.

Dahan

With the end of *vairab-puja* the *dahan* rite starts. The chief-mourner boils a small living fish, some rice etc., in an earthen can (*dahan-hanri*) in this ritual.

---

1. In practice *pindas* are offered usually upto five or six generations. In rare cases the Rabhas of the said settlements remember the names of the members of more than six ascending generations. It is also important to mention that the time of offering a *pinda*, the name and the *husuk* of the ancestor to whom the *pinda* is offered is to be uttered along with the Vedic *mantra*. This is done by the priest (Brahmin or Adhikari) who is previously told the name and the *husuk* of the ancesters. The priest at the same time suffixes the Hindu *gotra* Kaswapa following Yajur Veda. after the *husuk* because the Rabhas do not have *gotra*.

Labri Bhasan

In the meantime some of the paternal and maternal relatives of the deceased prepare a raft or float (*bhala*) with fives pieces of banana plant being pierced together through bamboo pegs. The chief-mourner with relatives, goes to the river. As he sinks under water, someone breaks the *dahan-hanri* on his head. The chief mourner gets up and sets the *bhala* afloat in the stream.

Purification

After these are over, the chief-mourner and the assembled persons bathe in the river for purification. The former throws the *paita* (sacred thread), the *sikei* etc. After bath they go back to the house of the deceased. The chief-mourner carries back with him the bamboo-container with *asthi* in it.

Before their entry into the house, the priest sprinkles sacred *tulsijal* on them and also on the different articles of the house for purification. The chief-mourner than digs a pit near the *tulsi-mancha* and buries the bamboo-container consisting of the *asthi*.

Dasa Bhojan

Thereafter, the chief-mourner takes *habishya* of fruits, sweets, milk etc. The assembled guests, relatives and others are entertained with a feast of *dasa* ceremony (*dasa-bhojan*) with *chida* (chapped rice), curd, molasses and salt.

C. KAMAN

Kheru

As among the Rajbansis, (Sanyal, 1965 : 120-121) among the Village Rabhas also on the 29th day of the mourning period the *kaman* or the final purificatory rite is observed. This *kaman* ceremony begins with the *kheru* i.e., shaving ceremony, in which the head of the male mourners and also their beard and moustaches are shaved and the nails pared off.

Parsha-Suddhi

After *kheru*, all of them, both male and female take bath and change their clothings. They no longer use the clothings used during the mourning period.

Further purification is done by touching a cow, cow dung, iron (generally a razor or knife or scythe), looking-glass, comb and fire along with the incantations uttered by the Brahmin.

D. KAM

Next day the *kam* ceremony i.e., the main obsequial ceremony is observed. It has two important rituals—(i) the *praschitta* and (ii) the *karma*.

Praschitta

The expiatory (*praschitta*) rite observed in this connection, is similar to that connected with *dasa* ceremony but in a somewhat elaborate way.

Karma

After *praschitta*, the *karma* (the obsequial proper) starts. The Brahmin starts the ceremony with the offering of different articles and the *pindas* to the ancestors and ancestresses on a bed of *kush* (*kush-brahmin*).

When all these are over the priest sprinkles *santi-jal* consecrated water) on every body who bows and pays homage to the ancestors and ancestresses. The chief-mourner takes all the *pindas* in a *kalar-donga* and throws the same at a distance.

Obsequial Feast

A feast of chapped rice, molasses, salt and curd is given to all at the end. This ends the funeral ceremony. From this day onwards the mourners and their family members lead a normal life, as they are socially clean.

It is important to mention here that the Rajbansis of this area perform their funeral ceremony in an identical way as that done by the Village Rabhas. They also employ the same Brahman or the *adhikari* for this purpose. Sanyal describes the procedure as similar (1965 : 118-120).

The Livelihood Pattern : Inter & Intra Community Linkages

8

THE LIVELIHOOD PATTERN : INTER AND INTRA COMMUNITY LINKAGES

Traditional Occupation

Cultivation has long been the traditional occupation of the Rabha (Martin, 1838: III : 549; Allen, 1903:49-50; Friend-Pereira, 1912 : 141). From time immemorial, agriculture has been the main source of their livelihood. The Forest Rabhas admitted that long before they came under the Forest Department of the State Government, their fore-fathers used to practise *tanjia* i.e. shifting cultivation by slash and burn method. The settled agriculture with plough and yoke is not very old to them.

The Village Rabha elders recalled that in their society too, shifting cultivation (*tanja*) was in vogue long ago. The whole area was covered with dense forest. People used to cultivate after clearing the area by that crude method. They have been practising the settled agriculture for a long time.

That the Rabhas of this district used to practise the shifting cultivation, like the Garos (Playfair, 1909 : 34 ; Nakane, 1961 : 29), the Khasis (Gordon, 1914 : 88 ; Nakane, 1961 : 102) and the Meches (Gruning, 1911 : 62), is available from an early account stating that they used to 'cultivate land with *gogo* or bill-hook' in early days, and thereafter took up *jotes* and started using plough and other implements similar to those used by the Rajbansis (Sunder, 1895 : 77). In this connection, Gruning in his Gazetteer, writes, "they have recently began to abandon their nomadic habits and rough system of cultivation by *jhuming* and to settle down and till the land in ordinary way" (Gruning, 1911 : 34). Friend-Pereira also mentions that the Rabhas used to practise a crude method for cultivation of rice (Friend-Pereira, 1912 : 141).

Besides cultivation, hunting was also an old practice of both the Forest and the Village Rabhas. As they used to live in or around the forest (still now they live within or outskirts of the forest) their habit for hunting grew in natural course.

The works for the development and maintenance of the forestry is also an old occupation of the Forest Rabhas. Buchanon also found the Rabhas as workers of the forest as early as 1810 (Martin, 1838 : III : 549), so also Allen in 1903 (1903 : 49-50).

Weaving was a traditional occupation of the Rabha women. Buchanon found all the Rabha women knowing to weave. (Martin, 1838 : III : 549).

Land-Tenure System

Since the operation of the first settlement in Western Duars in 1871, the tenure system of the area, as discussed in the Sunder's Settlement Report (Sunder, 1985 : 118-119) gave rise to four categories of tenure-holders or tenants, of whom *jotedar* and *chukanidar* were the tenure-holders directly under the Government, while *adhiar* and *dar-chukanidar* were tenants directly under the former and the latter categories of land-holders respectively.

After the commencement of the West Bengal Land Reforms Act in 1955 and in successive period, two types of tenure-holders are recognised at persent in the district of Jalpaiguri, so also at Madhya and Dakshin Manasi ; and these are *jotedar* and *adhiar*. The *adhiars* are of two types—one who cultivates land of only one *giri* or *jotedar* on share basis, is known as *adhiar* or *halua*, while the other, the *proja*, *jan* or *utungkara proja*, who cultivates land of more than one *giri* on share basis.

The latter class becomes *halua* to that *jotedar* with whom he resides and *proja* to all other *jotedars* whose land he only cultivates on share basis.

The *jotedar* has every right on the land he possesses. "He is a tenant with a heritable and transferrable title in his holding vested in him" (Sunder, 1895 : 118). On the other hand, the *adhiar* or *halua* has no right on the land. What he can do, is to cultivate the land of the *jotedar* and give him a definite share of what he produces. In the past he was absolutely under the mercy of the *jotedar*. He could stay with the *jotedar* and cultivate his land so long the latter was pleased with him. The *jotedar* had the power to expel the *adhiar* from his land. At present though most of the Rabha *adhiars* are non-registered, their conditions have much been secured through the safe-guards provided by the laws in the recent years.

Among the Rabhas of the Reserve Forest *bastees* the stated tenure-system is not found. Here the Forest Department of the Government of West Bengal is the owner of the land. This department has allotted some area of cultivable and homestead land to the official forest labourers temporarily in lieu of the labour rendered by these labourers to this department for the development and maintenance of the forestry. Further, some of these forest labourers who thus receive the land from the forest authority let out some portion on the basis of 50 : 50 share to their fellow *bastee*-dwellers (all Rabhas) who are not official forest labourers.

Present Economic Conditions : Working and Non-Working Units

The Rabhas engage themselves in different occupations. The frequency of the non-working units. In the forest *bastees* the number of workers for forest work is officially fixed. The Forest Department have fixed 81 Rabhas from 81 households of Purodha *bastee* as official forest labourers. They have also fixed 28 and 30 Rabhas from 28 and 30 households as official forest labourers from Nalgarh and Kamala *bastees* respectively. But it is usually seen that though the quota is fixed still a a larger number of the Rabhas from each *bastee* work as the forest labourers and enjoy the same facilities, meant for the official labourers. But the Village Rabhas are not employed as the forest labourers. The number of working and non-working units in these two types of settlements is thus variable. In order to show the difference in number of working and non-working units in the Rabha households of the *bastees* and villages, data from Purodha *bastee* and Madhya Manasi village in this regard, have been compared in Table 2. In Purodha *bastee* workers engaged as forest labourers and cultivators have been dealt with separately.

From the Table 17 it is seen that in Purodha the number of workers employed as forest labourers is much less in comparison with those engaged in cultivation. While males are exclusively employed as forest labourers, in cultivation both males and females take part. In the said *bastee* while the maximum number of workers in a household engaged as forest labourers is three, for cultivation there are as many as six workers in a household. But in Madhya Manasi the maximum number of working members is five. In Purodha and in Madhya Manasi the maximum number of households (59.81%) and (70.37%) respectively, send single worker for labour, but for cultivation the maximum number of households (43.93%) sends two workers.

From 107 Rabha households in Purodha 152 individuals go in for forest labour during non-agricultural season giving an average of 1.42 workers per household, though officially there are 81 recognised labourers ; and these 152 workers share the total wage actually meant for 81 workers. These 152 workers belong to the group of 15 to 59 group (total individuals of this age-group being 180). On the other hand, in cultivation 287 persons (43.03% of the total) inclusive of the members of both sexes, remain engaged, giving an average of 2.70 workers per household. Each Rabha household of Purodha sends more workers for cultivation.

The 54 household of Madhya Manasi send 88 workers, with an average of 1.63 workers per household. This average is much lower than the average worker per household engaged in cultivation (2.70) but a little above the average in labour (1.59) in Purodha *bastee*. The reason behind this is that the number of Rabha women in Purodha engaged in agricultural pursuits is more than those of the Madhya Manasi. Many Rabhas women of Madhya Manasi feel ashamed of taking up work outside their house. The general feeling is that 'the womenfolk should not work before the eyes of the male-folk, especially the unknown'. This feeling has developed among them during the last two decades following perhaps their contact with the Hindu castes.

Occupation

The majority among the Rabhas, according to 1971 Census are cultivators (Table 18). The number of those who work as agricultural labourers comes next followed by those who rear livestock etc. The exact number of Rabha working units employed as forest labourers is not available from 1971 Census. However, according to the Forest authorities of the Buxa and Cooch Behar Forest Divisions, in 1926 there were 564 and 470 forest labourers who worked in these two forest divisions of which 207 (36.70%) and 204 (43.40%) respectively were the Rabha labourers.

The Forest Rabhas, remain engaged mainly in two occupations—labour (both waged and non-waged) and cultivation along with some other subsidiary work such as fishing, hunting, weaving etc. Those who are not official labourers of the forest, do share-cropping in the land of the forest labourers and also earn wages by labour (forest work).

In contrast with their forest dwelling congeners, the Village Rabhas are not forest labourers. They remain busy in multifarious occupations, such as cultivation (in own hand), share-cropping, labour, service, fishing etc. But they are predominantly agriculturists. Out of 54 households of Madhya Manasi, 45 (83.33%) do some sort of cultivation ; and of these only 31 (57.41%) have their own land. Of these 31 land-owning households only 10 derive income only from their own. Of the different types of occupations, only four types are found among the Rabhas of Purodha. As against this, 17 types of occupations are found among this people of Madhya Manasi as shown in Table 19. While in Purodha the maximum number of households (75.70%) depend on 'cultivation and

TABLE 17

Distribution of Workers in Rabha House-holds

Sl. No.	No of Workers in a household	Purodha Bastee In Labour (Forest) Households engaged No.	%	Workers engaged No.	%	In Cultivation Households engaged No.	%	Workers engaged No.	%	MADHYA MANASI Households engaged No.	%	Workers engaged No.	%
1	2	3	4	5	6	7	8	9	10	11	12	12	14
1.	Single Worker	64	59.81	64	42.10	7	6.54	7	2.44	38	70.37	38	43.18
2.	Two workers	29	27.10	58	38.16	47	43.93	94	32.95	7	12.96	14	15.90
3.	Three workers	10	9.35	30	19.74	33	30.84	99	34.50	3	7.56	9	10.23
4.	Four workers	—	—	—	—	18	10.28	44	15.33	3	7.56	12	13.64
5.	Five workers	—	—	—	—	5	4.67	25	8.71	3	7.56	15	17.05
6.	Six workers	—	—	—	—	3	2.80	18	6.07	—	—	—	—
7.	No working member	4	3.74	—	—	1	0.94	—	—	—	—	—	—
	TOTAL	107	100.00	152	100.00	107	100.00	287	100.00	54	100.01	88	100.00

TABLE 18

Occupation Pattern Among the Rabhas, Census 1971

State/District	Total Population			Total Workers		Cultivators		Agricultural Labourers		Livestock Forestry Hunting & Plantation etc.		Mining & Quarrying	
	P	M	F	M	F	M	F	M	F	M	F	M	F
West Bengal													
Rural	2444	1153	1291	587	214	414	126	73	54	36	33	—	—
Urban	22	15	7	13	1	—	—	—	—	—	—	—	—
Jalpaiguri													
Rural	342	167	175	67	48	24	4	10	20	31	24	—	—
Urban	1	1	—	1	—	—	—	—	—	—	—	—	—
Cooch Behar													
Rural	1891	957	1034	429	157	387	122	36	26	—	9	—	—
Urban	—	—	—	—	—	—	—	—	—	—	—	—	—

State/District	Manufacturing Processing, Servicing, & Repairs: Household Industry		Other than Household Industry		Construction		Trade & Commerce		Transport		Other services		Non-workers	
	M	F	M	F	M	F	M	F	M	F	M	F	M	F
West Bengal														
Rural	2	—	—	—	—	—	—	—	—	—	62	1	566	1077
Urban	—	—	2	—	—	1	—	—	1	—	10	—	2	6
Jalpaiguri														
Rural	—	—	—	—	—	—	—	=	—	—	1	—	110	127
Urban	—	—	—	—	—	—	—	—	1	—	—	—	—	—
Cooch Behar														
Rural	2	—	—	—	—	—	—	—	—	—	4	—	428	877
Urban	—	—	—	—	—	—	—	—	—	—	—	—	—	—

labour', in Madhya Manasi the most frequent occupations are (i) cultivation and (ii) share-cropping and labour each having a frequency of 18.52%. In Purodha the 'share-cropping and labour' has the next higher frequency (19.63%) but in Madhya Manasi the second position is held by 'cultivation and labour' (12.96%) followed by 'Labour only' which has a frequency of 11.11%. All in all, the people of both settlements have three main occupations viz., cultivation, share-cropping and labour. The majority of these 88 earners of the Madhya Manasi village (Table 17) depend on land. They cultivate either their own land (40.91%) or land of other land-owners on share (*adhi*) basis (19.32%). A good number of the Rabha workers (27.27%) also depends on labour while 9 persons out of 88 earners (10.23%) are engaged in other services.

Similarly among the members of both sexes of the Rabhas of this village, majority depend on land, though some of them (males) have labour or service as the main occupations. The same trend of occupational pattern is noticeable among the Rabhas of Dakshin Manasi (Table 20). But in their case there is only one service-holder (male). No female labourer is found. They do not have any other source of income. Table 19 shows the distribution of different Rabha households of Purodha and Madhya Manasi according to sources of income.

TABLE 19

Distribution of Rabha Households by Their Occupation

Sl. No.	Nature of occupation	Purodha Bastee		Madhya Manasi	
		No. of house-holds	%	No. of house-holds	%
1.	Cultivation only			10	18.52
2.	Cultivation and Share-cropping			1	1.85
3.	Cultivation and labour	81	75.70	7	12.96
4.	Cultivation and Service			2	3.70
5.	Cultivation and Business			1	1.85
6.	Cultivation, Labour and Business			2	3.70

Sl. No.	Nature of oceupation	Purodha Bastee No. of house-hold	%	Madhya Manasi No. of house. holds	%
7.	Cultivation, Share-Cropping and Service			1	1.85
8.	Cultivation, Labour and Service			3	5.56
9.	Cultivation, Share-Cropping and Labour			3	5.56
10.	Cultivation, Share-Cropping, and Labour and other occupation*			1	1.85
11.	Share-Cropping only	3	2.81	—	—
12.	Share-Cropping and Labour	22	20.56	10	18.52
13.	Share-Cropping and other occupation			2	3.70
14.	Share-Cropping and Service			1	1.85
15.	Share-Cropping and Labour and Service			1	1.85
16.	Labour only	1**	0.93	6	11.11
17.	Labour and Service			2	3.70
18.	Labour and Fishing			1	1.85
	Total	107	100.00	54	99.98

* Other occupation includes medical practice, cart-driving, plumbing, fire-works making etc.

** She works in different households of the *bastee* and thus earns her livelihood.

In connection with the occupation of the Village Rabhas, it may be pointed out here that at Madhya Parkota (an adjoining village) there are nine Rabha households who eke out a living by a new profession of basket making. They have taken up this as the primary occupation in recent years. They learnt this craft from Hindus like the Doms.

The Village Rabhas do not go to work in any industry, mines, collieries, and such other places, or in tea estates, for earning cash money during agricultural slack season as many other tribals do. "The Duars people do not leave the district at any time for work" commented Sunder (1895 : *op. cit.*).

Some features about the economic conditions of the diffe-

TABLE 20

Distribution of the Village Rabha workers according to the Nature of Work

Categories of occupations	Madhya Manasi						Dakshin Manasi					
	Male		Female		Total		Male		Female		Total	
	No.	%	No.	%	No.	%	No.	%	No.	%	No.	%
Total Workers	70	100.01	18	100.01	88	100.01	54	100.00	15	100.00	69	100.00
I. Cultivation	30	44.29	11	61.11	42	47.73	25	46.29	4	26.67	29	42.03
II. Share-Cropping	16	22.86	1	5.56	17	19.32	10	18.52	5	33.33	15	21.74
III. Labour	13	18.57	5	27.78	18	20.45	14	25.93	—	—	14	20.29
IV. Service	9	12.86	—	—	9	10.23	1	1.85	—	—	1	1.45
V. Fishing	1	1.43	—	—	1	1.14	—	—	—	—	—	—
VI. Business	—	—	—	—	—	—	1	1.85	—	—	1	1.45
VII. Other Occupations*	—	—	1	5.56	1	1.14	3	5.56	6	40.00	9	13.04
		100.01		100.01		100.01		100.00		100.00		100.00

*Other Occupations include cart-pulling, plumbery, medical practice, etc.

rent communities with whom the Village Rabhas live in close associations and on economic interactions are narrated here. And as such a brief discussion is made here regarding the occupations of the different communities of the village of Madhya Manasi.

In this village, of the fifteen different communities inhabiting eleven (the Oraon, the Namasudra, the Rajbansi, the Muchi, the Bairagi, the Sutradhar, the Mahishya, the Saha, the Kumar, the Napit and the Muslim) depend mainly on the land (own cultivation and/or share-cropping). Labour is their second major occupation, except in case of the Napit community who equally depend on labour and hair-cutting, the Mahishya on service, and the Bairagi on both labour and carpentry. Though the main occupation of the Malos is fishing, but a good number of them also depend on share-cropping. The main occupation of the Brahmin is *jajmani* and of the Barvi and the Jugis, labour, though a good number of the Baruis are found to choose cultivation and business as their primary professions and that of the Jugis, cultivation.

From the analysis of the occupations of different communities of Madhya Manasi it is also evident that most of the occupational castes have slid away from their traditional occupation and adopted new one (Das, 1968 : 34-35). They came here from East Pakistan (now Bangladesh) and settled here almost in penniless condition, and as a result of this distressed economic condition and facing a new environment they, possibly, could not have carried out their own profession but earning the livelihood by new means for their mere survival. And that is why a good number of the Malo, the fishing caste, adopted other means, the majority of the Muchis are not cobblers; the Jugis, the weaving caste, have given up weaving, many Sutradhars, the carpenters, have followed the same path with the Jugis, the Kumars are not following their traditional occupation of earthen pot-making, and so on. So among these castes the traditional occupation is fast disappearing. This is persisting as the primary source of income among a few only but in some other cases it is considered as a subsidiary means.

Land Holding

The size of the land-holdings of the Forest and the Village Rabhas is very small. Comparatively, the Forest Rabhas have larger holding. It may be important to mention here that while the Village Rabhas have absolute right over the land they own, the Forest Rabhas are not the actual owners of their land. Forest Department of the State Government is the owner in the real sense.

1. CULTIVABLE LAND

A. Forest Rabhas

The total Rabha households of Purodha, Nalgarh and Kamala *bastees* are 107, 35 and 40 respectively. Of these 81 (75.70%) in Purodha, 28 (80.00%) in Nalgarh and 30 (75.00%) in Kamala have been officially treated as forest labourers' households by the Forest Department of the Government of West Bengal.

These households are provided the cultivable and homestead land. In these three *bastees* the remaining households do not have their 'own' land. (The 'own' land in the said three *bastees* means land given to the official forest-labourers by the Forest Department on contract basis for their service given to the said department. The term 'own' has been used here because these forest labourers think this land as their 'own' as they are enjoying the land concerned for generations). At Purodha *bastee* 78 (96.30%) households out of 81 have 3.50 acres of land each, while the remaining three households (3.70) have 7.0 acres of land as they belong to the *mandal* (Headman) of the *bastees*. 19 (76.00%) out of the 25 sharecropper households of this *bastee*, have *adhi* land varying between 1.0 to 2.50 acres, while the rest 6 (24.00%) between 2.50 to 3.50 acres. At Nalgarh *bastee* there are 28 'land-owning' households, of which 27 (94.43%) have 2.50 acres of land, while only one household, being the household of the *mandal* (headman) possesses double the area of the land, i.e. 5.0 acres. Remaining landless households are share croppers, and the area of the land they cultivate on share basis varies from 1.0 acre to 2.50 acres each.

Similarly, at Kamala *bastee* 29 (96.67%) out of 30 'land-owning' households, have 2.50 acres of land while only one household, that of the *mandal*, has double the area of land. The landless households, who live on *adhi*, cultivate 1.0 acre to 2.00 acres of land each.

It is important to mention here that in addition, each official forest labourer gets some area of land (approximately 2 acres) from the First and the Second Year Plantation areas for cultivation. Therefore, if this area of land (2 acres approximately) is included, the individual holding increases to a bigger size.

It may be pointed out here that the Forest Rabhas are also allowed to cultivate in the First Year and Second Year Plantation areas. They may cultivate vegetables, cotton etc. in the intervening space between two rows of plantations (one row of plantation is about 6 ft. away from the other). Each official labourer gets about one acre of land each, and in this land they can cultivate for two years only without damaging the plantations. As such they use hoe etc. and not plough drawn by bullock.

B. Village Rabhas

In Madhya Manasi as stated earlier, 31 Rabha households out of a total of 54, have own land and the rest 23 households (42.59%) have no land of their own. Of the total land-owning households (Table 21) majority (54.84%) have land ranging from1.0 acre to 3.0 acres, and 77.42% of these households have land below 5.1 acres. Only two households have more than 15.0 acres of land, of which one having 25.0 acres whereas the other 22.00 acres.

On the other hand, only 20 Rabha households (37.03%) of this village are share-croppers, though 6 of them also have small area of land of their own. The size of the land cultivated on share basis by the majority of these households (60.00%) varies from 1.0 acre to 3.0 acres, and none cultivates above 5.1 acres of land.

In Dakshin Manasi (Table 21) only 22 (37.29%) Rabha households, out of a total of 59, have their own land, of which the highest frequency (45.45%) goes to those below 1.0 acre of land. And 19 (86.36%) of these households have below 5.1 acres of land. Only one household has more than 15.0 acres of 'own' land.

The majority of the households (52.54%) of this village, posseses *adhi* land as they are devoid of their 'own' land. Of them 87.19% have *adhi* land between 1.0 acre to 3.0 acres, and all of them have below 5.1 acres.

TABLE 21

Distribution of the village Rabha householders by their Land Holdings (Own & Shared)

Size of Land-holding (in Acre)	Madhya Manasi Number of Households having		Dakshin Manasi Number of Households having	
	Own land	*Adhi* Land	Own Land	*Adhi* Land
Below 1.0	2 (6.45)	6 (30.00)	10 (45.45)	2 (6.45)
1.0 to 3.0	17 (54.84)	12 (60.00)	7 (31.82)	27 (87.10)
3.1 to 5.0	5 (16.13)	2 (10.00)	2 (9.09)	2 (6.45)
5.1 to 10.0	2 (6.45)	— —	2 (9.09)	— —
10.1 to 15.0	3 (9.68)	— —	— —	— —
Above 15.0	2 (6.45)	— —	1 (4.55)	— —
Total	31	20	22	31

(Figures in bracket indicate percentage)

2. HOMESTEAD LAND

A. Forest Rabhas

In the three forest *bastees* only the official forest labourers have been given homestead land, while those who are not forest labourers, do not have this type of land but live on the land of the forest labourers of the respective forest *bastee*. Each of the forest labourers' household of the three *bastees*, has been given 0.50 acres of land for this purpose. But, as they have provided homestead land to their non-forest labourer relatives and friends, the average homestead land per household has gone down to 0.38, 0.40 and 0.38 acres respectively in the three forest *bastees*.

B. Village Rabhas

Among the Rabhas of Madhya and Dakshin Manasi 31 (57.41%) and 28 (47.46%) households respectively have homestead land of their own. They do not have fixed area of homestead land and the average per household possession of homestead land by these household is 0.21 and 0.20 respectively. Those who have no homestead land of their own, live on the land of other persons (Rabha or non-Rabha).

3. Average Land-holding

The average per household possession of different types of land by the Rabhas of the three settlements, Purodha *bastee* Madhya and Dakshin Manasi (The average holding of the Rabhas of Nalgarh and Kamala *bastees* was not available) shows a distinct variation (Table 22). In Purodha the average per household holding of own-cultivable land, including let-out (*adhi*) land is 2.75 acres. The average per household of *adhi* land is 0.53 acre and those of homestead and fallow land are 0.38 and 0.12 acre respectively. The Purodha Rabhas do not possess 'other types' of land. In Madhya and Dakshin Manasi villages the average size of land-holdings among the Rabhas is not very large. Again, between the Rabhas of these two villages, the size of different types of land, except the *adhi* land, is higher in the former village. While among the Rabhas of the former village the average size of cultivable land per household owned (including the area let out on *adhi*) is 2.66 acres, in the latter village it is only 1.59 acres. In the case of *adhi* land the Rabhas of the former village possess only 0.95 acres, while in the latter village it is a bit higher in size (1.09 acres). If the let out land is taken into account, the Rabhas of former village have let out 1.31 acres per household, for *adhi* on an average; but in Dakshin Manasi it is only 0.24 acres. Thus Table 21 and Table 22 reflect that the Rabhas in general, have very low acreage of land holding per household. As this small size of land holdings (a good number of households do not have any land) cannot produce enough to meet their basic requirements, they are compelled to take loan or adopt other occupations (for Village Rabha only). Comparatively the economic condition of the Forest Rabhas is a little better than that of their congeners living

TABLE 22

Distribution of different types of Land (Average per household) held by the Rabhas

Settlements	Total house-holds	Total Popu-lation	Nature of Holdings	Area of Cultivable land (in acre) Owned			Total *adhi* land taken	Area of non-cultivable land (in acre)		
				Self-Culti-vated	Let out	Total		Home-stead land	Fallow land	Other Types*
1	2	3	4	5	6	7	8	9	10	11
Purodha			Total	237.09	56.48	293.57	56.48	40.50	12.90	—
	107	667	Average per household	2.22	0.53	2.75	0.53	0.38	0.12	—
Madhya Manasi			Total	72.65	70.97	143.62	51.11	6.39	19.22	13.53
	54	307	Average per household	1.35	1.31	2.66	0.95	0.12	0.25	0.25
Dakshin Manasi			Total	78.93	15.00	93.93	64.26	5.73	8.00	4.78
	59	291	Average per household	1.34	0.24	1.09	1.09	0.10	0.14	0.08

*'Other types' includes all types of land except those mentioned in the table. It includes primarily the bamboogroves, orchard, grassland and pasture land etc.

in the villages. This is because of their additional income from the First and the Second years' Plantation Areas, daily labour, together with the other facilities granted to them by the Forest Department which the Village Rabhas lack.

Jotedar-Adhiar Relation

The Forest Rabha share-croppers (who are the non-forest labourer class) do cultivate the land of the land-owing Rabhas of the settlements in simple *adhi* system i.e. the production is shared on 50 : 50 ratio. The seed, manure etc. are given by the land owners. If the share-croppers who are either relatives or neighbours of the land-owners, do not possess any bullock, they hire the bullock from the land-owners or from any other person, and clear up the rent after harvest. The share-croppers take some paddy (8 to 10 maunds) as interest-free loan from their masters and repay the same after the harvest.

On the other hand, the *adhi* system prevalent among the Village Rabhas is similar to what is found in the whole of the Alipurduar Sub-division (Western Duars) of the district of Jalpaiguri. For a long time, the Village Rabhas have been living in this part of Western Duars in close proximity of the Rajbansis and also some other communities like the Meches. They are the dominant caste groups of the area. The landless Rabhas were sometimes employed by the Rabhas, the Rajbansi and other community land-owners, and in the similar way the Rabha *jotedars* also let out part or whole of their land to the Rabha, the Rajbansi and other community share-croppers. This employer-employee relation caused wide socio-economic interactions amongst the Rabha, the Rajbansi and some other ethnic groups. It had thus left a marked impression on the social organisation of the Rabhas of West Bengal specially on that of the Village Rabha section.

The present tenure system, as it exists in Jalpaiguri, provides two classes of tenure-holders—the land owning class (*jotedar*) and the share-cropping class (*adhiar/halua and jan/proja*). The land-owners and the share croppers have contractual obligation as provided in the West Bengal Land Reforms Act of 1955. This act (Chapter-II, Section-16-1 A and B) states that the produce of any land cultivated by a *bargadar* or *adhiar* shall be divided between the *bargadar* and the person whose land he cultivates : (a) in the proportion of 50 : 50 in a case where plough, cattle, manure, and seeds necessary for cultivation, are supplied by the person owning the land, (b) in the proportion of 60 : 40 in all other cases. Earlier the *adhiar* of this tract used to get some extra facilities for example, an advance of 'two *bis* of paddy' (about 12 maunds) without any interest (as *bhuta, bhuti* or *bhutali*) to tide over the time until they got their share after reaping (Sunder, 1895 : 119). Further, the *adhiar* used to get *panji-jhara* i.e. all the paddy that fell off or lay on the ground where *panji* or stacks of paddy were kept, and his wife, *pathna-jhara* i.e. the paddy that remained scattered on the courtyard during the process of winnowing when the straw and dirt were being removed after threshing (*op. cit.*). Moreover, the *jotedar* was bound to pay the *pana* (i.e. rent of the bullock) to the *halua* if the former could not supply the same. But the condition was reverse with the *halua*. He was not to pay the *pana* (*op. cit.* 120). Again the *jotedar* had to provide the *adhiar* with the homestead land.

Before independence most of the areas of the district of Jalpaiguri, particularly of the Western Duars, were thinly populated, and it was not very difficult for the *adhiars* or *halua* to get land from the *jotedars* for cultivation on share-basis. Rather, it was difficult for the big *jotedars* or *dhanis* to get sufficient number of *adhiars*, and as such a fair size of land of these *jotedars* remained fallow for most part of the year or remained under forest. 'He has often considerable difficulty in keeping his labourers ; the demand for agriculture labour is so great that a man who is dissatisfied with his employer, can always get work elsewhere..." (Grunning, 1911 : 33). And that is why these *jotedars* used to keep their share-croppers around their houses by giving free homestead land and also to maintain a cordial relation with them and to provide them with other facilities mentioned elsewhere. The *adhiars* or *halua* also in their turn, usually lived with the same *jotedars* and maintained similar relation.

Some *jotedars* and *haluas* developed close relation among

them. In some cases the relation was so cordial that the *jotedar* relieved the *halua* of the advance (*bhutti*) or loan as the latter was unable to repay. In some other cases the close relationship led to the establishment of even the nuptial relation. On the contrary, the inability to repay the advance or for some other reasons, relations, between the *giri* and the *halua* were found to be strained in some cases. As conflict grew up it was not unusual to find both falling apart.

After independence in 1947 a large number of people came to this tract from East Pakistan (Now Bangla Desh) and also later on from Assam to be settled in this area. Initially there were some conflicts and clashes between the old and the new groups of people, (the old settlers used to call these refugees as *bhatias* contemptuously i.e. men from low country) but the refugees later on secured stability as they learnt to live with them. With the march of time, some of the refugee communities, mainly the Sahas, the Jugis, the Kayasthas, the Brahmins and the Goalas placed themselves in dominant positions in the political, social, economic and other spheres. The Sahas of Uttar Manasi and the neighbouring villages gradually took over the control of the trade and business. The agriculturists among the refugees, such as the Namasudra, the Mahishya, the Kaibarta and also the Jugis displayed praiseworthy skill and efficiency in the field of agriculture. As a result, the group of old settlers gradually became dependent on the refugees in the economic spheres. On the other hand, the agriculturist Rabhas lagged behind the refugee agriculturists in their struggle for economic survival. In the field of agriculture the refugee agriculturists did a better job than the *adhiar* of the Original Settlers Group, as a result many members of the latter group took up economic activities other than agriculture. Changing over to other occupation was no easy job. Some of them sold their property under economic stringency, and that is how they became landless.

The *jotedars* of the Original Settlers' Group, in their turn began to realise the increased value of the cash money. They started employing more and more the cheaper refugee cultivators in year to year contract (*jan* or *proja*). In doing so they not only profited from the more quantity of yield but also substantially reduced their obligations of providing inputs such as *bhuti*, *panji-jhara*, *pathna-jhara*, free homestead land etc. which they used to provide to the original share-croppers. In many cases *panji-jhara*, and *pathna-jhara* had already been stopped. The *pana* for both parties had been introduced notwithstanding objection from the *adhiar*. The *pana* was earlier given by the *jotedars* only in the event of their inability to supply the *adhiar* with one bullock. The *adhiars* now-a-days have to put up with this lest their contracts should be terminated.

So, one important reason for the waning of interest of the land-owning class (*jotedars*) towards their cultivators class (*adhiars* or *halua*) is the occurrence of conflict and consequent loss of interest between them. This was so because (a) labour was cheaper than before, (b) price for the produce sold was higher, (c) gradual increase of cost of living, etc. This situation is not so widely noticeable among the Forest Rabhas as among the Village Rabhas. The difference is only of degree.

The economy of the Village Rabhas has been severely affected as also their social and religious life. The *jotedar-adhiar* relation deteriorated still further. Before the refugees came cultivation was the only occupation of the Rabhas of of these two villages, and the Rabha *adhiars* were wholly employed by the *jotedars* of the area who belonged to the Rabha, the Rajbansi, the Mech and the Oraon communities. These Rabha *adhiars* cared little for the employment in cultivation because they were the only people to be employed. They made no effort to move out for employment. They depended entirely on the *jotedars* for their livelihood. Social, religious and political interactions were also set in through help, co-operation and even through different social and religious festivals. Such interactions were also noted between the Rabha *adhiars* or *haluas* and the Rabha *jotedars* who offered the same facilities to their share-croppers.

The situation changed after independence. The agro-based life of the Rabhas of these villages slowly moved in different directions.

Many of the Rajbansi, the Rabha and the Oraon *jotedars* of this area, who had earlier given land to the Rabha *adhiars* for cultivation, had already changed over to refugee agriculturists because of their skill in yielding more crops. Many Rabha share-croppers of these villages were either replaced or were given a smaller area of land for *adhi* than before. Many of them are also not getting even the earlier facilities. Thus many of them have become unemployed or underemployed proletarians and set out in search of some other means for survival. Some have been fortunate enough to change to other occupations such as daily labour, service, basket-making etc. But many of them are still unemployed. The working force is very low among them and the income is much below the subsistence.

The Forest Rabhas are comparatively a little better off, except, of course, the problem of their own population growth and the rising cost of living. Otherwise the situation is not as bad as that among the Village Rabhas. Against this background an assessment has been made in Table 23 on the interaction of the Rabha *jotedars* and *adhiars* in respect to land.

TABLE 23

Distribution of different communities to whom the Rabha land-owners have let out land and from whom Rabha *adhiars* taken land on *adhi* in Madhya Manasi

Sl. No.	Rabha land-owners let out land on *adhi* to			Rabha share-croppers take land on *adhi* from		
	Community	No.	%	Community	No.	%
1.	Rbbha	8	53.33	Rabha	12	60.00
2.	Rajbansi	2	13.33	Rajbansi	4	20.00
3.	Refugee	4	26.67	Refugee	3	15.00
4.	Rabha & Refugee	1	6.67	Rabha & Refugee	1	5.00
	Total	15	100.00		20	100.00

Table 23 shows that the land owning Rabhas of Madhya Manasi Village have given their land on *adhi* mainly to their own community people (55.33% of the cases) and some to the

Rajbansis, still in 26.67% cases they have preferred the refugees exclusively. The Rabha land-owners have tended to favour the refugee peasantry. On the other hand, the Rabha share-croppers, have taken land mainly from the Rabha land-owners (60.00%). Some have, of course, taken land on *adhi* from the Rajbansi (20.00%) as also from the refugee (15.00%) land owners. It thus indicates the shift of dependence from their own people and the Rajbansis to the refugees. This occurred slowly after independence.

The Rabha share-croppers of the forest *bastees* cultivate land of their Rabha relatives and neighbours of their respective settlement. Similarly, the Rabha land-owners of these *bastees* give land for share-cropping to their Rabha relatives and neighbours of their respective settlement. This is not only because of the prevailing Forest laws and other restrictions of the Forest Department but also because of their feeling of solidarity with their own people.

Indebtedness

Due to their low income and the rising cost of living the Rabhas particularly those who are landless, face acute economic crisis and remain in debt. An *adhiar* "is in a chronic state of debt" (Sunder, 1895:119). They usually take loan from village *mahajan* at a high interest. The *mahajans* here are the main lending agencies. The poor Rabhas are always made to toil for thcm. In Madhya and Dakshin Manasi and also in Purodha the refugees mainly play the role of the *mahajans.* Once a Rabha "gets into the clutches of this Indian Shylock, it becomes extremely difficult, to extricate himself from this grip" (Roy, 1951 : 203). Thus a time comes when he has little to offer to pay back the loan except his services, because "the paltry initial debt goes on swelling enormously by a process" which a poor, illiterate, helpless Rabha can never understand. Still, they have to accept

> "loan either from the land-lord himself or from a money -lender, the rate of interest is enormous; they go on paying interest year after year, yet there are cases, where they are still in debt after having paid the capital back three

> times over by way of interest. The poor man 's labour is practically forfeited until he one day purchases his freedom by selling the land which he built up by the sweat of his brow. And this is added one to the number of proletarians in our land who have nothing to sell except their labour " (Bose,1967:178).

The Constitution of India has assured economic promotion of the Scheduled Castes and Scheduled Tribes and protection from social injustice and all forms of exploitations (Article-46). There is also suititable legislation for the protection of the tribals from the claws of the money-lending agencies. Yet the network of activities of these money-lending agencies is so pervasive that it is very difficult for the Rabhas and many other tribals to get rid of them.

Like other tribals, in their cases too, "the factors which are mainly responsible for the miserable income . . . are small land-holdings, old technique of cultivation, infrequent use of fertilizers, and general ill-health" (Das & Raha, 1963:73). The other reason which is true for the Forest Rabhas, is "their own improvident habits and their lamentable love for liquor". Their immoderate attraction for *chakat* (rice-bear) reduces a fair amount of rice they get from their field.

> "when the debtor gets old or takes to drinks, the money-lender sets to work to squeeze him depriving him gradually of all his cattle, his wife 's ornaments and other property (Gruning, 1911:100).

The latter reason is not much strong among the Village Rabhas.

> "Due to their long contact with the dominant Hindu castes in whose influence and pressure, the present day (Village) Rabhas have given up this habit of liquor to a great extent" (Das & Raha, 1967:55).

Our study (Table 24) shows that among 107 Rabha households in Purodha, 58 (54.20%) have taken loan from various sources. Of these 58 households 43 (74.14%) have taken paddy loan, while 15 (25.86%) cash loan. Among them the average per household cash loan is Rs. 31.29 while that of paddy loan is 34.64 kg. The usual rate of interest charged for the cash loan is 25% to 50% of the capital and that for the paddy loan is 50%.

Like the Forest Rabhas of Purodha, the Village Rabhas of Madhya Manasi balance their deficit budget also by taking loan (by *bhuti*, *muli* etc.). Out of the total 54 households of the village, 34 (62.96%) have incurred loan from different sources. The average cash and paddy loans per household are Rs. 78.64 and 62.68 kg respectively which are definitely much higher in amount than those incurred by the Forest Rabhas of Purodha *bastee*. The rate of interest is also much higher than that given by the Purodha Rabhas. It varies from 50% to as high as 200%.

The maximum number of households of the Rabhas of Purodha have taken paddy loan from their own community people and the next higher frequency goes to those who have taken loan from Janjogi Grain-Gola. (Table 24). Regarding the cash loan, the Rabha households of this *bastee* have taken the same mainly from the Oraons. In Madhya Manasi the Rabha households usually borrow paddy from the refugees, the Rabhas and the Rajbansis and borrow cash mainly from the refugees and the Rajbansis.

Howali System

Among the Rabhas, mutual co-operation in different areas of life, particularly the economic co-operation is found. Often the Rabhas are seen to help one another by offering their labour free of cost, in exchange of similar help. In the field of agriculture, a Rabha is often found to seek help from neighbours and relatives who agree to help him. For this help one pays nothing in cash or kind except offering food of *chakat* only. This help is reciprocal. The same sort of reciprocity in co-operation is also found in house-building and other activities. It covers social and religious ceremonies also. The characterstic of this mutual help is that this is of a localized type and is found to exist within the settlement or

TABLE 24

Type of Money-Lending Agencies from whom the Rabhas have taken Loan

Sl. No.	Name of the sources from whom the Rabhas have taken loan	Purodha Bastee					
		No. of Rabha Households taken loan by					
		Paddy only		Cash only		Total	
		No.	%	No.	%	No.	%
1	2	3	4	5	6	7	8
1.	Rabha	17	39.54	—	—	17	29.31
2.	Rajbanshi	4	9.30	3	20.00	7	12.07
3.	Oroan	7	16.28	7	46.67	14	24.13
4.	Marwari	—	—	—	—	—	—
5.	Government	—	—	—	—	—	—
6.	Co-opertive Graingola	11	25.58	—	—	11	18.97
7.	Refugees	—	—	—	—	—	—
8.	Rabha & Refugee	—	—	—	—	—	—
9.	Refugee & Government	—	—	—	—	—	—
10.	Rajbansi & Refugee	—	—	—	—	—	—
11.	Rabha & Co-op. Grain-Gola	—	—	—	—	—	—
12.	Otner Sources	4	9.30	5	33.33	9	15.52
		43	100.00	15	100.00	58	100.00

		Madhya Manasi No. of Rabha Households taken loan by						TOTAL	
		Paddy only		Cash only		Both Paddy & case			
		No.	%	No.	%	No.	%	No.	%
		9	10	11	12	13	14	15	16
1.	Rabha	3	21.43	2	13.33	—	—	5	14.71
2.	Rajbansi	2	14.29	4	26.67	—	—	6	17.65
3.	Oraon	—	—	—	—	—	—	—	—
4.	Marwari	—	—	2	13.33	—	—	2	5.88
5.	Government	—	—	2	13.33	—	—	2	5.88
6.	Co-operative Graingola	1	7.14	—	—	—	—	1	2.94
7.	Refugees	4	28.57	3	20.00	5	100.00	12	35.30
8.	Raha & Refugee	2	14.29	6	6.67	—	—	3	8.82
9.	Refugee & Government	—	—	1	6.67	—	—	1	2.94
10.	Kajbansi & Refugee	1	7.14	—	—	—	—	1	2.94
11.	Rabha and Co, op. Grain Gola	1	8.14	—	—	—	—	1	2.94
12.	Other Sources	—	—	—	—	—	—	—	—
		14	100.00	15	100.00	5	100.00	34	100.00

within the hamlet. The Rabhas of a settlement (village or a forest *bastee*) is found to have such co-operation. They usually do not extend this help outside their own settlement.

Though the *howali* system is still present among the Rabhas in general, but this system among the Village Rabhas, shows the sign of declination. While social solidarity is the main integrating force behind the preservation of this system among the Forest Rabhas, the introvert forces and money-mindedness due to the influence of cash and market economy are pushing this system to degeneration among the Village Rabhas.

Change in the Rabha Economy

The economy of the Village Rabhas has undergone some important changes during the last few decades. The economy of the Forest Rabhas has, however, maintained somewhat a stable pattern. The change in economy among the Village Rabhas is two-fold :

(1) There has been change from shifting cultivation, and hunting to settled cultivation ; and

(2) There has been change from settled cultivation to some cash earning jobs like service, waged (cash) labour etc.

Earlier, they used to engage themselves in *tanjia*. Later they leaned towards settled agriculture under the influence of the Koches or the Rajbansis. This change was significant as it provided the turning point in the history of Rabha culture. The change over to settled cultivation has brought in its wake a number of cultural changes. The most important is the individual right over the land i.e. the formation of personal property as in case of the Garos (Nakane, 1961 : 90-91; Burling, 1963 : 305-307) and the Khasis (Chattopadhyay, 1960 : 27-28 ; Nakane, 1961 : 102). The Rabhas gradually realized its importance. They wholeheartedly directed their efforts to agriculture and allied activities. Their interest in cultivation was so keen that they disapproved any other occupation as the source of their livelihood. Only a very few persons of the Rabha community did take up other occupations. Even the forest labourers among the Rabhas had (and still have) agriculture as the primary source of income. Their interest in the agriculture is borne out by the following local proverb which is in currency among the Village Rabhas, the Rajbansis and others.

Uttam Krishi, Madam Ban
dhik chakri, bhik nidan

(Cultivation is the best, trading comes next. Service is damned, begging is the worst.)

So the Village Rabhas have faced the same kind of change as has been faced by many tribal communities of India.

> "There has been a tremendous change in the economic environment of primitive tribes in India. The semi-nomadic tribes, who lived on fruits and roots and occasional *jhuming* (shifting cultivation) of their forest clad environment, have become permanent cultivators (Majumdar, 1950 : 70).

The Village Rabhas continued to live with settled agriculture as their main occupation until recently when they found that this was not enough to keep their body and soul together. Their difficulties arose from the growth of their population, their growing desire for cash money, and thirdly the heavy population pressure in their area due to the influx of the refugees after independence. As a result of this multiplication of population, the land has been fragmented. Naturally it has reduced the size of land-holding in a Rabha household. The population increase has not been accompanied by the increase in the number of jobs for adult males. These eventually resulted in the economic crisis in an agro-based Rabha household. This crisis has thrown many Rabhas into unemployment, while some others had taken up such diverse jobs as service, business, basketry, etc. A Rabha with a small size of holding of the cultivable land, finds his inability to meet his basic needs unless he looks for some supplementary source of income. He breaks his age-old practice of agriculture and seeks some other jobs. Another reason for the change of occupation of the Rabhas is their growing need for cash money for making purchase of different things. The earning of wages in cash is therefore, considered often important even to those who have cultivable land.

Now-a-days almost every Rabha household, even of the land-owners, thinks it important and necessary to earn wages in cash. At least they have realised the utility of cash wages, and as such many Rabha household send at least one or two members to some occupations other than cultivation. A service is the strong expectation among many literate Rabhas, at least those who have read even upto class VII or VIII or so. They are averse to going over to industrial areas outside their own locality as seasonal migrants.

As there was almost no industry (except the tea industry) in the domain of the Rabhas, it becomes hard to find suitable employment avenues. Fortunately, some developmental works started there in recent years. The works of the railway tracts (metre-guage) were started in 1948 and of the broad-guage in 1962. The community Development works at Kumargram police station started functioning in 1958. Further, after the Chinese aggression in 1962, dcvelopmental works, such as construction of roads etc., have been taken up in this area. But only a few Rabhas could get employment in development works.

Besides the above changes, some other changes are also found in the Rabha economy. Some old occupations of the Rabhas have been discarded. Hunting, which was a very attractive occupation of the Rabhas, is not found to be pursued as widely as before. Very rarely they go for hunting. The Forest Rabhas do it despite the prevalence of the wild life preservation and protection rules. The ceremonial hunts, *phafsani*, held in the last day of the month of *pous* (December) and *bisamoy*, held in the last day in the month of *chaitra* (April) have almost been abandoned by the Village Rabhas though the Forest Rabhas maintain it. One reason why hunting has fast disappeared from the Village Rabhas is because of the strict forest rules and also the Hindu influence. Change has also occurred in the traditional occupation of the Rabha women. Weaving was a major occupatlon among

Rabha women. It continues among the Forest Rabhas to some extent but the Village Rabhas do not pursue it any more. Only a few old women and two or three adult women (who received training from the Eri-culture Training-Cum-Production Centre at Uttar Manasi organised by the Scheduled Castes and Tribes Welfare Department of the State Government) know weaving. Against this a number of the Forest Rabha women has acquired skill in weaving and spinning.

The level of education is very low among the Rabhas. Some of them with some education, have been able to secure employment in public and private organisations. With the opening of the vocational training by the Scheduled Castes and Scheduled Tribes Welfare and some other departments of the State Government, a few Rabhas have received the opportunity to choose new profession for earning livelihood.

The Rabha society has thus shifted from their traditional economy based on shifting agriculture and hunting to settled agriculture i.e., from an unstable and insecured economy to a stable and secured economy of plough cultivation. This change is noticeable among both the Forest and Village Rabhas. As the fragmentation of the land is not very severe among the Forest Rabhas (mostly they are employed by the Forest Department in the successive periods and as such they get land from the Forest Department and as they meet up their need for cash money by waged-labour given to the Forest Department, and as they did not feel the pressure of the refugees and face economic crisis caused thereby), there has been no further shift of economy from agriculture and labour to some other jobs among the Forest Rabhas. Further the strict rules have prevented them from taking different jobs.

The village Rabha, on the contrary, are facing the chill blows of the above problems, and as a result they are now looking around for some jobs only to get rid of the impending defeats in the struggle for existence. Tne characteristic of this mutual help ls that this is of a localized type and is found to exist within the settlement or within the hamlet. The Rabhas of a settlement (village or a forest *bastee*) is found to have such co-operation. They usually do not extend this help outside their own settlement.

Though the *howali* system is still present among the Rabhas in general, but this system among the Village Rabhas, shows the sign of declination. While social solidarity is the main integrating force behind the preservation of this system among the Forest Rabhas, the introvert forces and money-mindedness due to the influence of cash and market economy are pushing this system to degeneration among the Village Rabhas.

Market and its Impact

The present market or *haat* at Uttar Manasi which has its tentacles over a very wide area at present, was born in earlier part of this century, when a few Rajbansi, Rabha and the Mech thought of establishing a *haat* (local weekly market). The banyan tree which then Rabha leader planted at the centre of the market, is still there. At that time a few Rajbansi, Rabha and the Mech used to come to this market to sell their produces like rice, milk, curd etc., and some Rajbansi, Rabha and the Mech used to come to purchase. Later on a tea stall was also started. That was the humble beginning of the present-day very big *haat* at Uttar Manasi.

The market started growing very slowly at the beginning. In late forties it took some shape as a number of shops mostly grocery shops, tea stalls and stationery shops belonging mostly to non-indegenous people, came up. Besides these shops which remained opened most of the days during a week, there were temporary shops for vegetables, spices, rice, cosmetics etc. which remained opened only once a week. The timing was between ten in the morning to two and three in the evening. Nobody dared to keep the shop open after three in the evening because of the menace of the wild animals like the tiger, elephant, hyena etc.

The market at Uttar Manasi flourished actually when the refugees started coming to these areas. Among the refugees, particularly the Saha, were professionally the businessmen. So on coming to these areas, they forthwith realised that this was the very virgin place to start with their profession. They established more and more shops and gradually got themselves involved in both retail and wholesale business in this area. At present, a very good number of shops are owned by the Saha and in the market economy of Uttar Manasi and even in the nearby *haat*, particulary the daily transactions, they have established themselves. That means the control of the indegenous people like the Rajbansi, the Rabha and the Mech over the Uttar Manasi market has gone out of their hand. Now the migrant people like the Saha, some other Bengali refugees, the Marwari and some other people have gaind control over the market economy of the area.

With the growth of the market at Uttar Manasi and also in the neighbouring areas, particularly after 1955 when these markets were actually flourished, the Rabhas involved themselves in the market economy mainly for want of cash. They come to the market in order to sell their produces to get cash ; and this cash has allured them to turn their attention towards cultivation of cash crop also which so long was almost non-existent among them. The market also made them interested of the various modern goods like cosmetics, stationery, metal utensils, furniture, clothings, garments, foodstuff, fancy goods etc. hitherto unknown to them. The attraction of these articles has more and more increased their demand for cash. And the more their interest for these articles and thereby more their demand for cash increased, the more they get dependent on different Hindu castes including the Rajbansis as well the Bengalee refugees, particularly those who are landowners and money lenders for waged labour and loan respectively. It is thus seen that for the Rabhas of Madhya and Dakshin Manasi, the market at Uttar Manasi played a very important role in bringing them closer to the various Bengalee Hindu castes and thereby causing immense changes in their culture. Another very significant change that the market economy has brought in the life of the Rabhas is to make them self-interested. They now think of their own and of their family only. It has also made the male-folk more important in the society and made them dominant and authoritative. It has also established closer relation between father and son rather then any other relatives, thereby increasing the importance of patri-kins.

Their shift from shifting cultivation to settled cultivation—and the growth of market and cash economy in their land have distinct impact on their life style. These have drifted the

Village Rabhas very close to the various Hindu caste groups, particularly the Rajbansi in the earlier times and the refugee Hindus in recent years. In fact these two shifts have made the Village Rabha dependant more on these Hindu Caste economically. As a result of this economic dependence, they started imbibing many cultural traits from the latter. And with the acceptance of many cultural traits first from the partrilineal Rajbansis and then from the patrilineal refugee Hindu castes, their traditional matrilineal traits, got either weakened or lost, causing a distinct drift from a matrilineal system towards patriliny. The impact of market and cash economy on their culture is also similar. This have made their males more dominant, authoritative and more individualistic bringing in the identical changes in their culture. And it is particularly true for the Village Rabhas. In case of the Forest Rabhas, this is not distinct. It is true that the Forest Rabhas also accepted settled agriculture to replace shifting cultivation but they never were dependant on the Hindu castes, the Rajbansi and others, because of the forest laws. Influx of the refugees also did not take place in their *bastees*. Moreover market economy does not have that impact on them. As a result the Forest Rabhas could retain their traditional matriliny to a significant extent even these days and do not show much movement towards patriarchalization.

The Social Control : Pattern and Activities

9

THE SOCIAL CONTROL : PATTERN AND ACTIVITIES

The Village Council among the Forest Rabhas

The village council among the Forest Rabhas is known as the *marab son*. The Panchayati Raj System of today has not come among them. The word, *marab son* means 'Council of Elders' (*Marab*=man, *Son*=aged). This council of elders consists of the elderly and able persons of the *bastee* (number not fixed) headed by the *mandal* (official head man) who is also the traditional head man (*pare*). As the *para* (traditional chief), the headman of the *bastee* acts with limited power. He has to act according to the direction of the *marab son*. But in the capacity of the *mandal* (official headman) he has more powers given to him by the Forest Department of the Government of West Bengal, and under which he supervises the work of the Forest labourers and contrals them. As the *pare* he does not get any extra facility but as the *mandal* he gets some more acreage of land from the Government (actually double the area of land that a forest labourer gets from the Forest Department).

However, the *marab son* of a *bastee* as stated earlier, consists of a number of members who are selected from the elderly and intelligent persons of the *bastee*. There is no hard and fast rule in regard to the selection of the members of the council or the number of members. Old, sick, deformed, ignorant and very young persons are avoided; otherwise any aged man of the *bastee*, who is a Rabha, is eligible to become a member. But the selection of a member is entirely dependent on the decision of the council. The *deasi* and the *dhami*, the priests, are also members of this council by virtue of their position in their society.

This council judges the intra-*bastee* disputes. Usually the social and religious offences are tackled by this council. But any offence which arises by violating any forest rule or due to murder, theft, injury or such other reason, is referred to the forest authority,

When any social or religious offence takes place in a *bastee* or if any Rabha complains against some one to the *pare*, the latter summons the meeting of the council on a day suitable to the majority of the members. All the members of the council are informed regarding the place, time and date of the meeting. The parties to the suit, are also asked to attend.

The meeting of the council generally takes place on the courtyard in front of the house of the *pare* or any suitable place selected earlier. A glass of *chakat* (rice-beer) is served to each member of the council; the cost of rice-beer is borne by the parties involved in the suit. After that the meeting starts. the council hears the complaint from the plaintiff and the replies and explanation of the defendant's side. Having heard both sides, the council members consult amongst themselves and judge the case. Thereafter, the judgement is given. The person, if found guilty, is usually fined. In case of severe offence, he is excommunicated also.

When a dispute take place between two or more *bastees* i.e. in case of *inter-bastee* dispute, the meeting of the joint council of different *bastees* is called. In this meeting members who are the *pare* of different *bastee* councils, attend. The meeting usually takes place either in the *bastee* of the plaintiff or of the defendant. In this case the *bastee*, where the meeting takes place, supplies the *chakat* to the members. After hearing, a long discussion takes place. The case is decided thereafter.

If this council cannot reach a decision in one meeting, successive meetings are summoned for the purpose. The verdict may be fine or excommunication or both if found guilty. Sometimes, the case of a serious intra-*bastee* socio-religious offence is referred to such inter-*bastee* council also. One of such cases is cited here.

'The incident took place sometimes in 1965 at Kangan *bastee* under Chillapata Range of Cooch Behar Forest Division. When Phuli Darboth, widow of late Latu Panchibak of this *bastee* became pregnant, one Birsa Tirki, an Oraon who used to work in their field, was held responsible for it. The council of Kangan *bastee* took strong exception to this affair and found Phuli guilty of the breach of the Rabha social custom. Birsa then admitted his fault, paid a fine of Rs. 200/- and 100 kg. of paddy and went on staying in the *bastee* severing all connection with Phuli.

But the Rabhas of different neighbouring *bastees* became serious in this affair. They decided in an inter-village council meeting that Kangan *bastee* had done a great offence in disposing of such an illegal act in such a light way. The council passed a verdict that if Kangan *bastee* council did not expel the Oraon man from the village (the woman might stay in the *bastee* after proper atonement) within a fortnight, all the member-*bastees* would socially beycott the Kangan *bastee*. Birsa was expelled from the *bastee* immediately. Phuli was forced to live in this *bastee* and through some purificatory rites, she expiated for her fault and lastly became one with them'.

At present the past of the *pare* as also the *mandal* among the Forest Rabhas is not handed down from father to son. It is selective like that of the *dhami* or the *deosi*. But in old days it was hereditary. The daughter's (heiress) husband used to succeed the office previously. Now the most efficient person is selected for the post. For the post of the *pare* the *marab sen* selects a suitable candidate if the present *pare* dies, or is unable to work due to illnes or some other reasons or leaves the *bastee* for ever or commits some serious offence etc. The *mandal* ship is selected by the Forest authority.

Evidently the Forest Rabhas still hold their traditional political organisation. There has however been a remarkable change in the rule of succession of the headmanship. Though the office of customary headman (the *pare*) was hereditary (father to daughter's husband), this rule of succession is now broken by the indication of a new administrative post of the *mandal*. Earlier the Forest authority used to select the *pare* as the *mandal*. Now as the Forest authority exercises influence to select the *mandal* from the forest *bastee*-dwelling Rabhas and as the *mandal* has more economic power over the *pare*[1] the Rabhas find it suitable to select the *mandal* as the *pare*. Thus the office of the customary secular headman (the *pare*) has been tied to the newly created administrative headman (the *mandal*) to form the secular head, the *pare* of the *marab son* (village council) and also administrative or official head (the *mandal*) of the *bastee*.

The Forest Rabha political organisation has little influence of the modern politics. The main reason is the prevalence of the strict forest rules which restrict the agents of the different political parties to enter into the *bastees* and spread their ideologies. The other reason is that the Forest Rabhas show less interest in coming in contact with the people of the villages, town etc. Of course, they have their own trade union which has control over their official activities.

The Council of the Village Rabhas

Like the present-day Forest Rabhas, the Village Rabhas once had the council of elders (*marab son*) functioning in its full strength. It used to control all the socio-religious affairs among the Rabhas living in a village. Previously the Rabha villages in this district were peopled with a few other communities like the Rajbansis, the Meches, and the others. Each of the communities had its own community council which

1. When a waged work is to be done, the authority only orders the *mandal* to complete the work within a specific period. The *mandal* selects the number of people to be required for this job, and distributes the wages given to him by the authority in lump. The *mandal* also supervises the work of the labourers and exerts authority on them.

looked into the affairs of its own community. But the inter-community conflicts were judged by a village-council formed by the members from all the communities.

This situation prevailed till independence in 1947. The situation started changing thereafter. After independence this area continued to face a heavy influx of the refugees from East Pakistan (now Bangla Desh) who settled in this area. These refugees belong to different Hindu caste people and of different ideologies. With the influx of the refugees the area began to develop new channels of communication, trade and business and new social and political systems. Later on many developmental projects were started by the Government, such as the road and the railway communications, community development works etc. New ideas and agencies with new political beliefs penetrated into the area. All these exerted great pressure on the Rabha village organization which started loosing its solidarity to a great extent. In the wake of all these and particularly with the introduction of Panchayati Raj system, the traditional political organization of the Village Rabhas began to face a new crisis. And in this it lost almost all its power, authority and integrity.

At present the council of elders is not very important and significant in the life of the Village Rabhas. What is still found is only the relics. It cannot exert its power and control over the Rabhas of the village. Cases are found where the Village Rabhas have ignored the decision of their own *marab sen.* Their own village council could neither prevent Ganga Kantran from marrying a non-Rabha nor could it collect any fine from them or could outcaste them.

Now-a-days only in a few cases the Rabha elders of the Village council meet together to discuss same matters having socio-religious bearings. But in most of the cases it is seen that a Village Rabha shows less interest in what happens to his fellow villagers. While among the Forest Rabhas, a social or religious offence affects the whole *bastee* among the Village Rabhas it effects only one or a few households.

At Kumargram area, the first Panchayat system came into being in 1961 and the election of members was completed between April and June of that year. With the introduction of the Panchayati Raj system, the *marab son* among the Village Rabhas has lost much of its importance. At present they sometimes go to the *gram sava* (village Panchayat) instead of the *marab son* or call some of the members of the *gram sava* to attend the meeting of the *marab sen*. These *gram sava* members of Panchayats often take active part in the meeting of the *marab son* and judge the cases.

In the *Kamakhyaguri Anchal Panchayat* which is constituted of eight *gram savas* from seven villages, including *gram savas* of Madhya and Dakshin Manasi, the entire Rabha community is represented by a Rabha from Madhya Manasi. He also represents his community in many other statutory organisations of Alipurduar Sub-division and also of Jalpaiguri district.

MODERN POLITICAL TREND

Forest Rabhas

The Forest Rabhas live in somewhat secluded area. Their *bastees* are usually situated within the Reserve forests. As such outsiders are generally prohibited to enter into the Reserved forests under the prevailing forest protection rules. Moreover, there is the danger of assault by the wild animals. People usually avoid going to the forest *bastees*. As such the agents of various political parties do not prefer much to go to the forest dwelling Rabhas and influence them with their respective ideology except during the time of election. The Forest Rabhas, on the other hand, do not frequently go to the villages, towns and market places outside the forests, except on the weekly market days, when they come in contact with people of other areas. For all these reasons the Forest Rabhas do not seem to be much aware of the present day political trends of the country. Another reason is that economically as well as socially they are less dependent on the people of other communities living outside the forest. Their present economic condition is comparatively better than that of the Village Rabhas, and they hanker less for the modern amenities. Further, they generally prefer to relate their difficulties (if any) to the forest authorities (the Beat officer or the Range Officer) rather than to outsiders. Moreover in their *bastees* there is none who is much aware of the modern political trends and has interest in these. None of the *bastee* dwellers listens to radio regularly and reads newspaper (they cannot read or write). So in absence of these media, they get little information of the present political world. All these have probably, made them less interested or even disinterested in the present day political activities and situations.

Recently in some areas a section of the labourers has started a movement to secure some more facilities from the Government. Some political parties have taken active part in this movement to strengthen it. This movement seems to have been directed towards extracting some extra facilities from the Government.

Village Rabhas

The Village Rabhas of the district of Jalpaiguri received the exposure to modern political forces as early as 1939. These forces percolated through reformative religious movement. This movement was first planned and propelled by the Hindu Mahasava, a politico-religious organisation of this country and later on by the Congress (Indian National Congress).

The Hindu Mahasava sought to prevent the tribals like the Garos, the Maches, the Rabhas and such others from adopting Christianity. The Congress and some other revolutionary parties (such as the Anusilan Samity, the Jugantar group etc.) who fought for the freedom of the country, inspired these Rabhas in the political idealism. The Congress, of course, took the lead in this respect. In 1940-41 the then local Secretary of the National Congress at Alipurduar Sub-division, picked up a Rabha leader and inspired him to become a member of the Congress to fight against the British. Some other Congress leaders also took initiative to inspire him and his compatriots to work for the Congress in the freedom movement. The Rabhas took this chance. In lieu of their active part in the freedom movement, they wanted the assurance from these political parties to accept them as the Hindus. All these parties were agreed to this proposal, and these Rabhas got the moral support from them.

Being inspired by the Congress and other parties and

organisations, who were fighting against the British rule in India, many Rabhas, mainly the Village Rabhas, of Kumargram and Alipurduar police stations of Jalpaiguri district and of Tufanganj police station of Cooch Behar district, took active part in the freedom movement and were imprisoned or otherwise punished for the same. Even after independence many Rabhas still work for the Congress. The Rabhas, in general, support the Congress, though recently some of them have been influenced by the idealism of the Communist Party of India (Marxist) and of the Revolutionary Socialist Party (R.S.P.) etc. Some Rabhas of the two villages studied, take active part in different political movements organised by these parties.

The political idealism was to some extent responsible for intensification of their desire for the Hinduization. They wanted to get a place in the Hindu society. When they came in touch with the political parties and organisations, one of their motto was to win the support of these parties and organisations towards their movements for the Hinduization. This was started under the auspices of the Hindu Mahasava.

So, the Village Rabha get inspiration to a great extent to carry on their movement of the Hinduization. The Rabhas of Madhya and Dakshin Manasi under the charismatic leadership of Sri D.N. Das (Kantran), who was a very prominent figure in the whole of Alipurduar Sub-division, even in the district of Jalpaiguri and others, took active part on the freedom movement of India. These people have made them conscious about their position in the society and have contributed towards improving their social status and position. Some have started looking to their position and condition in the light of the modern liberating political ideologies infused in them by different political parties.

The World of Supernaturals : Beliefs and Practices

10

THE WORLD OF SUPERNATURALS : BELIEFS AND PRACTICES

Religion:

In the primitive world religion is thought to be the

> 'ideas, attitudes, creeds and acts of supernaturalism which includes all that is not natural, that which is regarded as extraordinary, not of the ordinary world, mysterious and unexplained and unexplainable in ordinary terms' as Norbeck puts it. (1961:11).
>
> 'Religion is a cultural universe' and
>
> 'is verily a universal feature of human culture, not because all societies foster a belief in spirit but all recognize in some form or other awe-inspiring, extra-ordinary manifestation of reality' (Lowie, 1936:XVI). MaxMuller held the view that religion sprang from spontaneous emotional reactions of wonder, awe and fear evoked in men by natural phenomena.

Impressed by these powerful and inexplicable forces...primitive men reacted with the emotional attitude and behaviour (Norbeck, 1961:19). The primitive world tries to take a number of measures conjointly in order to expel the action of the evil and to save them from the impending danger, and this action of the primitive people gives them a feeling of oneness and unites them together to fight the forces of evil and danger coming from different internal and/or external agencies. In all primitive or tribal societies of the world, religion is very important and the whole community stands for the religion. They have a deep rooted feelings for their own religion and for their world of deities and spirits.

They always move together to ward off danger by performing certain rites, rituals, festivities or through some magical means. The primitive people unitedly observe these for their safety, security and prosperity as they firmly believe that the religion only can help them achieving these. They would get bumper crops, better hunts, more children, good livestock etc. if they can appease their concerned deities and spirits.

Though "the present day Rabha religion may be characterised as a mixed type of Hinduism and animism" (Das & Raha, 1967 :130) still an important difference is noticed in the religion of the two Rabha divisions of Jalpaiguri district—the Forest Rabhas and the Village Rabhas. This difference is in the degree of admixture of the Hinduism with the traditional animism of the Rabhas. The religion of the Forest Rabhas includes some characteristics of Hinduism in the midst of traditional animism. The Village Rabha religion is much alike the Local Hindu religion in so far as beliefs, practices and ideas are concerned. The traditional animism is less significant here. It is absorbed in the fold of the dominant Hinduism of the Village Rabhas. Among the Forest Rabhas the traditional religion on the otherhand, is the dominating feature. The Rabhas of both sections say they are the Hindus and they practise Hinduism. That most of them practise Hinduism is further evidenced from the returns of 1971 Census which clearly states that 98.42% of the total Rabha population of West Bengal are Hindus. Similarly, 99.71% of total Rabha population of the district of Jalpaiguri and 97.99% of the total Rabha population of the district of Cooch Behar have embraced Hinduism. The same picture been given by the Census of 1961 which reveals that 98.91% (5,987) of the total Rabhhas of west Bengal (6,053) declared themselves as the Hindus, besides 0.97% as Christians and 0.12% as Buddhists (Datta-Gupta, 1968: 168-189). It gives the general view that the majority of the Rabhas declared themselves as the Hindus.

The number of people turning to Christianity is not that significant though in the recent years it has much increased. It is curious to note here that the Census do not record a single Rabha of this district as animist, though the religion of the present day Rabhas, especially of the Forest Rabha section, shows the presence of animism at a high degree. The animism is not visible unless one does go deep into their religious beliefs and practices. Animism is stated to be the attribution of a soul to the natural objects and phenomena. It will be found that religion of the Forest Rabhas is deeply woven with the animistic beliefs, and practices.

It is a fact that besides Hinduism and animism the influence of any other religion such as Christianity, Buddhism, Islam etc. was not at all significant in the life of the Rabhas of West Bengal. This is proved not only from the figures of the Census of 1961 and 1971 but also the data collected through the extensive field investigation carried out by me throughout the district. In recent years of course, a good number of the Rabhas showed their inclination towards Janjogi religion and Christianity, particularly to Christianity.

The same thing is also noticeable among the Rabhas of the three neighbouring districts of Assam where the majority of the Assam Rabhas reside. Among the total 49,217 Rabhas of Goalpara district of Assam according to 1961 Census, 49,004 (99.57%) have declared as the Hindus (Pakyntein, 1965:409). In Kamrup district the same Census returns that 43,721 (99.91%) out of a total of 43,758 Rabhas as the Hindus (Pakyntein, 1964a:387). On the other hand, in Darrang district, though a good number of Christian Rabhas (1,589 or 14.89%) according to 1961 Census, are found to reside, still out of a total of 10,673 Rabhas in this district 9,084 (85.11%) have stated to profess Hinduism (Pakyntein, 1964b:329). It clearly proves that the Rabhas have an earnest will to become the Hindus.

From the early accounts, some idea about the Rabha

religion of the old days may be obtained. Though these early account writers differ in their views, most of them generally agree that the Rabhas show an inclination towards Hinduism. Regarding the Rabha religion Hodgson in 1849 stated, "I look upon the Rabhas as merely the earliest and most complete converts to Hinduism" (1849 : 712). Later on even in 1880 he persisted in his earlier view (1880 : 115). Martin referring to Buchanon-Hamilton, states that the ground work of the Rabhas is quite similar to that of the Pani-Kooch who 'has not adopted the Brahminical religion" (Buchanon-Hamilton, 1810 : 215 ; Martin, 1838 : 547). But after nearly 150 years Majumdar finds the Pani-Koch group to have 'adopted such an amount of Sanskritization that they have definitely come under the fold of Hinduism' (1967 : 70). Hunter believes that the Rabha religion is a mixed religion of animism and Hinduism. He states, "their religion is a curious mixture of belief in their own demons and good spirits, and in Hindu Gods, whom they also worship after their own fashion" (1876 : 37). That they were 'on the road to Hinduism', was marked by Gait (1892 : 232), Waddel, on the other hand. marked that though the Rabhas were in the process of Hinduism still the influence of the Hinduism was very obscure even less legible than that found among the Koch (1900 : 65). Endle also found that the animist Rabhas were inclined to Hinduism. His opinion is that "the general type of the Rabha religion is distinctly animistic, but one or two of the higher sub-divisions, especially the Patis, are said to show a leaning towards Hinduism of the *Sakta* form (1911 : 84-85). Allen on the other hand, found the bulk of the tribe professing animism (1902 : 142). But in some other account he reports about the presence of a tinge of a Buddhistic form of doctrine in the Rabha religion (1903 : 51). Friend-Pereira's view is quite similar to that of Allen. He finds the Rabhas as pure animists. "Even their most Hinduised section, the Pati Rabhas, never represent their host of gods and demons by images or pieces of stones or other natural objects", he said in support of their animism. But he also could not trace any tinge of Buddhistic impression in the Rabha religion (Friend-Pereira, 1912 : 144).

So it is seen from the early accounts that the Rabhas from a very early time, felt the essence of dominant Hindu religion and started modelling their religion with the Hindu religious elements.

This also holds good in case of the Rabhas of West Bengal. Though their religion is a mixed form of animism and Hinduism, still a section of them who lives in the villages, is more advanced on the road to the Hinduism (Das & Raha, 1967 : 131). The other section, the forest dwelling Rabhas, has still retained in less-altered form of the traditional religion; of course, even in their religion recent introduction of the traces of Hinduism are also noticeable.

The Forest Rabha Religion

The present day Forest Rabhas are the worshippers of various spirits and natural objects. They worship spirits of various rivers, springs, forests, hills, wild animals and other natural objects. In their *bastee*-altar (*baidam*) which is usually situated within the reserve forests, they construct miniature temples where these spirits are believed to reside. Though this section of the Rabhas has a large number of deities and spirits, their chief deity is Rishi (Raha, 1963 : 29). But there is a controversy among the early account writers whether Rishi is a male or female. While Buchanon-Hamilton, Martin and Dalton are of opinion that Rishi is a male one and his wife is Charipak (Martin, 1838 : 547 ; Dalton, 1872 : 87). Sunder's view is that Rishi, a female deity, is the wife of Juggo and is "considered to be the Greatest of these two deities" (1895 : 76). For this reason a Rabha man has to submit himself to a Rabha woman in all matters. "Her whims and fancies are law to him" (Sunder, 1895 : 76). Among the Pani-Koch too, the principal deity is Rishi. Rishi, for the Forest and the Village Rabhas, is a male deity and is also known as Mahakal. But Sunder considers them as two different deities (*ibid*). "Rishi and his wife are the Gods that are worshipped throughout Assam as the Buraburi, though under Brahmanical influence in most place the Buraburi are now worshipped as if they are Shiva and Durga" (Dalton, *ibid*). In this connection it may be said that in the district of Jalpaiguri Shiva is also considered as

Mahakal. Buchanon, Martin and Dalton are of opinion that Rishi and his wife live in heaven (*rongkorong*) (Martin : *ibid* : Dalton : *ibid*).

Among the Forest Rabhas a long bamboo pole represents Rishi. This bamboo pole has two branches on two sides of its free end from which are hung cotton threads in which small lumps of cotton are tied. This bamboo, usually planted in the courtyard in front of the house, is known as *zerphak*. Sunder expresses the same view (Sunder, *ibid*). But Allen is of the opinion that Rshi is represented by a pot of rice on a bamboo platform. Probably Allen's view is not correct. Among the Rabhas of this State two earthen pots of rice placed on the northern side of the platform of the store, are represented by Rungtuk and Basek respectively. The Village Rabhas call Rungtuk as Thansiri also following the Rajbansis. Rungtuk and Basek are the two daughters of Rishi or Mahakal Rishi is an old one and very powerful, and that is why the Rabhas, especially tne Forest Rabhas, worship Him in all important social and religious ceremonies. Rungtuk and Basek are household deities and considered as the deities of wealth like Lakshmi of the Hindus.

Besides the above deities, the forest Rabhas have several other spirits which denote different natural objects such as rivers, streams, hills, forests, wild anmals etc. Some of these spirits are Bura-Garam (spirit of the river and forest, Garam), Bura Tabak (spirit of the river, Tabak), Bura Dima (spirit of the river Dima), Bura Par Thakur (spirits of the river, forest and *bastee*. Paro), Bagh Raja and Bagh Sanyasi (spirits of the tigers), Bura Torsa and Gabur Torsa (spirits of the river, Torsa), Salkumar Raja (spirit of the Salkumar forests), Benia Raja (spirit of Bania beat), Rajdundi (spirits of water), Baska Raja (spirit of the hills), Jalbak (spirit of cholera) etc. So this shows that the Rabhas worship a large number of spirits of the natural objects like mountains, rivers, streams, forests, wild animals etc. Slde by side the Rabhas also worship some kings as saints or spirits such as Bhot Raja (king of Bhutan), Nalraja (king Nala) etc. Besides, there are three other deities, Portani, Maitani and Michik-bai who are considered as the deities for the children. Of these three, Portani is considered as a child catcher. She is worshipped so that she does not catch and kill any child. The other two deities are known to be the spirits for child welfare. These spirits are invoked after child-birth or when a child suffers from illness. It is interesting to observe the similarity between Portani and the Buddhist Tantric goddess Hariti, as the latter is also known as the stealer and killer of child. The other two have the similarity with the Hindu deity, Sasthi, who is worshipped as the giver and protector of tbe child. The forest Rabhas have adopted some deities in recent years such as Lakshmi, Shiva and Mahakal etc. These Hindu deities are worshipped in their own method. No Hindu Brahmin is employed nor any Brahmanical method of worship has been adopted. Among this section of the Rabhas the *deosi* and the *dhami* are the traditional community priests. The former is known to be superior because only he is entitled to worship Rishi or Mahakal, the supreme deity. The worship of all these deities and spirits is done in their traditional way with the offerings of several articles and *chakat* (rice-beer) and sacrifice of certain animals and fowl. Tne worship of idols or any morphic figures is conspicuously absent.

The Village Rabha Religion

The religion of the present day Village Rabhas may be called a mixed type of religion, a mixed form of animism and Hinduism. The Village Rabha religion of today is well on its way to Hinduism. They worship the deities of the Hindu pantheon. "Kali, Shiva, Kamakhyam, Narayan, Sitala, Gangadevi etc., are the important deities worshipped. Besides these, there are other deities and spirits such as Rakal, Biskarma, Bishari, Masan, Bara Thakur, Surkumi, Murla, Jalmasan, Gabur etc. (Raha, 1963 : 29 ; Das & Raha, 1967 : 132). They worship the Hindu deities alongside the spirits of different natural objects.

Besides the above the Rabhas also have many other deities and spirits, *Nur-bai* is accepted as the deity for the welfare of the parturient woman and the new-born child. This deity has the similarity with the goddess Sasthi of the Bengali Hindus. Bulua Ray is a very malevolent spirit. Some particular place in the forest known as *talai-dam*, is its abode. Adult males and females are often possessed by it. Dokal is another malevolent spirit. It causes various types of stomach disorders. The evil soul of any dead person is known as the Joura. Gang-raja is the deity for agriculture. He is worshipped in a part of a cultivable land in the month of *aswin* (September-October). He is worshipped for bumper crops. But the Rangdani Rabhas of Assam on the other hand, have different sets of the deities (*bai*). Deities among them are of two types (i) deities whose rites are annually performed by the villagers jointly for the general well-being of the village. These deities are called Hason Bai (deities of the land) (ii) Deities causing different types of ailments. These deities are propitiated only when occasion arises. These deities are called Bai Kakkai (deities which bite) (Friend-Pereira, 1912 : 144).

Though many Village Rabhas have Thansiri or Rungtuk but the majority of them do not have Basek. They do not plant *zerphak* like the Forest Rabhas. Besides Thansiri, some of the Rabhas of these two villages have extra *thakurghar* (temple for the deities) or sometimes *laksmighar* (i.e. abode of Lakshmi, Goddess of wealth and prosperity). But every Village Rabha household has *tulsi-than* or *tulsi-mancha* (sacred Basil altar) which is considered as the abode of gods like *Balaram* (brother of Lord Krishna), *Lord Krishna* and *Lord Narayan* etc. The *tulsi-mancha*, is an elevated earthen altar with Basil plants grown in it. The Forest Rabhas do not have such *tulsi-mancha*. Like the Forest Rabhas and the Rajbansis, (Sanyal, 1965 : 134-137) the Village Rabhas worship deities and spirits of different natural objects such as the rivers, forests, hills etc. viz. Tista Buri (spirits of the river, Tista), Torsa Raja (spirit of the river Torsa) etc. They also worship Kali. But the most important goddess of the Rabha of the two villages is Kamakhya. The Rajbansis of the area also have identical deities and spirits. Sanyal refers to the similar deities and spirits being worshipped by the Rajbansis of the North Bengal (*ibid*, 134-150)

The Rabhas of the two villages observe different religious festivals such as the *balarampuja*, the *nisakali puja*, the *janmastami*, and the *radhastami*, the *bisharipuja*, the *Kalipuja*, the *shivpuja*, the *laksmipuja*, the *satya narayanpuja* etc. in the same way as done by the local Rajabansi by employing Brahmin (Assamese) or *adhikari* (Rajbansi Brahmin) (*ibid.*, 133-139). They do not employ the *deosi* or *dhami*, their own community priest as are done by their brethren living in the forest *bastees*, because they do not have the *deosi* and the *dhami*. The similar method of worship is followed in their case as is followed in case of the local Hindu castes.

It is difficult to say how far the Rabhas have imbibed the Brahmanical conceptions connected with the various deities and festivities. Most of the Rabha inhabitants are ignorant of these. They have developed these by imitating the local Hindus, especially the Rajbansis. For example, Lord Balaram and the *balaram puja* (festival in which Lord Balaram is invoked), Goddess Manasa and the *mansa puja* (festival in which Manasa, goddess of snakes is invoked), the *Janmastami* and the *radhastami* (in which Lord Krishna and Radha are paid homages) etc., are taken from the Rajbansis. But the *lakshmipuja* (festival of Goddess Lakshmi) the *satya narayan puja* (festival of Lord Narayan) etc. have been imbibed from the higher caste Hindus.

So unlike the congeners living in the forest *bastees*, the Village Rabhas have replaced much of their traditional religion by the local Hindu religious beliefs and practices. The Forest Rabhas have still retained their religious tradition to the great extent. However below we give some more details about some of the deities of the Rabhas of West Bengal.

Runtuk and Basek

Runtuk and Basek have taken the most important place in the Rabha pantheon of deities and spirits. These two deities also known to the Rabhas as Dhan-Lakshmi, are their household deities. In general these deities are known as Thansiri or Ghar-deo. Thansiri means *sthaneswari* or *sthanshree* i.e. deity of the place. The Rajbansis and the Bodo also have household deity called Thansiri. The Bodos also call it Mainao. But the method of worship is quite different from one group to another.

The abode of Runtuk and Basek is in a bamboo platform by the side of the paddy store in the north-west part of the northern most room. This bamboo platform is known as *ching sang gang*. The head of the household lives in this room. These deities do not have any morphic figure. A red coloured earthen pitcher full with paddy represents the deity Runtuk. On the neck of this pitcher one egg of the hen i.e. *tou cho* (*tou*= hen,che=egg), is kept. When this pitcher is purchased, a Rabha does never bargain with the potter. Whatever the latter wants as price of the pitcher, is given. But the pitcher must be without any spot or crack.

The traditional priest, *deosi*, counts the auspicious day for the foundation of these deities. The worship connected with the foundation of the deities, always takes place at the night of the brighter half of the month. Various articles like incense, vermilion (*sindur*), cotton (*carpas*), ball made of rice flour, rice beer, pig, pieces of new white and red cloth, *atap* (par boiled) rice, banana etc. are required for this purpose. Besides offering the above articles, chicken or pig is also sacrificed. The place of sacrifice is situated very close to the door for entering into the kitchen of the house. At the time of sacrifice the *deosi* utters the following *mantra* (incantation)

Hal Jal Ji Neu
Hal Jal Ji Nai
Sona Nogou Na Bau
Sona Noktang Na Oau
Hatti Rai Tasay
Ghora Bau Tasay
Hal Jal Ji Neu
Hal Jal Ji Nai

(Runtuk, Basek, you are two sisters; Runtuk, I am offering you a house made of gold. Basek, I am offering you a house made of silver. Be kind to us. Do not get angry with us and go away on an elephant; do not go away angrily on a horse. Oh Goddess Runtuk ! Oh Goddess Basek ! be kind with us). But the offering of *chakat* is the most vital part of the ceremony. The *deosi* sits on the bamboo platform and worships the deities. The day of foundation of the deity in the house is observed with worship and festivity every year. Every evening the deity is propitiated with lamp and burning incense.

On the occasion of any social or ritual ceremony these two deities are always worshipped first. After marriage when the newly married couple goes from bride's house to groom's house or vice versa, they must pay their homage to these deities. After harvest or when they first eat the new rice these deities are worshipped with pomp. The Rabhas make vow to these deities in case of any danger, disease or sufferings in the house.

Basek is considered as the sister and companion of the Runtuk. She is also represented by a smaller earthen pitcher which is kept on the right side of the pitcher represented by Runtuk. Identically this pitcher is also filled with rice up to the neck and an egg of hen is kept on this rice. The pitcher is wrapped with red and white cloth pieces. Vermilion is also painted on the pitcher.

Michik Bai

Goddess Michik Bai is worshipped for the welfare of the children as already stated. The worship is undertaken by the *deosi* in the evening by offering *atap* rice, flowers, some sweets and by burning incense. One cock and one hen are sacrificed. Offering of *chakat* is also very important. Rishi and Mahakal are also worshipped. After the worship the *prasaḍ* (offerings) is first of all given to the child for whose welfare this worship has been made. Then the same is given to all others. During puja the *deosi* utters the following incantation.

Dohai Mama Byolni
Dohai Bantorni
Dohai Amburi Dohai Amburi
Dohai Jinnyani
Dohai Mama Byolni
(Maternal uncle Byolni bless him
Banterni bless him
Mother Amburi bless him

Jinnyani bless him
Bless him uncle Byolni)

Nur Bai

In the Rabha society Nur Bai is worshipped as the deity of child welfare. In case the expectant mother or the child suffers from any disease, this deity is worshipped in the evening of any day in the same room where the expectant mother or the child is lying. A *zerphak* is also erected there. The *deosi* worships the deity by offering *atap* rice, ripened banana and *chakat*. Usually a duck or a pigeon is sacrificed and the blood is sprinkled there. Then most of the sacrificed bird is cooked with *atap* rice and offered to the deity. Then the *huli* (medicine man) treats the child with the burning incense to cure him.

Bulua Bai

Bulua Bai is one of the malevolent deities of the Rabhas. This spirit may possess any male and female and harm them. The *huji* can only determine if a man or a woman is possessed by Bulua Bai or some other spirit. The typical expressions and behaviour of the man/woman possessed indicate that he/she has been possessed by Bulua Bai. To cure him/her the *huji* performs various magical rites like *telpara* (magical means by oil), *jalpara* (magical means by water). And to remove the influence of this spirit the *huji* performs a *puja* in the near-by Forest. The spirit does not have any figure. A small bamboo with branches (*pahla*) is treated as the deity as the Rabha believe that this deity looks like a bamboo. The male Rabhas take this bamboo and go to the forest where the *huji* worships it with offerings. Then after taking the offered articles they start for the village silently without looking back. They believe that if they look back or talk, the spirit may accompany them. Bulua Bai is a male deity and has two sisters as his companions. They are Pania and Gancha. They are also worshipped along with Bulua Bai.

Dekal

Dekal is one of the spirits of the Rabhas for which people

suffer from various stomach troubles. When a man suffers from acute stomach trouble the *huji* instructs for a worship of this spirit. The relatives of the patient construct a platform (*chadang*) made of bamboo splits (*haplak*) where various offerings including rice, vegetables, entrails of the chicken or pig are kept for the spirit. Then the *huji* invokes the spirit. After the worship they throw all these materials on the field without taking the offerings which are forbidden to eat.

Joura kal

Joura is the spirit of the dead man. It is always a malevolent one. *Huji* can determine if somebody is possessed by this spirit through some magical rite (*jhar-phuk*). In order to appease this spirit, an altar is made in the western side of the living room where the spirit is worshipped with the offerings of the powdered rice and *chakat* and sacrifice of a chicken. Nobody takes the offerings.

Gang Raja

When the sweet smell of the autumn paddy is blown through the air all over, the Rabha peasants worship Gang Raja for a bumper harvest. In one evening in the month of *aswin* (September-October) they worship this spirit in the paddy field. They construct a bamboo platform (*chadang*) where they worship with rice, banana, etc. and also sacrifice a duck which are offered to Gang Raja along with the *chakat* by the *huji*.

Rishi Jaga

Rishi and his consort Jaga are considered as the supreme deities. Rishi is also known as Mahakal and is considered as equivalent to Shiva of the Hindu pantheon. Rishi and Jaga do not have any morphic figures and are worshipped in different socio-religious crises. They are sometimes worshipped inside the living room on the bamboo platform (*ching-sang-gang*) where there are Runtuk and Basek. A small bamboo having a number of branches with small balls of cotton hung from these branches is kept standing. This is called *zerphak* which symbolises the deities. Worship is performed by the *dhami* by offering articles like *atap* rice, banana. curd, chapped rice (*chida*) etc. Sometimes, depending on the nature of crisis, a chicken or a pig is sacrificed. Worship also takes place on the courtyard in front of the house where the *zerphak* is planted.

Socio-Political and Socio-Religious Movements

Like many tribal societies in India (Singh, 1973), the Rabhas cf West Bengal were also involved in movements at different time and juncture of their life. Their desire to get a place in the local Hindu society was a long-standing one, still their actual movement for Hinduism began as early as 1939. Though a detailed account on this movement among the Rabhas has already been discussed elsewhere (see Raha *et al,* 1978:50-55), we like to incorporate a brief account of these movements here considering their important relevance to the socio-religious life of these people. In fact the Rabhas were involved in two different movements; one that is Hinduisation movement which began, as already stated, in early 1939, and the other, the Janjogi movement started during 1960. While the Hinduization movement was geared up with the aim of getting admission into the Hindufold and thereby raising their social standing' (Raha *et. al*, 1978) and was started by the Rabhas themselves though of course, inspired by the non-Rabhas, the Janjogi movement on the other hand, was started by the non-Rabhas to bring the Rabhas into their fold by baptising them into their faith and idealism. While the Hinduisation movement was mainly sponsored by the Village Rabhas, the Janjogi movement was restricted to the Forest Rabhas only. The basic difference beween these two movements was that while the Hinduization movement of the Village Rabhas was basically a social mobility movement, the Janjogi movement was basically a religious movement mixed with the principle of social reformation and these movements had created a good deal of enthusiasm among these simple folk which were hitherto unknown in their life'. (Raha, et al, *ibid*).

The Hinduization Movement

The Hinduization movement among the Viliage Rabhas

though reached its peak in 1939, had actually a very humble beginning in 1930. During this year a group of the Rabhas inhabiting Bhorea village under Tufangunj Police Station of Cooch Behar district thought of becoming Hindu and thereby securing a place in the local Hindu society. For a long time they were aspiring for this status. They had seen how the local Koch or the Rajbansis started the Kshatrization movement and secured a place in the Hindu society. They had also seen how the Koch could shake off their tribal or primitive status and secured a place in the Hindu society through such a movement. Such movements provoked the Rabhas of Bhorea to venture in the similar line which they thought might help them to land in their secured goal. In their multi-ethnic village where they were living with different Hindu castes including the Rajbansis, they were discriminated and looked down upon by their Hindu co-villagers. But this discrimination and social distance created by the then conservative forces among the local Hindus, could not force them to give up their desire for a justice, a fair position in the western Duars' society. Rabhas instead of becoming disheartened they activated their movement more and more and therefore their desire for reaching the goal was aggravated.

> "But they were being socially discriminated and looked down upon by their Hindu/Hinduized compatriots, and the prevailing social climate had infused in them an ardent desire to upgrade their social position so that they may receive a fair deal from their co-residents" (Raha et al, 1978).

But the thing was not so smooth-sailing. The conservative forces were not so easily to bent down upon and accept the request of the people who were so long kept in the bottom. Rather the demand of the Rabhas for a higher social status tightened the attitude of these forces towards the Rabhas who started hitting the Rabhas back.

> "Things became worse when the Rabhas aspiring for higher status, wanted to attend the *harisabha* (temple of the Lord

> Hari organised by the Hindu) which has obviously a move on their part to socially equalise them with the Hindus, but were prevented from doing so. This humiliated them. It became more acute when Sri Bhabendra Nath Choudhuri, a Hindu saint, declared that the Rabhas were Hindu and so they not only possessed the right of attending *harisabha* but also had the genuine right of receiving the services of the Brahmans and barbers." (Raha et al : *ibid*)

Shri Choudhuri's feelings for the Rabhas and support for them was not only to uplift them from their low position in the ladder of social hierarchy, but the main reason was 'possibly to detract them from being swayed by the strong wind of conversion of the local tribal into Christianity'. (Raha et al : *ibid*) During this time Christian missions were quite active in this region. Different tribal groups like the Mech, the Santhal, the Oraon, the Munda and others of this area were baptised to Chrisianity by the Christian missionaries. They were also trying to convert the Rabhas to Christianity. So when the Rabhas saw that a section of the Hindus was trying to bring them in the Hindu fold in spite of the opposition from the other section, the enlightened Rabhas thought not to miss this opportunity. They felt that if they could avail themselves of this opportunity, they might be successful in their aim. So they held meetings, discussed the issue and decided that this opprtunity should not be missed. Accordingly they adopted the following resolutions.

I. The Rabhas should get the status of Sudra.
II. They should give up drinking liquor and rearing pigs and fowl.
III. They should get the surname Sarania (Roy Choudhuri, 1970 : 89).

After this decision a good number of the Rabha families of this village 'purified' themselves through some rituals (*yajna*) and declared themselves as the 'Hindu Rabha'. They faced some difficulty in getting priest (*adhikari*), Brahman and barber who have important role in the Hindu rituals. At that time no

Rajbansi *adnikari*, no Brahman and no barber agreed to serve these 'Hindu' Rabhas. 'So one Hepak Rabha was initiated by Shri Bhabendra Nath himself and was raised to the status of *adhikari* of the Rabha and a barber was secured from Assam ; . . ." (Roy Choudhury : *ibid*). But thing was not that smooth sailing.

> "The after-effect of this move was not very promising. The Rabhas of Barasalbari (P.S. Tufanganj) and Kamakhyaguri (P.S. Kumargram), who are numerically stronger, declined to accept the converts in their society and the Rajbansis, whom the Rabhas are imitating, and the other Hindu castes also refused to accept them as Hindu. Moreover, the Rabhas, in general, were poor and were dependent on the Rajbanshis. The latter do not rear pigs and fowl due to their social custom. They gave them to the Rabhas for rearing and got their stipulated shares. On becoming 'purified', that source of earning was closed. The Rajbanshis also became deprived of the special arrangement when the Rabhas refused to rear pigs and fowl. It was due to this that other Rabhas and Rajbanshis opposed it. Consequently eight out of ten Rabha families left Hinduism within two years of their first purification and went back to their age-old customs." (Roy Choudhury, *ibid*).

Due to this opposition from the Rajbansis and other Hindu castes, particularly from their own people, the Rabhas who were keen for becoming Hindus, suffered from a temporary set-back. Though many of them gave up 'Hinduisms' they adopted on becoming 'purified', but their thirst for 'Hinduism' did not subside. It was a temporary recession. Their desire for Hinduism was rekindled again after a lapse of a few years only.

> "It was to the credit of Sri Dhaneshwar Bhattacharya, a Hindu social reformer, that the Rabha Hinduization movement received a jolt and was again set in motion around 1939-40. This social reformer took up the mission of getting the Rabhas acknowledged as Hindus on a war-footing basis when he heard that the Rabhas around

Manasi and Barasalbari would prefer to embrace Christianity if their adoption to Hinduism was denied. However, this task was not at all a smooth-sailing-affair as there was continued resistance from the Hindus as well as from the conservative section of the Rabha tribal group itself. The job appeared to be harder when 'the British Government and the Christian Missionaries also went against him' (Raha, 1970 ; Raha et al : *ibid*).

During thc lull of these five or six years the Rabhas of those villages who earlier showed their opposition against the Hinduization movement of the Rabha, now started showing some interest towards it. Shri Dhaneswar Chakravarty came to know it. He tried to pursue the Rabhas of these villages after having a detailed discussion with them. From the outcome of the discussion he realised that unless he had a verdict from some authority he might not be successful in coverting the Rabhas to Hinduism. The converted Rabhas might not be accepted either by other Rabhas or by the local Hindus like the Rajbansis. So

> 'facing the opposition Sri Bhattacharjee sought for advice from the then Royal *Pandith* (*dwar pandith*) of Cooch Behar royal family who gave him the directive that the communities like the Rabhas, the Garos, the Meches, the Koches and such others might be transformed into the Hindu, and the water from them could be acceptable if proper expiation was done as they were untouchables previously. Then he started this movement among these people with the fresh energy and enthusiasm. He performed several *yajna* in different places, such as Bara Salbari and Bandijelous under Tufanganj Police Station of Cooch Behar district, Madhya Manasi and Daldali-Hemaguri under Kumargram Police station and Jasodanga under Alipurduar Police Station of Jalpaiguri district where after elaborate rituals and expiatory rites, the Rabhas became Hindu ceremonially. Sri Bhattacharjee took two other Brahmans (Assamese), Hridinath Debsarma and Mohit Kumar Debsarma and two barber (Assamese Napit),

Ghanashyam Seal and Nidhiram Seal for performing different social and religious ceremonies among the Rabhas. The present Brahmins (Assamese) Dhaneswar Chakravarty and his brother, Raneswar Chakravarty came to this place after a few years when Hridinath Debsarma and Mohit Kumar Debsarma left the villages. In this way the Rabhas became Hindus, got the services of the Brahmin and the barber' (Raha, 1970 : 453).

At that time the Pandits in the court of the Maharaja of Cooch Behar were considered as the sole authority on Hinduism and socio-religious rules and regulations of the Hindus.

On receiving the verdict in favour, Shri Bhattacharya arranged purificatory ceremony in different villages inhabited by the Rabhas. The first village where such a purificatory ceremony took place, was Barasalbari (Bochamari) which was preceded by a meeting in which the following resolutions were passed.

(1) Within one month from this day we shall give up pork, chicken and liquor and enter into the Hindu community according to the Shastras. From this day we shall perform all the rites and ceremonies according to the Shastras. From now we shall not perform the rites connected with death and marriage and other ceremonies as we did so long. We shall practise the manners and customs of the Sudras of the Hindu community and receive (the services of) Brahmin priests and barbers.

(2) Our original custom that the daughter would inherit the property of the father is detestable ; so we decide together that the son shall inherit the father's property. For this a petition has to be submitted to the Maharaja of Cooch Behar, so that the son might be accepted as the successor of the father's property instead of the daughter.

(3) In obedience to the injunction of our religious preceptor, we shall construct one *harimandir* (a house

for the worship of the deity, Hari and for the assembly of the devotees to sing religious songs in the name of Hari) in a convenient place in every village. Every month, once or more than once, as occasion arises, we shall assemble in that *harimandir* and hold discourse on religious matters. We shall obey all the precepts of the Shastras in matters connected with religion and in this we shall follow what our preceptor tells us to do.

(4) If there is a quarrel or difference of opinion among ourselves, we shall bring in our preceptor and have it decided (or compromised). In all matters we shall follow the order (advice) of the preceptor. We shall not do anything against his orders.

(5) We shall accept the Brahmin, whom the preceptor selects as our priest. When necessity arises, he shall arrange for a barber. In obedience to his instruction, we shall accept barber, Brahmin and Babaji (*Adhikari*) (whose social status is lower than that of the Brahmin priest).

(6) We accept Srijukta Dhaneswar Bhattacharya of Taluk Bhatibari of Pargana Katibari, P.S. Alipur Duar, Dt. Jalpaiguri, as our preceptor. We shall obey him in all respects in religious matters and not otherwise.

Signatures of different villagers — 2nd Magh, 1347 B.S.

(Roychoudhury, 1970 : 90-92)

It was decided that any breach of these directives from the part of anybody, would be dealt severely. Any Rabha found guilty of violation of these directives would be excommunicated and he would have to perform expiatory rituals for re-entry. However, Shri Bhattacharya with the help of three Brahmins and two barbers of Assamese origin, 'undertook the purificatory ceremony which includes *yajna* also among the Rabhas an 28th *chaitra* (March-April) 1347 B.S. (1940) in the village Barasalbari in order to aecept the Village Rabhas in the Hindu society. The Rabhas thus purified, took the surname 'Das'.

Later on a meeting was held under the chairmanship of Shri Bhattarcharya and the following resolution was taken.

"In pursuance of the meeting held on Wednesday, the 2nd Magh, 1347 B.S., we have become purified that day by a Brahmin in the presence of the gentlemen present are overleaf and our castemen who have put in their signatures below have promised to be purified very soon like ourselves. In pursuance of their promise we have become purified today.

1347 B.S.—28th Chaitra, Friday
Priests :
Sd./1. Sri Lalit Chandra Deb Sarma
2. Sri Hari Nath Deb Sarma
3. Sri Baneswar Bhagabati
Barber :
Sd./1. Sri Sidhiram Sil
2. Sri Chanaram Sil

After the purification in Barasalbari the Rabhas of Kamakshyaguri were also purified in the same way on the 18th of Jaistha (April-May), 1348 B.S. (1941). A meeting was also held in Kamakshyaguri and it was resolved that

1. In accordance with the decision of the meeting held on the 2nd Magh, 1347 B.S. in Bachamari (Barasalbari), we the inhabitants of Kamakshyaguri (whose signatures are given below) have become purified today. From this day onward we shall perform rites and ceremonies as the Sudras of the Hindu community do. We shall perform all the spiritual, ancestral, and other rites and ceremonies of the Hindus. If we do otherwise, we shall have to do penance and undergo fresh purification.
2. We agree that we shall perform all our future rites and ceremonies with the help of two priests (a) Srijukta Lalit Chandra Deb Sarma and (b) Srijukta Harinath Deb Sarma, who are present at the time of purification.

3. We shall be purified by Srijukta Dhaneswar Bhattacharya of Chatibari village. We accept him as our religious preceptor. All religious observances will be performed according to his instruction.

18th Jaistha, 1348, B.S. (1st June 1941)
Sri Dhaneswar Bhattacharya
Sri Baneswar Bhagabati
Written by
Sri Rudra Singh (Mech)

Thereafter such type of purificatory ceremony to admit the Rabhas in the Hindu society took place in different Rabha inhabited villages of Alipurduar Sub-division of Jalpaiguri district and Tufangunj Sub-division of Cooch Behar district.

While analysing the various movements among different tribal people, Mahapatra observes,

> "Social movements of chiliastic or massianic kind, primarily aimed at increasing their ethnic unity, purity and prosperity through a reformed religion . . . in their later phase got politically oriented . . . often ending in a violent clash with the British power. As the National Congress carried its campaigns into the interior of India, the participants of these originally non-political, non-national movements were taking part in anti-Britlsh demonstrations' (1972 : 404).

The same thing happened wlth the Rabhas.

> "During the years of the Rabhas' struggle for acquiring Hindu status, the National Freedom Movement was simultaneously going on. Several political parties were already active in this part of country and could mobilise the people against the British. The activities of the 'Anushilan Samity' (a revolutionary group of Bengal) had already created much anxiety to the colonial administration and the people's anti-British sentiment was growing fast. However, the anti-British wave that swept the entire North Bengal in these days, had very little or no impact on the Rabhas who

remained largely aloof from this at that time and were primarily interested in getting Hindu status for which they were striving hard. Nevertheless the Rabha sentiment did not escape the notice of the local political activists who came forward to derive political benefit out of their social aspiration. The Hindu Mahasabha backed the Rabha cause and Sri Baneshwar Bhattacharya was deputed to explore the feasibility of bestowing Hindu status on the Rabhas. The local unit of the Indian National Congress in particular, was successful in conveying their message to the Rabha mass mainly through some local elites, particularly through Sri Daben Das, a Rabha. Sri Das was already popular among the Rabhas to a great extent as a stage actor of local folk theatre. Sri Das did an excellant job in mobilizing the Rabhas for freedom movement. However, the Rabha enthusiasm in the Freedom struggle culminated in the incident when a large number of the local Rabhas led by Sri Das and others took part in active anti-British demonstration in various places of Alipurduar Sub-division, particularly at the Kumargram Police Station which culminated in the Police firing. Many Rabhas courted arrest while some of them were injured in this action. Thus the Hinduization movement among the Rabha which initially started as a local social mobility movement, was later on involved in the greater freedom struggle too, mainly due to the sympathetic attitude as well as assurances of the various political parties for fulfilment of the social objective of the Rabhas, which they were trying to achieve through the Hinduization movement." (Raha et al, 1978 :).

The Janjogi Movement

One *Param Pita Tribouddha Gundhari Janjogi Baba* is the originator and propagator of the Janjogi religion. It originated in 1960 and was first preached at Purodha *bastee*. Later on Rabhas of some of the other forest *bastees* also accepted this new religion. This religion prohibited drinking of liquor and discarded any easy-going life. It also discouraged worship of deities and spirits and prescribed hard work leading to self sufficiency and economic prosperity. At the beginning due to fear of being destroyed, the Rabhas of some forest *bastees* accepted this religion (Raha, et al, 1978 :). The simple Rabhas accepted this religion only to avert their destruction. But when they realised that the story of destruction of those who did not embrace this new religion was a false one, and when they felt that it was difficult for them to accept the rules of the Janjogi religion, particularly to disregard their own pantheon of deities and spirits, and to abstain from drinking, many of the Forest Rabhas who were baptised to this new religion, started leaving it in favour of their traditional religion. As a result the Janjogi religion persists only among a few Rabhas of some forest *bastees*, these days.

It is interesting to note here that while the Hinduization movement involved the Village Rabhas, the Janjogi movement restricted only to the Forest Rabhas. This movement 'though apparently religious in nature, had objective of social reformation too, characterised by the rejection of certain traditional customs and practices and at initial stage met some success'. (Raha, et al, 1978). The type of movement may be termed as 'revisionary' as this was 'organised for the 'improvement' or 'purification of the culture or social order to get rid of 'evil' or 'low' type of customs, beliefs or institutions of the people.' (Mahapatra, 1972 : 400). The Hinduization movement among the Village Rabha on the other hand, was meant to achieve a status in the Hindu society which involved 'a significant discontinuity in social affiliation and cultural orientation, as is characteristic of a 'revolutionary' movement''. (*ibid*).

> "It is particularly interesting to note that the Hinduization movement which was initially a non-political and an exclusively social movement, presented, a political colour with the Rabha participation in the larger National Freedom movement in the latter phase. And in this changing character of the movement too, the basic social aspiration of the Rabhas operated decisively."

Another interesting point to be noted here is that the Hinduization movement helped the Village Rabhas to come closer to the patriarchal Hindu society and to adopt many patrilineal Hindu characters to replace their traditional matrilineal norm. But in case of the Forest Rabhas rejection of the Janjogi religion by them helped them to restore their matrilineal tradition.

The Summing up : The Rabha's March for a New Tradition

11

THE SUMMING UP : THE RABHA'S MARCH FOR A NEW TRADITION

In the foregoing chapters I have tried to analyse the various aspects of the culture of the two ecological groups of the Rabhas of West Bengal—the Forest dwelling Rabhas and the village inhabiting Rabhas, giving particular emphasis on the change of their culture. This comparative study reveals that while the change in the traditional matrilineal Forest Rabhas culture is not that significant, the culture of the Village Rabhas depicts marked changes due to various factors, and these changes have resulted in the formation of an altogether different type of social system—from matrilineal to patrilineal one, though traces of the traditional metriliny is still in existence proving their past matrilineal base.

The study reveals that the two ecological sections of the Rabhas—the Forest Rabha and the Village Rabhas—consider themselves as belonging to the same Rabha i.e. the Koch Rabha group though they admit the cultural and linguistic differences between them. The present day difference in habitat of these two sections of the Rabhas is of course there but even the present day Village Rabhas acknowledge that once in the past their settlements were also covered or surrounded by the forest as was the condition of the Duars in the past, and they had the same type of isolation as is prevalent in the forest settlements of the present day, if not more.

The study shows that the forest *bastees*, situated inside the Reserve Forest areas, are somewhat isolated due to the prevailing forest rules which prohibit the entry of the outsiders. Those forest *bastees* where the Rabhas live, are mostly inhabited by the Rabhas only and are as such, culturally homogeneous. The same degree of cultural homogeneity is not found among the Rabhas living in the village where various Hindu castes, the Muslims and the other tribal people also inhabit in their neighbourhood. Unlike the Forest Rabhas who have been living in semi-isolation without experiencing the effects of the immigration of outsiders, the VIllage Rabhas are in close association with the Rajbansis, the Meches, the Oraons and others since remote past. During pre-independence period they had close relation with the local Rajbansis ; but after independence they came in touch with a large number of immigrants, the refugees from East Pakistan (now Bangladesh) belonging to different Bengalee Hindu castes, who came and settled here permanently. In several domains of their cultural life, the Rabhas and the various Hindu castes, especially the Rajbansis of the villages, have common interests. They act together in pursuance of a common and complementary aim. As a result of the inter-dependence in different spheres, the present day Rabha culture reflects a clear picture of borrowing of the non-Rabha rather of the Rajbansi cultural elements, which is due mainly to their long and intimate contact with these people, particularly the Rajbansis. The rapid development of the cash and the market economy and also the implementation of the new administration, new legislations including new land reform acts, new educational systems, and a number of constructional and developmental schemes etc., including communication and transport systems have also direct impact on them, thereby bringing varied degree of changes in their culture.

As a result of their cultural homogeneity, little impact of the cash and the market economy and lack of regular contact with the outside world due mainly to the semi-isolated condition of their habitat, while the Forest Rabhas have still preserved their traditional matrilineal culture to a considerable extent, the Village Rabhas for their regular and intimate interactions with various patrilineal Hindu castes, particularly the Rajbansis, and for the rapid development of the cash and market economy due mainly to the unprecedented heavy influx of the Hindu refugees from the then East Bengal (now Bangladesh) in their area and also for various other reasons stated above, have chosen the path of changes ; and these changes are taking them away from their traditional matrilineally based social system to provide a new patrilineally based one. They have replaced and are still replacing many of their traditional matrilineal culture traits by those borrowed from the local patrilineal Hindus. The Forest Rabhas too, are changing in the similar direction. But their extent and rate of change is undoubtedly lower and slower.

The Rabha community of this State is directly divisible into a number of social segments or clans, known as the *husuks*. The origin of the *husuk* and the sub-*husuk* (*neoya husuk*) indicates that the *husuk* organisation of the Rabhas had a matrilineal base. The *husuks* are exogamous, and a good number of them are totemic in nature. The main function of these *husuks* is to control the marriage system. Though the Forest Rabhas observe this rule of *husuk* exogamy strictly, the Village Rabhas, in recent years, have relaxed this rigidity a little. Because of the rule of the matrilineal descent of the *husuk*, marriage in the mother's *husuk* is strictly forbidden among both the sections of the Rabhas. The Forest Rabhas can marry in the father's *husuk*. But the Village Rabhas, following the Hindus of the area, are now-a-days inclined to prohibit marriage in father's *husuks* also. Besides the main function of the *husuk* among both sections of the Rabhas to regulate marriage, as already stated, the *husuk* among the Forest Rabhas also has control over the property in the sense that they never allow their property to go to a member of different *husuk*. In their case though the individual has actual right over the movable property and assumed right over the immovable property, the right is transmitted to the proper inheritor within their *husuk*. And this has been possible because of the prevalence of the matrilineal descent and inheritance and matrilocal residence. They see that no body from different other *husuk* inherits the property and also as far as possible they see that the property remains within the same family. But because of the patrilineal rule of inheritance and patrilocal residence among the Village Rabhas, the property cannot be retained within the *husuk*. As the property (both movable and immovable) is actually owned by the Village Rabha father and inherited by the Village Rabha sons, who have different *husuks* (sons get their mother's *husuk* due to matrilineal descent and parents have different *husuks* due to clan exogamy) the property among the Village Rabhas passes from one *husuk* to another.

As for totemism, some of the Rabha clans are totemic in nature, while others are non-totemic. The Forest Rabhas still follow the prohibitions against the totemic objects, but some of the Village Rabhas show reluctance in observing the same. This is due to their contact with the HIndu castes among whom no such clan organisation and totemism are present.

Another characteristic of the Rabha *husuk* organisation is the presence of some independent sub-*husuks* called the *neoya husuks*. These *neoya husuks* might have formed probably due to the over population and their growing importance. Moreover, in the *husuk* organisation of the Village Rabhas, a new *husuk* or better to say a Hindu *gotra*, Kaswap, has been introduced. This is because of the marriage of a Rabha man with a Rajbansi girl who had Kaswap as her *gotra*, and following the matrilineal descent their children got their mother's *gotra*.

It is none-the-less important that the Village Rabhas call these *husuks* as their *gotra* following the local Hindus, especially the Rajbansis. In marriage or in funeral ceremony, the priest who is an Assamese Brahmin or a Rajbansi *adhikari* gives them Hindu *gotra*, Kaswap, as these ceremonies are done in the same method (*yojur vedic*) as is followed by the Hindu castes of North Bengal and Assam. But it is interesting to say that this *gotra* conception has not yet entered into the culture of the Forest Rabhas.

In the expression of kinship the Forest Rabhas follow their traditional terminologies and the Village Rabhas use the local Rajbansi terms. The younger generations of this section (the Village Rabhas) have almost forgotten their traditional terminologies. The kinship pattern of the Forest Rabhas reflects the importance of the members of one's matrilineage. They are considered more intimate than the members of the patrilineage. Among the Village Rabhas certain members of both lineages have equal importance and intimacy. The Forest Rabhas for their uxorilocal type of residence, live and also continue to do so with their matri-kins. The Village Rabhas live with the relatives of their father for the prevalence of the virilocal residence. The relationship shows that in the life of an unmarried male among the former section of the Rabhas his *ningosas* have the influence and after marriage, his wife's *ningosas*. In case of the unmarried and married males of the latter section of the Rabhas, the influence of some of the *jukus* is apparent, and the *ningosas* do not have any significant influence on them. In the life of an unmarried as also of a married woman in the Forest Rabha society, her own *ningosas* and not the *jukus* do always have influence, but the condition is different in the case of Village Rabha woman. So long she remains unmarried, some of her own *jukus* and *ningosas* have influence but after marriage when she goes to her husband's house, she goes under the control of some of her husband's *jukus* and *ningosas*. Women in Forest Rabha society have more liberty than those in the Village Rabha society.

The Rabhas of this district in general, have medium sized households. The Village Rabhas have more attraction for the nuclear family than the Forest Rabhas. The extended type of households in both the sections has the next higher frequency. While the Forest Rabhas have more uxorilocally extended households, the Village Rabhas have the reverse type. In their case virilocally extended households dominate over the uxorilocally extended ones. In general the Forest Rabha households have matri-kin orientations, while the Village Rabha households are mostly patri-kin oriented. Most of the Forest Rabha households are similar to those of the Garo or the Khasi, while the households of the Village Rabhas are in general, akin with those of the Rajbansis or of any patrilineal community. The Forest Rabha parents prefer to live with their married daughter with or without her husband like the Garos, the Khasis, the Pnars and other matrilineal communities. The Village Rabha parents on the other hand, like to live with their married son with son's wife and children, like the Rajbansis or any other patrilineal community. But in a few Village Rabha households both married son and married daughter are found to reside with or without their respective spouse and children proving the fact that the Village Rabhas are in a transitional phase.

Though in many respects the households of the two sections of the Rabhas show differences, they have common feature in one respect. Among both sections, the households with members belonging to the generation of self and one descending generation of self have the highest frequency.

A comparison of the development cycle of the households of the two sections shows the persistence of the traditional uxorilocality and matri-kin orientation in Forest Rabha households, and a distinct shift from uxorilocality and matri-kin orientation to the virilocality and patri-kin orientation in the Village Rabha households though in the past as the developpment cycle reveals, the latter also had uxorilocality and matri-kin orientation in their households.

The conception of what constitutes as property differs between the two sections of the Rabhas. The Forest Rabhas consider only the personal belongings as their property, while the Village Rabhas consider both movoble and immovable articles as property. This difference is borne from fact that in case of the Forest Rabhas the land, the house and the other constructions are not their own, but actually belong to the Forest Department of the State Government. The forest authority only permits them to enjoy these temporarily in exchange of their labour rendered to this department on year to year contact. The Village Rabhas, on the other hand, have absolute right over their land, house, other constructions and also on their personal belongings. The rules of inheritance and succession are also different in these two sections of the Rabhas.

Among the ForestRabhas the property (movable) is owned by the females and the rules of inheritance for movable property, follow the female line (mother-daughter; preferably the youngest one). The immovable property is assumed to be officially owned by the father (though actually these are owned by the Forest Department) and the same is inherited by the daughter's husband from the father. In the case of Village Rabhas the property, both movable and immovable, is owned by the males, and the rules of inheritance follow the male line (father-son) mainly. In the case of the Village Rabhas changes have occurred on account of the influence of the Hindu castes, mainly the Rajbansis. But deviation from this rule in certain cases among the Village Rabhas is met with where mother-daughter or mother's brother-sister's son is matrilineal rule of inheritance, has been followed which may be considered as the relics of their matrilineal past. That the Village Rabhas also had the matrilineal mode of inheritance in the past, is proved from the genealogies. Further one interesting and important point is required to be mentioned here is that in case of the Forest Rabhas the rules of inheritance of property follow the rule of inheritance of the household deities, Runtuk and Basek. That means the inheritor/successor of the household deities will be inheritor of the property. And in this case inheritor is usually the daughter, rather the youngest daughter. But among the Village Rabhas for their patrilineal rule inheritance of property and patrilocal residence, this principle has lost its importance.

The Forest Rabhas follow their traditional system of birth and infancy rituals, regulations and restrictions. But the Village Rabhas have adopted the Local Hindu (Rajbansi) method of birth and infancy rituals which are quite different from those of their forest dwelling brethren. It is interesting to note that while the Forest Rabhas desire more for a female child, the Village Rabhas on the contrary, seek for a male child though none of them show apathy for the child of the other sex. During the first pregnancy the Forest Rabhas worship their own deities, but the Village Rabhas pay their homage to the Hindu goddess Shasthi. When the labour pain starts they call local midwife. Sometimes the Village Rabhas called in a trained midwife or the pregnant woman to the near-by Health Centre. Bnt thls is not done by the Forest Rabhas. When the labour pain of a pregnant Village Rabha woman starts, the midwife worships sixteen mother goddesses (*solomatrika*) ; all the sixteen goddesses are Hindu goddesses. This is not so in case of the Forest Rabhas. The rituals performed after the pollution period is over among the Forest Rabhas are their traditional ones but the Village Rabhas celebrate Hindu rituals in the same way as are observed by the Rajbansis.

It is thus seen that the Forest Rabhas still observe their traditional birth rituals while the Village Rabhas have adopted the local Hindu birth rituals as followed by the Rajbansis.

Identically the Forest Rabhas perform their name giving and first feeding of rice ceremonies in their traditional way but the Village Rabha follow the local Hindu way of giving names and first feedings of rice ceremony as is done by the Rajbansi.

The dormitory system (*naksa*) is in existence among the Forest Rabhas only but not among the Village Rabhas among whom dormitory system is totally non-existent since long.

It is thus proved that the Village Rabhas have chosen these local Hindu (Rajbansi) method of birth end infancy rituals in order to move a step ahead towards patriarchalization and to secure a place in the local Hindu society.

In so far as marriage is concerned, the Rabhas in general, practise endogamy i.e. they marry within their own community. Among the Forest Rabhas this rule is strictly observed, but amomg the Village Rabhas this rule has been violated in a number of cases and marriages with other communities such as the Rajbansis, the Saha, the Goala, the Mech and others have taken place. While the Forest Rabhas consider the marriage with other communities as a social offence, the Village Rabhas do not go that far ; rather they consider it a matter of prestige to get married with the Hindu castes.

The Rabhas prefer monogamy, but no bar exists against plural marriage. The frequency of polygyny is very low ; polyandry is prohibited. Like the polygyny, the frequency of the sororate and the levirate types of marriages among both the Forest and the Village Rabhas is extremely low. They usually prohibited marriage with the wife's elder sister and with the deceased younger brother's wife.

Among the Forest Rabhas, the cross-cousin marriage is present, but it is not at all common. The parallel cousin marriage is altogether absent. The Village Rabhas, following the Rajbansi and some other Hindu castes of the locality, avoid both types of cousin marriages. Besides the above types of marriages, there are some other types such us marriage by service, marriage by exchange etc., present among them but these are not common.

The Village Rabhas like many other Hindu castes, marry at a comparatively lower age. In comparison to the Village Rabhas, the Forest Rabhas marry in a comparatively higher age-group. Adult marriage is the rule among them.

The bride-price or the bridegroom-price (dowry) is absent among the Forest Rabhas. But the system of bride-price is present among the Village Rabhas. It is, however, not practised by all. In recent years some Village Rabhas have demanded bridegroom-price (dowry) following some Hindu castes.

As for the pre-marital residence, the Forest Rabhas prefer *bastee* endogamy i.e. marriage within the same *bastee*, in a majority of the cases. The Village Rabhas do not do so. The Rabhas generally select the house of the bride as the place of marriage. Among the VIllage Rabhas the house of the husband's parents is accepted as the place of marriage in a good number of cases.

The pattern of residence among the two sections of the Rabhas gives strikingly different features. While the Forest Rabhas form a temporary duolocal residence before finally forming the uxorilocal or the neolocal residence, the Village Rabhas usually form the virilocal residence after marriage. Another interesting point is that while the Forest Rabhas prefer *bastee* endogamy i. e., unilocal village residence, the Village Rabhas like the virilocal village residence.

Divorce is common among the Forest Rabhas. It is not favoured by the Village Rabhas. Similarly, remarriage is also common among the Forest Rabhas, it is seldom practised by the Village Rabhas.

Among the Rabhas cremation of the dead bodies is the general rule. While this rule is followed perfectly among the Forest Rabhas, it is supplemented by burial among the Village Rabhas among whom the poorer section mostly goes for burial as cremation is costlier. Moreover during the main agriculture operations, particularly during transplantation period, the Village Rabhas opt for burial to cope up with the heavy agricultural activities. The Forest Rabhas have specific place for cremation, the same is not fixed in case of the Village Rabhas among whom any place on the bank of the river, canal etc. serves the purpose of disposing the dead body. The various rites and rituals performed by the Forest Rabhas during disposal of the dead and also during post-disposal period, are quite different from those present among the Village Rabhas. While the Forest Rabhas follow mostly their traditional customs in this regard, the Village Rabhas on the other hand, follow the customs practised by the local Hindu castes, particularly the Rajbansis in-to-to. While the Forest Rabhas employ their own priest in different functions, among the Village Rabhas the Brahmin and barber perform the death rituals. But one interesting point is that till these days the female relatives of the dead perform some important rituals before the dead body is disposed among both the Forest and the Village Rabhas. But in case of the latter section of the Rabhas the females of the younger generation have little idea about such rituals. They have almost forgotten these.

The post funeral rites, that is, rites observed after the disposal of the dead body, are quite elaborate among the Village Rabhas and are performed in the same way as are done by the Rajbansis and other Hindu castes of the area. But among the Forest Rabhas these are not so lengthy and absolutely different from those practised by the Rajbansis and other Hindu castes. According to them they follow their own traditional methods. Thus it is clear that while the Forest Rabhas follow their mortuary rites and ritual according to their own customary rules, the Village Rabhas have adopted the Hindu (local) way.

The present-day Rabha economy shows a distinct change from that it was in the olden days. The traditional economy of shifting cultivation, hunting and gathering has given place to settled cultivation with plough. The stability of the latter type of economy has been widely realised. The Rabhas have probably adopted this from the Rajbansis from whom they have learnt the method of settled cultivation with plough along with many other things. The adoption of settled cultivation brought about changes in their culture. As the population multiplied and the land got divided, it became difficult for the Village Rabhas to continue this economy. They were forced to seek other economic pursuits to supplement their income and more desire for cash money. As a result some Village Rabhas are found to be engaged in different wage earning jobs, like service, business etc. This became possible after the opening of the communication system and starting of various developmental works in the area. The other section, the Forest Rabhas, on the other hand, did not suffer as much, and their need for cash if fulfilled by the labour they put in against cash payments works under the Forest Department. The strict forest protection and preservation rules and their Service Rules do not allow them to accept other jobs, excepting undertaking their own agricultural works and selling some of the production.

In the pre-independence era the Village Rabhas, living in the neighbourhood of the Rajbansis for generations, remained economically dependent mostly on the Rajbansis. After independence a large number of refugees came and settled in this region. Some of the Village Rabhas began to depend on them. This economic dependence on the Hindu Castes compelled the Village Rabhas to depend socio-culturally on the former thereby acquiring many cultural traits from the former, which ultimately helped them in their movement for a place in the Hindu society by rejecting traditional matriliny. But the Forest Rabhas were much less dependent on the Hindu castes. Another important feature is that the Forest Rabhas employ their women in different agricultural pursuits. Some Village Rabhas have now started considering it below their dignity to allow their womenfolk to work in the field. The attitude seems to have been acquired from the local refugee Hindus most of whom do not allow their women to work in the field. But this restriction does not prevail among other tribals like the Mech, the Oraon, the Santal and others and even among the forest dwelling Rabhas.

Thus though the present-day economy of the Rabhas shows distinct shift from their traditional shifting cultivation, the Forest Rabhas continue with their Forest works and agriculture while the Village Rabhas due to the pressure from the internal and/or external forces, have to adopt diverse economic pursuits particularly cash earning jobs. The opening and expansion of markets in their areas and transaction with cash economy have made them more and more conscious about them and made the economic pursuits more male man-power oriented. The involvement of males in decision making economic pursuit has given rise to the Village Rabhas households masculinity and more authority to the male folk, particularly to the patri-kins, which helped the Village Rabhas to move towards patriarchalization. This is not so in case of the Forest Rabhas.

Another remarkable point required to be mentioned here, is the inter-ethnic linkages. The traditional agro-based relation of the Rabhas with the Rajbansi and their traditional economic dependency on them suffered a set-back when there was heavy influx of the Bangalee Hindu refugees from East Pakistan (now Bangla Desh). Many of these refugee for their expertise and skill in agriculture, could replace the Village Rabhas as share-croppers in the land of the Rajbansi making the Village Rabhas further dependent on the refugees, thus escalating their mobillity towards patrilineal Hindu pole. Among the Forest Rabhas no such influx of outsiders happened as they never were dependent on the Rajbansis or any other Hindu Castes nor there was any influx of refugees in their area. So for these and for many other reasons so much of change in their traditional matriliny is noticed.

The traditional village council or council of elders (*marab sen*) still persists among the Forest Rabhas only, the same among the Village Rabhas has almost been replaced by the statutory panchayat system. Here only a relics of *marab sen* is seen. Only in a very few cases the Village Rabha elders assemble together to discuss about some very important social or religous issues. Even in those cases also the elders, particularly the members of the statutory village panchayat (*gram sava*) are also invited to attend. The latter who mostly belong to the Rajbansi or other Bengalee refugee even take part in the deliberations and help the body to come to conclusion. Among the Forest Rabha the situation is quite different. The *marab sen* works in full swing and no statutory panchayat system exists there. The outsiders are also not allowed to participate in the deliberations. They also have traditional means to solve the inter-*bastee* dispute. But the mechanism to solve inter-village dispute among the Village Rabha is not that strong.

The interference of the political parties in the forest *bastee* is much lower than that among the Village Rabhas among whom the impact of different political parties is much more. In fact they are experiencing the activities of different political parties much before independence, almost from late thirties. The influence of the political parties also indirectly helped the Village Rabhas in their movement for Hinduism and thereby patriarchalism.

In religion, difference is obvious among different sections of the Rabhas. The Forest Rabhas mostly follow animism, and worship spirits and demons of different natural objects such as rivers, springs, forests, hills etc., the Village Rabha religion reflects both Hinduism and animism in a curiously mixed combination. While on one hand, they worship different Hindu gods and goddesses like the Rajbansis, on the other, they invoke the spirits of different natural objects like their forests dwelling brethren. The Forest Rabhas are purely non-idolaters, but the Village Rabhas, following the local Hindus, have become partially idolaters. The Forest Rabhas participate in a number of festivals connecting the worship of most of their deities and spirits and none of these festivities are the Hindu festivals. The village dwelling Qabhas on the other hand, take part in a number of festivals, most of which are connected with the worship of the Hindu gods and goddesses. The Forest Qabhas do not participate in the festivities of the local people, particularly of the Hindus, the Village Rabha directly or indirectly participate in the religious festivals of the local Hindus, both the Rajbansis and refugee Hindus. Their earnest desire to become Hindus compelled the Village Rabhas to involve intimately into the Hinduization movement since long, the Forest Rabhas had no such desire. They of course, involved in the Janjogi movement but that is sheer out of fear. Later on many of them discarded this religion. And Christianity they have embraced in recent years only for getting certain benefits, mainly economic. But Janjogi or Christianity could not influence the Village Rabhas and deviate them from their will to become Hindus.

Thus while the Forest Rabhas in general have still preserved their tradition to a great extent the Village Rabhas have imbibed a good amount of the local Hindu cultural elements (mainly of the Rajbansi castes) and are on the way to Hinduization. While traditional matriliny still persists among the Forest Rabhas in a high dergee the Village Rabhas have chosen the process of patriarchalization by adopting the cultural traits from the patrilineal Hindu castes and also due to the influence of various internal and/or external forces.

Thus we see that a major section of the Rabhas of West Bengal is transforming their social system from one type to another, from the matrilineal to the patrilineal social system.

Bibliography

BIBLIOGRAPHY

Adam, L. (1947) Virilocal and Uxorilocal, *Amer Anthrop*. Vol. 49.

Aiyappan, A. (1944) *Iravas and Culture Change*, Madras.

*Allen, B.C. 1902 *Census of India, 1901, Vol. IV. Assam, Pt. I. Report*, Shillong.

*Allen. B.C. (1903) *Assam District Gazetteer* Vol. III. Goalpara.

Ali, A. (1935) *The Spirit of Islam.*

Baines, A. (1912) *Ethnography* (*Castes and Tribes*), Calcutta.

Banerjee, S. (1963) Pnar Kinship System. *Bull. Anth. Sury. India*. Vol. XII, No 3—4

Banerjee, S. (1964) Residence Pattern among the Pnar, *Bull. Anth. Sury. India*, Vol. XIII, No. 1-2.

Bareh, H. (1967) *The History and Culture of the Khasi People.*

*Barua, B.K. (1951) *A Cultural History of Assam*, Nowgang.

*Barua, H. (1956) *The Red River and the Blue Hill*, Gauhati.

*Barua, J.K. (1951) The Rabhas (in *Tribes of India.* Pt. II Published by Bharatiya Adimjati Sewak Sangh, Delhi).

*Basu, S.K. & Raha, M.K. 1974 *Kamakhyaguri* (Special saries No. 15) Calcutta.

Bertrand, G. (1958) *Secret Land where Women Reign*, London.

*Bhattacharya, P. (1931) *Kamrup Shasanabali* (in Bengali) B.S. 1338

Bishi, K. (1956) Uttar Banger Stri-achar (in Bengali) (in *Benglar* 1363 B.S.
Stri-achar. Ed. Indira Debichoudhurani)

*Boileau, H. 1892 *Report on the Census of the District of Jalpaiguri, 1891*, Calcutta.

Bose, J.K. (1941) The Garo Law of Inheritance (in *Anthropological papers No. 6*. Calcutta University), Calcutta.

Bose, J.K. (1947) Culture Contact among the Garos of Eastern Bengal (unpublished Ph. D., dissertation).

Bose, N.K. (1967) *Culture and Society in India*, Bombay.

*Boverly, H (1872) *Census of India, 1872, Vol. I.*

Broom, L. & J.I. Kitsuse 1955 The validation of Acculturation: A Condition to Ethnic Assimilation. *Amer Anthrop*. Vol. 57, No. 1

*Buchanon-Hamilton F. (1810) *An Account of the District Rangpur*, London.

Burling, R. (1956) Garo Kinship Terms, *Man in India*. Vol 36, No. 3

Burling, R. (1958a) Garo Avuncular Authority and Matrilateral Cross-cousin marriage. *Amer Anthrop*. Vol. 60.

Burling, R. (1958b) Cross-Cousin Marriage among the Garo of Assam. *Man* Vol. LVIII, No. 1.

Burling, R. (1963a) *Rangsaggri : Family and Kinship in a Garo Village*, Philadelphia.

Burling, R. (1963b) Garo Kinship Terms and the Analysis of the Meaning, *Ethnology*, Vol. 11. No. 1.

Burman, U.N. (1963) *Rajbansi Kehatriya Jatir Etihas* 1370 B.S. (in Bengali) Jalpaiguri.

Chattopadhyay, K.P. (1939) Satakarni Succession and Marriage Rules. *J. Asia Soc. Bengal*. Vol. 2.

Chattopadhyay, K.P. 1941 Khasi Kinship and Social Organisation (in *Anthropological Papers* No. 6, Calcutta University), Calcutta.

Chattopadhyay, K.P. (1943) The Cultural basis of Rules of inheritance *Sci. and Cult*. Vol. 9.

Chattopadhyay, K.P. (1960) Some Changes in Khasi Culture, *J. Asiatic Soc. Beng*. Vol. II. No. 1.

*Choudhuri, H.N. (1903) *The Cooch Behar State and Its land Revenue Settlements*, Cooch-Behar.

Choudhuri, N. (1961) Acculturation of the Munda : A Study in Differential Change and Caste Formation (unpublished Ph. D. Dissertation).

Colson, E. (1958) *Marriage and Family among tod Plateau of Tonga of North Rhodesia*, Manchester.

Colson, E (1962) Plateau Tonga (in *Matrilineal Kinship* Ed. D.M. Schneider and K. Gough) California,

Costa, G. (1954) The Garo Code of Law. *Anthropos.* Vol. 149, No. 5-6.

*Dalton, E.T. (1872) *Descriptive Ethnology of Bengal,* Calcutta.

*Das, A.K. (196)8 *Trends of Occupational Pattern through generations in rural areas of West Bengal* (Special series No. 10) Calcutta

Das, A.K. & M.K. Raha (1964) *The Oraons of Sunderban* (Sp. series No. 3) Calcutta.

*Das, A.K., and Raha, M.K. (1967) *The Rabhas of West Bengal* (Special series No. 9) Culcutta.

*Das, A.K. and Raha, M.K. (1968) Cooch Bihar Adibasi. *Smaranika.* Cooch Behar (in Bengali).

*Das, A.K. Roychoudhuri, B.K. & Raha, M.K. (1966) *Hand-Book on Scheduled Castes and Scheduled Tribes of West Bengal.* (special Series 8), Calcutta.

*Das. B.M. (1956a) A Study of the work on the Head-Hair of The Pati Rabha. *J. Gauhati University,* Vol. VII.

*Das, B.M. (1956b) Rabha Kinship terms. *Man in India,* Vol. 35, No. 1.

*Das, B.M. (1956c) Physical characters of the Rabhas, *Man in India.* Vol. 36, No. 2.

*Das, B.M. (1957) Family Structure of the Rabhas. *Man in India* Vol. 37, No. 2.

Das, B.M. (1958a) Demographic studies of a Rabha village. *Vanyajati,* Vol. VI. No. 2.

*Das, B.M. (1958b) Blood-groups of the Rabhas. *Man in India,* Vol. 38, No. 3.

*Das, B.M. (1958c) Story of King Dahan. *Assam Tribune,* 22.6.68.

*Das, B.M. (1958d) A note on Child-mortality among the Rabhas. *J. Gauhati University,* Vol. IX. No. 2.

*Das, B.M. (1960) *Ethnic Affinities of the Rabhas.* Gauhati.

*Das, B.M, & P. Uzir. (1959) Relative Length of the First and the Second Toes of the Rabha Foot. *J. Gauhati, University,* Vol. X. No. 2.

*Das, B.M. and P. Uzir (1960) Inter-Spaces in Rabha Foot. *J. Gauhati, Univ.* Vol. XI. No. 2.

Das, T.C. (1945) *The Purums : an old Kuki Tribe of Assam*, Calcutta.

Das, T.C. (1961) Nature and extent of social change in tribal society of Eastern India. *Socio Bull.* Vol. II.

Das Gupta, P.K. (1966) Family among the War Khasi, *J. Ind. Anthrop Soc.* Vol. I.

*Datta, S.P. (1969) Rabha Speech : a preliminary study (in *District Hand-Book of West Bengal, Jalpaiguri, 1961 Census* by B. Roy, Appendix V).

*Datta Gupta, J. (1967) *Census of India, 1961 Vol. XVI. West Bengal and Sikkim*, Pt. V-A (ii)

Datta-Majumdar N. (1956) *The Santal: Study in culture change.* Calcutta.

Domant, G.H. (1880) Notes on the Locality and population of the tribes dwelling between the Brahmaputra and Nilgiri rivers *J.R. A.I.* Vol. XII.

Dube, S.C. (1947) The Economic life of the Kamars, *Man in India*, Vol. XXVII, No. 2.

Eggan, F. (1949) The Hopi and the lineage principles (in *Social structure* Ed. F. Eggan and M. Fortes).

Eggan, F. (1950) *The Social Organisation of the Western Pueblos.* Chicago.

Ehrenfels, B.O. R. (1941) *Mother-right in India*, Hyderabad.

Ehrenfels, B.O.R. (1954) Anthropological Background(of Matrilineal societies) (in the *Status of Women in South Asia*, Ed. Dr. A. Appadorai), Calcutta.

Ehrenfels, B.O.R. (1955) Three Matrilineal Groups of Assam, *Amer Anthrop.* Vol. 57, No. 2.

Elwin, V. (1947) *The Muria and their Ghotul*, Bombay.

——(1968) *The Kingdom of Youth*, Bombay.

Emeneau, M.B. (1938) Toda culture—thirty five years after : An Acculturation study. *Ann.Bhandarkar Orien. Res. Instt.* Vol. XIX. Pt. 11.

*Endle, S. (1911) *The Kacharis*, Calcutta.

Fair-Child, E.P. (1952) *Dictionary to Sociology.*

Fereira, J.V. (1965) *Totemism in India*, Bombay.

Firth, R. (1957) A note on Descent Group in Polinesia. *Man* Vol. 57, No. 4.

Forde, D. (1964) Double Descent among the Yako (in *African systemtof Kinship and Marriage* Ed. A. R. Radcliffe-Brown and D. Forde).

Fortes, M. (1949) Time and Social structure : An Ashanti case study. (in *Social Structure* Ed. Eggan, F. and M. Fortes) Oxford.

Fortes, M. (1953) Structure of Unilineal Descent Group. Amer, Anthrop. Vol. 45, No. 1.

Fortes, M. (1964) Kinship and Marriage among the Ashanti. (in *African System of Kinship and Marriage* Ed. A.R. Radcliffe-Brown and D. Forde).

Frazer, J.G. (1910) *Totemism and Exogamy* Vol. IV. London.

*Friend-Pereira, (1912) J.E. The Rabhas (in *Census of Assam. 1911, Vol. III, Pt. I Report*).

Fürer-Haimendorf, C. Von. (1938) The Morang System of the Koryak Nagas, Assam *JRAI* Vol-LXVIII

Furer-Haimendorf, C. Von. (1943) *The Reddis of Bison Hills*, Hyderabad.

Fürer-Haimendorf, C. Von. (1950) Youth Dormitories and Community Houses in India, *Anthropos*, Vol. XLV No. 1.

*Gait, E. A. (1892) *Census of Assam, 1891. Vol. 1 Report.*

*Gait, E.A. (1902) *Census of India, 1901, Bengal, Report.*

*Gait, E.A. (1963) *History of Assam* Revised 3rd Ed. by B.K. Barua and H.V.S. Murthy. Calcutta).

*Gangopadhyay, B. (1964) *Marriage Regulations amnog certain castes of Bengal.*

*Ghose Choudhuri, B.B. (1932) *Assam O Bangodesher Bibaha Paddhati* 1339 B.S. (in Bengali), Calcutta.

Goodenough, W.H. (1955) A Problem in Malaya Polynesian Social Organisation. *Amer. Anthrop.* Vol. 57, No. 1. Pt. 1.1.

Goswami, M. & Majumdar, D.N. (1967) Clan Organisation of the Garos, *Man in India*, Vol. 41, No. 1.

Gough, E.K. (1952) Changing Kinship Usages in the setting of Political and Economic change among the Nayars of Malabar, *J.R.A.I.* Vol. 82, Pt. I.

Gough, E.K. (1959) The Nayars and the definition of Marriage *J.R.A.I.*, Vol. 89.

Gough, E.K. 1962a Nayar : Central Kerala ; Nayar : North Kerala ; Mapilla : North Kerala, Tiyar : North Kerala (in *Matrilineal Kinship* Ed. D.M. Schneider and K. Gough).

Gough, K. (1962b) The Modern Disintegration of Matrilineal Descent Group (in *Matrilineal Kinship* Ed. D.M. Schneider and K. Gough).

Gough, K. 1962c Variation in Residence (in *Matrilineal Kinship* Ed. D.M. Schneider and K. Gough).

Gough, K. (1962d) Descent Group Variation among Mobile Cultivators (in *Matrilineal Kinship* Ed. D.M. Schneider and K. Gough).

*Grierson, G.A. 1903 *Linguistic Survey of India, Vol. III No. II*, Calcutta.

*Gruning, J.F. (1911) *District Gazetteer*, *Jalpaiguri*, Calcutta.

Gurdon, P.R.T. (1914) *The Khasis*, London.

*Hodgson, B.H. (1949) On the Origin Location, Number, Creed, Custom, Characters and Condition of the Kooch, Bodo and Dhimal people with a general description of the climate they dwell in *J. Asiatic Soc. Beng*. Vol. XVIII, No. II.

*Hodgson, B.H. (1880) *Miscellaneous Essays relating to Indian subjects*, London.

Hodson, T.S. (1911) *The Naga Tribes of Manipur*, London.

Hunter, W.W. (1876) *Statistical Accounts of the District of Jalpaiguri*, Calcutta.

Hutton, J.H. (1851) *Castes in India*, Bombay.

Iyer, L.K.A. (1909) *The Cochin Tribes and Castes*, Vol.1 No. II, Madras.

Jay, E (1961) Revitalisation movements in Tribal India (in *Aspects of Religion in Indian Society* Ed. L.P. Vidyarthi).

Kapadia, K.M. (1947a) *Marriage and Family in India.*

Kapadia, K.M. (1947b) *Hindu Kinship*, Bombay.

Karrandikar S.V, (1929) *Hindu Exogamy*, Bombay.

Kirkpatrick, C. (1965) *The Family as Process and Institution*, New York.

Kroaber, A.L, (1938) *Essays in Anthropology*, California.

Kunstadter, P.1963 A Survey on the Consanguine or Matrifocal Family. *Amer. Anthrop.* Vol. 65, No. 1.

Leach, E.R. (1961) *Pul Eliya : A Village in Ceylon*, Cambridge.

Linton, R. (Ed.) (1960) *Acculturation and the Process of Culture Change in seven American Indian Tribes*, New York.

Loeb, E (1964) Patrilineal and Matrilineal Organisations in Sumatra, *Amer. Anthrop.* Vol. 36, No. 1.

Lowie, R.H.L. (1936) *Primitive Religion*, London, George Routledge & Sons.

Lowie, R.H.L. (1953) *Primitive Society*, London.

*Mackenzie, A. 1884 *History of the Relations of the Government with the Hill Tribes of the North-East Frontier of Bengal*, Calcutta.

Madan, T.N. (1965) Family and Kinship : A Study of the Pandits of the Rural Kashmir, Bombay.

Mahapatra, L.K. (1972) Social movements among Tribes of India, in *Tribal situation in India* Ed. K.S. Singh.

Majumdar, D.N. (1967) Social Organisation of the Koch of Garo Hills, Assam (in *Common Perspective for North East India*, Ed. P. Das Gupta).

*Majumdar, D.N. (1968a) A Study of the Clan Organisation among the Rabhas, *Bull. of the Anth. S.I.* Vol. XVII No. 3.

*Majumdar, D.N. 1968b A Study of Religious Practices Among the Song Koch of Garo Hills. *Bull. of the Anth. S.I.* Vol. XVII No. 3.

*Majumdar, D.N. (1968c) An Account of Magico Religious Rites and Beliefs of the Rangdani Rabha, *Bull of Anth. S.I* Vol. XVII No. 3.

Mandelbaum, D.G. (1941) Culture Change among the Nilgiri Tribes, *Amer. Anthrop.* Vo. 43.

Mandelbaum, D.G. (1948) The Family in India (in *Family : Its Function and Destiny*. Ed. Anshen).

*Martin, M. (1838) *History, Antiquities, Topography and Statistics Eastern India*, Vol III, Calcutta.

Mayne, J.D. (1954) *Hindu Law and Usages*, Madras.

*McSwiney, J. (1912) *Census of India, 1911, Assam, Vol. III, Pt. I, Report.*

Mehra, J.D. (1953) Effects of Acculturation on the Garos of Boko, Assam, *Vanyajati* Vol. II, No. 1.

Mehta, S.S. (?) Women from the standpoint of Marriage, *J. Anth. Soc. Bombay* Vol. X.

Mills, J.P. (1937) *The Rengma Nagas*, London.

*Milligan, J.A. (1919) *Survey and Settlement Report of the Western Duars in the District of Jalpaiguri*, 1906-16, Calcutta.

Mitchel, J.C. (1963) Marriage. Matriliny and Social Structure among Yao of Southern Nyasaland (in *Family and Marriage* Ed. J. Mogey). Dharwar.

*Mitra, A. (1954) *District Handbook of West Bengal, Jalpaiguri, Census of India, 1951*, Calcutta.

Mukherjee, (1956) Garo Marriage and Kinship Organisation, *Anthropologist*, Vol. III, No. 1 & 2.

Mukherjee, B. (1958) Social Groupings among the Khasis of Assam, *Man In India*, Vol, 38. No. 3.

Mukherjee, B. 1961 Comparative study of the Kinship Systems of Six Matrilineal Tribes, *Eastern Anthropologist*, Vol. XIV No. 1.

Mukherjee, B (1962) Rajbansi Kinship system, *Bull. Anth. Surv. af India*, Vol. XI, No. 1.

Mukherjee, B. 1963 Socio-economic and Religious Organisation of the Rajbansis. *Bull Anth. Surv. India*, Vol. XII, No. 1 & 2.

Murdock, G.P. (1949) *Social Structure*, New York.

Nakane, C (1961) *Garo and Khasi : A Comparative study of the Matrilineal systems*. Paris.

Nakane, C(1963) The Nayar Family in Disintegrating Matrilneal system (in *Family and Marriage*, Ed. J. Mogey) Dharwar.

Nanjundayya, H.V. and Iyer, L.K.A. (1935) *Mysore Tribes and Castes* Vol. III-IV.

Niggermeyar, H. (1933) Totemismus in Vorderindien, *Anthrops.* Vol. 407. 1964.

Norbeck, Edward 1961 *Religion in Primitive society*. New Yor , Harpar & Row Publishers.

O'Dannel (1891) *Census of India*, Vol, III, V.

Oliver, D.L. (1955) *A Solomon Island Society : Kinship and Leadership among the Siuai of Bougainville*, Cambridge.

O'Malley, L.S.S. (1913) *Census of India, 1911*, Vol. V Pt. I Report.

O'Malley, L.S.S. (1943) *Indian Social Heritage*.

Orans, M. (1965) *The Santals : A Tribe in search of a Great Tradition*.

Pandit, N. (1976) Class conflicts or Elite conflict ? (Reviewed article) in *Economic and Political Weekly* Vol. XI No. 23.

Paul, G.P. 1956 The Place of Khadduh—the youngest daughter in Khasi and Synteng Society *Vanyajati*, Vol. IV, No. 2.

*Paul,S. (1970a) Hasang—Tokou: A Rabha Legend (in Bengali) *Dabi* Vol. 14 No. 1.

Paul, S. (1970b) Devi Michik Bai O Ekti Rabha Upakatha (in Bengali) *Dabi* Annual Vol.

Paul, S.(1970c) Rabha O Tader Devi Rantuk-Basek (in Bengali) *Jalpaiguri District Centenary Souvenir*. 1968-1969), Ed. Dr.C.C. Sanyal et. al.

Paul, S. (1971) Rabhader Ourdhyadaihik Kriya (in Bengali) *Dabi* Annual Volume.

Paul, S. (1972) Uttar Banger Gramin Prabachan (in Bengali) *Koushiki*, Vol 2 No. 11-12.

Paul, S. (1973) Rakhal Thakur O Annyanya Loukik Dev-devi (in Bengali) *Jathrik* Annual Volume, 3—4, pp—2-6.

——(1974) Paschim Duarser Lokachar (in Bengali) *Loksilpa* Vol-1, No. 3, pp. 3-5.

——(1975) Rabhader Achar-Achoron (in Bengali) *Banbani*, Vol. 17 No. 1.

——(1976) Rabhader Husuk (in Bengali) *Youth Festival Souvenir* pp. 12-18.

——(1977) Rabha Prasonga (in Bengali) *Dabi* Annual Volume pp. 1-5.

——(1978) Rabha Bibaha Riti (in Bengali) *Youth Festival Souvenir*.

——(1978) Rabhader Aharjya-Paniya O Madok Drabya (in Bengali) *Banmahal* pp. 35-41.

——(1978) Adivasi Rabha Samaje Pot Paribarton (in Bengali) *Dabi* Annual Volume pp. 1-8.

——(1978) Chor-Chormir Gan (in Bengali) *Koushiki* Vol. 8, No. 3-4. pp. 1-6.

——(1979) Rabha Lok Britya: Nitya Geet O Chara (in Bengali) *Jatrik*. Annual volume pp 1-10.

——(1980) Rabhader Paribar Sangatan (in Bengali) *Dabi* Annual Volume pp. 1-3.

——(1982) Uttar Banger Rabha Upajati (in Bengali) *Dabi* Silver Jubilee Volume. pp. 145-161.

——(1982) Rabha Bhasar Sankhipta Ruprekha (in Bengali) *Anarja* Annual Volume pp. 5-14.

——(1982) Uttar Banger Rabha O Mech Loknitya (in Bengali)

Uttar Banga Lok Jan Sanbad Hokahuk Festival Volume pp. 13-15.
——(1983) Uttar Bangar Loknitya (in Bengali) *Dabi*, Annual Volume. pp. 81-89.
——(1985) Rabha Loksangeet (in Bengali) *Dabi*, Annual Volume pp. 51-56.
——(1985) Bosini: Rabha Loknitya (in Bengali) *Lok Nakshatra* Vol. 36, pp. 3-4.
Paul, S. & Raha, M.K. (1967) Riddles from North Bengal, *Bull. Cul. Res. Inst.* Vol VI, No. 1 and 2.
Peal, S.E. (1893) The Communal Barracks of Primitive Races, *J.A.S.B.* Vol, LXI.
*Playfair, A. (1909) *The Garos*, London.
*Porter. A.E. (1933) *Census of India* 1931 Vol. V Pt. I Report, Bengal and Assam.
Rad-Cliffe Brown, (1964) Introduction (in *African System of Kinship and Marriage*, Ed. A.R. Radcliffe-Brown and D. Forde).
Radhakrishnan, S. (1927) *Indian Philosophy*, Vol. II. London.
Raha, M.K. 1963a Changes in the Magico-religious beliefs and practices of the Oraons. *Bull Cul. Res. Inst.* Vol. 1, No. 2.
*Raha, M.K. (1963b) The Rabhas of West Bengal. *Bull. Cul. Res. Inst.* Vol. I, No. 3.
Raha, M.K. (1964) Cultural Changes in Tribal Sunderban, *Modern Review*. Vol. C XVI, No. 5.
Raha, M.K. (1966) The Garos, *Bull Cul Res. Inst.* Vol. V No. 1. and 2.
*Raha, M.K. (1967a) A Note on the Rabha kinship Terminology *Proc. Ind. Sci. Cong.*
Raha, M.K. (1967b) Ceremonial friendship among the Rajbansis of Jalpaiguri, *Sci. & Cult.* Vol. 3, No. 2.
Raha, M.K. (1970) Social Organisation of the Rabhas of Jalpaiguri (unpublished Ph. D. Dissertation).
*Raha, M.K. (1972a) Youth Dormitory among the Rabhas, *Bull. of the Cul. Res. Inst.* Vol. IX No. 1 & 2.
*Raha, M.K. (1972b) Pashim Banger Rabha O Tader Samajer Dhara (in Bengali) *Bulletin of the Academy of Folklore*, Vol. I, No. 3 & 4.
* Raha, M.K. (1973) Rabha Kinship Terms : An Analysis (in

Journal of Indian Anthropological Society), Vol VIII, No. 2 (Abstract).

Raha, M.K. (1974a) The Rabhas of Western Duars : A Structural Analysis of a Changing Matrilineal Society, in the *Bulletin of Cultural Research Institute*, Vol. X, No. 1 & 2.

*Raha, M.K. (1974c) Folk Songs in Tribal West Bengal, in "*Sangeet Natak*" Journal of Sangeet Natak Academy.

*Raha, M.K. (1977b) The Husuk Organisation of the Rabhas of West Bengal. (Abstract) *Proceedings of the Indian Science Congress*, 64th Session.

*Raha, M.K. (1977c) Kinship Terms of a Changing Matrilineal Tribe, *Kerala Sociology*, Vol. V. pp. 52-61.

*Raha, M.K. (1978) Economics of the Rabhas, A Preliminary Note (Abstract) Proceedings of the Indian Science Congress, 65th Session.

Raha, M.K. (1978) Village Life in Western Duara (unpublished article).

Raha, M.K. (1967) Folksongs of the Tribals of West Bengal : An analytical study of continuity and change, in *Folk Music & Folklore : An Anthology* Vol. VI. Ed. H. Biswas.

Raha, M.K. (1980) Birth and infancy Rites among the Rabhas. *Bull of C.R.I.* Vol—14 No. 3 & 4 pp. 108-114.

Raha, M.K. (1982) The Rabhas of West Bengal, *Van Bandhu* Vol. 1. No. 5 pp. 3-5.

Raha, M.K., J.C. Das &S. Mandal (1976) Rabhader Samajik—Rajnaitik Andolan (in Bengali) in *Paschim-bander Adivasi Andolan*. Ed : A.K. Das & S. Mukhopadhyay.

Raha, M.K., J.C. Das & S.C. Mandal (1978) Socio-Political Movement among the Rabhas of North Bengal *Bull. of C.R.I.*, Vol. XIII, No. 3 & 4.

Raha, M.K. – J.C. Das (1982) Agrarian Relations in the Western Duars : Changing Patterns of Inter Community Ties. *Journal of Indian Anthrop*. Soc. Vol. 17 pp. 31-38.

Raha, M.K. & J.C. Das (1988) Some aspects of change in the Tribal culture of West Bengal (Society and Culture : Problems and Prospects) edited by A.K. Das, M.K. Raha and S.K. De (in press).

Raha, M.K. & S. Paul (1963) Deha-Tatwa : Songs of the

Baistom Baudias of North Bengal, *Folklore* Vol. XIV No. 3.

Raha, M.K. & S.K. Pal (1968) Chor Chornir Gan : A Typical Folksong from Western Duars, *Bull. C.R.I.* Vol. VI, No. 3 pp. 86-96.

Raha, M.K. & S.K. Paul (1969) Some Verses from Western Duars. *Human Events.* Vol. III, No. 7—8.

Raha, M.K., J.C. Das & S. Paul (1974) The Meches and Their Endi Silk Industry, *Jagriti,* Vol. XVIII No. 2.

Raha, M.K., J.C. Das & S. Paul (1975) Verses of Western Duars : An Eco-Cultural Analysis, Folklore, Vol. XVII No. 2.

Raha, M.K., J.C. Das, & R.S. Suri (1976) Social system in Western Duars Village, *Bull. Cul. Res. Inst.* Vol. XII No. 1 & 2.

Richards, A.I. (1940) Mother-right among the Central Bantu (in *Essays presented to C.G. Seligman* Ed. Evans Pritchard, G.E.).

Richards, A.I. (1940) *Bemba marriage and present economic condition.*

Richards, A.I. (1951) The Bemba of North-Eastern Rhodesia (in *Seven Tribes of British Central Africa* Ed. E. Colson and M. Gluckman).

Richards, A.I. (1964) Some types of family structure amongst the Central Bantu (in *African system of Kinship and Marriage* Ed. A.R. Radcliffe-Brown and D. Forde).

Risley, H.H. (1891) *Tribes and Castes of Bengal* (*Etnnographic Glossary*) Vol. I and II, Calcutta.

Rivers, W.H.R. (1932) *Social Organisation*, London.

*Robinson, W. (1849) *Notes on the Languages spoken by the various tribes inhabiting the Valley of Assam and its mountain confines.*

*Rowney, H.B. (1882) *The Wild Tribes of India*, London.

Roy, P. (1964) The Christianity and the Khasis. *Man In India*, Vol. 44, No. 2.

Roy, S.C. (1929) *Oraon Religion and Customs*, Ranchi.

Roy, Burman, B.K. (1967) *Cheltlat* (Monograph No. 3, Census 1961), New Delhi.

*Roy Choudhuri, B.C.(1970) Social Mobility Movement among the Rabha of North Bengal, *Man in India*, Vol. 50, No. 1.

Safa, H. I. (1965) The Female-based in public housing : a case study in Puerto Rico. *Hum. Organisation*, Vol. 24, No. 2.

Sanyal, C. (1965) *The Rajbansis of North Bengal,* Calcutta.

Sarkar, S. (1985) Banahasi Rabhader Jiban Prasange (in Bengali in *Desh*.

Schmidt, W. (1935) *The Origin and Growth of Religion : Facts and Theories,* London, Muthuen & Co. Ltd.

Schneider, D.M. (1953) Yap Kinship Terminology and Kin groups, *American*, Vol. 55 No. 2.

— –(1962) The Distinctive features of Matrilineal Descent groups (in *Matrilineal Kinship* Ed. D.M. Schneider and K. Gough).

Sen, B. et al (1969) Adibasi Andolaner Samasya Prasange (in Bengali).

*Shafers, R. (1953) Classification of the Northernmost Naga languages. *J. Bihar Res. Soc.* Vol 3 Pt. 3.

Singh, K.S. (1978) *Tribal Movement in India*, Concept Publication Delhi.

*Singh, R.R. (1968) The Rabhas of West Bengal by A.K. Das & M.K. Raha, (Review article) *Khadi-Gramodyog* Vol. XV No. 1.

Sinha, S. (1953) Some Aspects of Changes in Bhumij Religion, *Man in India*, Vol. 33, No. 2.

Sinha, S. (1956) The Acculturation of the Bhumij of Manbhum: A study in social class formation and ethnic integration (unpublished Ph. D. Dissertation).

Sinha, S. (1957a) The Media and nature of Hindu-Bhumij interaction. *J. Asiatic Soc-Beng*. Vol. XXIII, No. 1.

Sinha, S. (1957b) Tribal cultures of India as a dimension of a little tradition in the study of Indian civilization : A preliminary statement. *Man in India* Vol. 37, No. 2,

Singh, Jogendra (1973) *Modernization of Indian Tradition*, Thomson Press (India) Ltd. Delhi.

Srinivas, M.N. (1952) *Religion and Society among the Coorgs of South India*, Oxford.

*Sunders, D.H.E. (1895) *Survey and settlement Report of the*

Western Duars in the District of Jalpaiguri. 1889-1895. Calcutta.

Swift, M.G. (1958) A note on the durability of Malay Marriage, *Man*, Vol. 58, No. 208.

Sachchidananda, (1964) *Culture change in Tribal Bihar.* Calcutta.

Thurston, E. and K. Rangachari (1909) *Castes and Tribes of Southern India*, Vol. III and VII, Madras.

Turner, V.W. (1957) *Schism and Continuity in an African Society* Manchester.

Vidyarthi, L.P. (1963) *The Maler : A study in nature-man-spirit complex of a Hill tribe in Bihar.* Calcutta.

*Waddel, L.A. (1900) The Tribes of the Brahmaputra valley *J. Asiatic Soc. Beng.* Vol. LXIX Pt. III.

Appendices

APPENDIX 1

Earlier Accounts on the Rabhas

The earliest account on the Rabhas is that written by Buchanon—Hamilton (1810). He has described this community on the points like the distribution, tribal divisions, affinity, religion, magico-religious functionaries, inheritance of property, marriage, divorce, remarriage and education standard. He has touched each of these points in a few lines,

The same account of Buchanon—Hamilton was reproduced by Martin in his book Eastern India (1838 : 546-549) without any alteration.

In connection with only the affinity of the Rabhas, Hodgson, as early as 1849, wrote a few lines in one of his articles (1849 : 703-712). He wrote the same thing in another article also (1880 : 103, 105, 115).

Robinson also wrote a few lines on the affinity of the Rabhas (1849 : 216).

After Buchanon—Hamilton a comparatively detailed account on the Rabhas is met with in Dalton's book where he has mainly described the Rabha religion and costume with a short introduction in the beginning dealing with their habitat, divisions, cultural affinity with the Garos and Pani-Koch and some changes in the custom of the Pati Rabha section (1872 : 87, 92).

In 1879 in one of his reports Hunter mentions in a few lines, about the language, religion and tribal divisions of the Rabha community (1879 : 37).

Domant while discussing about the customs, manners etc. of the tribes dwelling between Brahmaputra and Mingthi rivers, stated the linguistic position, Hinduization, habitat, custom, population distribution, tribal divisions and affinity of the Rabhas in nut-shell (1880 : 223-235).

Mackenzie after a few years, considered the Rabha language only in a few lines referring its similarity with Mech and Kachari language (1884 : 549).

In the Census report of Assam of 1891 Gait has given a short description of the Rabhas. Within a few paragraphs he has described their affinity, language, internal divisions and social hierarchy (1892 : 232). In another book he has only mentioned a line or two about their language (1963 : 1, 6).

In his settlement report Sunder has devoted a chapter on the social and religious life of some communities of Jalpaiguri district. In that chapter he has written an account on the Rabhas under the headings, viz. castes, inheritance, marital relation, reproduction, child birth, homesteads, households, property, meals, narcotics, fire, clothing, weaving, ornaments, religion and deities, superstitions, agriculture, crops, watching of crops at night, agricultural implements, cattle, fishing, music, measures, diseases, medicine and funeral rites (1895 : 72-79). Though this account is written under the heading 'The Garos' still the pattern of culture described in this account, is absolutely similar to the culture of the Forest Rabhas but quite different from that of the Garos. It seems that Sunder might have misidentified the Rabhas with the Garo as in earlier days the Rabhas were often called the Garos. Similar is the case with Choudhuri's articles (1903 : 600-601).

After Sunder, Waddel in 1900 described their affinity and internal divisions in a few lines considering their similarities with the Totala or Dadiyal Kachari (1900 : 65).

In 1901 Census only a few lines have been mentioned regarding the Rabhas, considering them as belonging to the Bodo tribe. It traces its affinity with the Kacharis and describes their distribution in different parts of Assam (1902 : 142).

In the Linguitistic Survey of India, Grierson has dealt

mainly about their language through he has also described their affinity with the Bodo group of people. He has also mentioned some Rabha vocabularies in the said book (1903 : 102-105).

But Allen has given a brief account on the Rabhas in the District Gazetteer, Goalpara. He has covered their affinity, language, migration, population, social organisation, social hierarchy, settlement pattern and material life, marriage, funeral ceremonies and religion. He has touched all these points in a few pages (1903 : 49-51).

Anderson has only mentioned the affinity and language of the Rabhas in Grierson's book (1903 : 104-105).

In the Imperial Gazetteer of India it has only been mentioned that the Rabhas have a close relation with the Garos (1909 : 504).

In his book on the Garos, Playfair has described in a few lines, the origin, language, affinity and cradle—land of the Rabhas (1909 : 20-22). Endle on the other hand, has given a comparatively better account on this tribe covering in nut-shell the following points, viz. affinity, habitat, origin and tradition, language, Sub-divisions, social status, admission of a Kachari convert into the Rabha community, religion and relation to the sexes (marriage). He has also given some Rabha vocabularies (1911 : 83-85).

In 1911 Census of Assam McSweney has given a short description on the name-giving ceremony among the Totla Rabhas of Kamrup adding a line on the cause of illness (1912 : 77-78). But in the same report Friend-Pereira has written somewhat detailed account on these people covering different aspects of the Rabha life and activities. He has mentioned these in the following headings :

(I) Description of the Rabhas including the habitat, physical features, clothings and ornaments, food habit, food quest and their behaviour.

(II) Language;

(III) Social organisation, Government and Law ;

(IV) Marriage and Divorce ;

(V) Birth and initiation ceremonies ;
(VI) Death and funeral rites ;
(VII) Religion ; and
(VIII) Tradition and History (1912 : 141-145).

Simultaneously with Firend-Pereira's report, Baine's account was published. In this account the description of the Rabhas covering only the affinity and language of the Rabhas, has been dealt with (1912 : 129).

In 1931 Census report, Porter following the report of Rev. Victor J. White of Mymensingh, only states the names of the seven sub-tribes of the Rabhas and their position among different other communities (1933 : 463, 483).

A bit detailed account on this community has been written in an article by Barua. He has described this tribe in a few pages detailing their physical features, matriarchal characteristics like those of the Khasis and the Garos, their process of Hinduization, death ceremony, language, dress, occupations, their fascination about military services etc. (1951 : 35-38).

In 1960 the Department of Publication of the University of Gauhati Published a book "Ethnic Affinities of the Rabhas" by B.M. Das. The six chapters of this book contain the introduction, somatoscopic observations, somatometric characeters, blood-groups, finger prints and palm prints and ethnic affinities. The six appendices contain, (i) story of King Dadan, (ii) Family structure of the Rabha, (iii) A note on child mortality among the Rabhas, (iv) Rabha kinship terms, (v) A study of the whori on head-heir of the Pati Rabha and (vi) Relative lengths of the first and second toes of the Rabha foot (1960 : 1-149, xii). Besides the above, Das has also published a few more articles mainly on the physical anthropology of the Rabha of Assam, though there are a few articles also on the social life of them (1955a ; 1955b ; 1956a ; 1956b ; 1957 ; 1958a ; 1958b ; 1958c ; 1958d). A few articles are also written by him jointly with P. Uzir (1959, 1960).

Regarding the Rabhas of West Bengal a good number of articles and a monograph covering almost all the aspects of the Village Rabha culture of this State by A.K. Das and M.K. Raha (1967) have so far been published.

An article on the Rabha dialect of West Bengal has also been published in recent times by Datta (1969).

Besides the above authors, there are a few others who have mentioned something about the Rabhas in a few lines.

APPENDIX 2

List of the original Rabha Husuks, Neoya Husuks and Totemic objects*

Sl. No.	Original Husuks	Abbrevia-tions	Neoya Husuks	Abbr-eviation used	Totemic objects (if any)
1.	Banda	Ba			Milk and milk products.
2.			Bandadhai	Bd	
3.			Bandasusuk	Bk	Curd, Milk and a kind of insect called *Indipoka.*
4.			Bandasang	Bs	*Boal*, a type of fish.
5.			Banda-Bantao	Bb	Brinjal.
6.	Banang	Bn			*Karna*, a type of reptile.
7.	Bantao	Bt			Brinjal.
8.			Sajo-Bantao	Sb	Brinjal, a particular variety.
9.			Kokai Bantoa	Tb	
10.	Champak	Cp			
11.	Chinchet	Ch			Ginger
12.	Choru	Cr			Milk and curd.
13.	Choudai	Cd			
14.	Dangdong	Dg			

* The list is not exhaustive.

Sl. No.	Original Husuks	Abbreviation	Neoya Husuks	Abbreviation used	Totemic objccts (if any)
15.	Dalangsa	Dl			*Boal*, a type of fish.
16.	Dapar	Dp			
17.	Darbahasu	Db			
18.	Darboth	Dr			Banyan tree.
19.	Dedoi	Dd			
20.	Durunga	Dn			Peacock and Peahen.
21.	Haiphang	Hp			Yeast
22.	Hardak	Hd			
23.	Hengsarang	Hg			
24.	Here	He			
25.	Kama	Ka			
26.			Kamachitam	Ck	
27.			Kamamochat	Km	Rat
28.			Kamaraba	Kb	
29.			Kamarasanji	Kj	*Boal*, a type of fish.
30,			Kamachikram	Kh	
31.	Kantran Kn				
32.			Hedam Kantran	Hk	*Dauk*, a kind of bird
33.			Hasak Kantran	Sk	*Kora* or *Pankouri* a kind of bird.
34.	Kara	Kr			
35.			Karabojidol	Kd	
36.			Karachandal	Kc	
37.			Karatablet	Kt	
38.			Karahtong	Kg	
39.			Karalepa	Kl	
40.			Kara-Lombok	Kk	
41.	Kaswap	Kp			This is a Hindu *gotra*.
42.	Kencham	Ke			
43.	Lavong	Lv			Ginger
44.	Lengbarai	Lb			
45.	Lengsa	Ls			
46.			Lengsakumar	Lr	
47.	Logobakt Lokobak	Lg			*Boal*, a type of fish.

Sl. No.	Original Husuks	Abbreviation	Neoya Husuks	Abbreviation used	Totemic objects (if any)
48.	Lombak	Lk			Ginger, *Boal*, a kind of fish.
49.	Moiji	Mo			*Simal Alu*, a kind of edible tuber.
50.			Moijibhobra	Mb	*Boal*, a kind of fish.
51.			Moijibhog	Mg	
52.			Moijidong	Md	*Boal*, a kind of fish.
53.			Moijinai	Mn	
54.			Moijipran	Mp	*Boal*, a kind of fish.
55.			Moijisampar	Ms	*Beth*, a type of creeper
56.			Moijinakal	Mk	
57.	Mositak	Mt			Deer
58.			Sumir Mositak	Ma	Deer, a particular variety.
59.	Negenang	Nn			
60.	Nogman	Nm			
61.	Nogra / Nogora	No			
62.			Gobitanji-Nogora	Ng	
63.			Hatong-Nogora	Nh	Earth worm.
64.			Kaksani-Nogora	Nk	
65.	Prandom	Pd			
66.	Pomrei	Po			Tortoise
67.			Pomreimandu	Pm	Tortoise, a particular species.
68.	Panchibak	Pb			*Duaki* and *Kora*, two types of bird.
69.			Panchibak-ganjinang	Pg	
70.	Kangoa	Ra			
71.	Rongdom	Rd			

Sl. No.	Original Husuks	Abbreviation	Neoya Husuks	Abbreviation	Totemic objects
72.	Rongot	Rg			
73.	Sarjinang	Sj			
74.	Sumbri	Sm			
75.	Tangoi	Tg			*Shol*, a kind of fish. (if any)
76.	Uni	Un			*Bhatipakhi*, a kind of bird.
77.			Uni-Brahman	Ub	
78.			Uni-Chandal	Uc	
79.			Uni-Chatama	Um	*Indi*, a kind of insect.
80.			Unichitan-barai	Ut	Peacock and Peahen.

APPENDIX 3

Composition of the Rabha Households

Sl. No.	Composition of the households	Settlements							
		Pars bastee	Andu bastee	Kandal Bastee	All forest bastee	Madhya Manasi	Dakshin Manasi	All villages	All settlements
1.	Widow (single member)	1	—	—	1	—	2	2	3
2.	Widowed parent with unmarried children	2	—	3	5	8	5	13	18
3.	Hu, Wi with/without umCh	43	12	10	65	29	38	67	132
4.	Either or both parents with umCh, mDa, with/without DaHu, DaumCh	20	7	8	35	4	2	6	41
5.	Either or both parents with umCh, mSo, mDa with/without their spouses and umCh	10	7	4	21	—	2	2	23
6.	Either or both parents with umCh, mSo with/without SoWi and SoumCh	6	3	1	10	7	4	11	21

7. Either or both parents with umCh, mDa, DaHu, DaumCh, DamDa, with/without Da DaHu and Da DaumCh	1	—	—	1	—	—	—	1
8. (w) Mo, mDa, DaHu, DaumCh, mSo, DamDa, Da DaHu, Da DaumCh	1	—	—	1	—	—	—	1
9. Hu, Wi, UmCh, WimSi with/without WiSiHu and WiSiumCh	2	—	1	3	—	—	—	3
10. Hu, Wi, umCh, WiBr with/without WiBrWi and WiBrumCh	—	2	1	3	—	—	—	3
11. Hu, Wi, umCh, HumBr with/without HuBrWi and HuBrumCh	—	—	1	1	—	1	1	2
12. Hu, Wi, umCh, HumBr with/without HuBrWi and HuBrumCh with HuMoMo	—	—	—	—	—	1	1	1
13. Hu, Wi, umCh, mDa, DaHu, WimYoSi, WiYoSiHu	—	1	—	1	—	—	—	1
14. Hu, Wi, umCh, mSi, mDa, with/without DaHu and DaumCh with WimYoSi, WiYoSiHu, WiYoSiumCh	—	1	—	1	—	—	—	1
15. Hu, WiumCh, mSo, mDa with/without DaHu and DaumCh with Wi (w) ElSi, Wi (w) ElSiSo	—	1	—	1	—	—	—	1

16. Hu, Wi, umCh, HuYoSiumCh	—	—	1	1	1	—	1	2
17. Hu, Wi, umCh, WiumYoBr	1	—	—	1	—	—	—	1
18. Hu, Wi, umCh, WiumYoSi	1	—	—	1	—	—	—	1
19. Hu, Wi, umCh, WiElSiumSo	1	—	—	1	—	—	—	1
20. Hu, Wi, umCh, HuumYoSi	1	—	—	1	—	—	—	1
21. Hu, Wi, umCh, HuMoYoBrSo	1	—	—	1	—	—	—	1
22. Hu, Wi, umCh, HuMoYoSiSo	1	—	—	1	—	—	—	1
23. Hu, Wi, umCh, WiMoYoSi (d) So	1	—	—	1	—	—	—	1
24. Hu, Wi, umCh, mDa, DaDa, DaumCh, WiElSiumSo	—	—	1	1	—	—	—	1
25. Hu, Wi, umCh, mDa, DaHu, DaumCh, DaHuumYoBr	—	—	1	1	—	—	—	1
26. Hu, Wi, umCh, mDa, DaHu, DaumCh, HuMoYoS i(w) Da	—	—	1	1	—	—	—	1
27. Hu, Wi, umCh, mDa, DaHu, DaumCh, HuYoSiHu MoSiumCh	1	—	—	1	—	—	—	1
28. Hu, Wi, umCh, mDa, DaHu, DaumCh, mSo, SoWi, SoWium-YoBr	—	—	1	1	1	—	1	2
29. Hu, Wi, umCh, mSo, SoWi, WiumYoBr	1	—	—	1	—	—	—	1
30. Hu, Wi, umCh, mSo, SoWi, HuElBrumDa	—	—	—	—	—	1	1	1
31. Hu, Wi, umCh, HuSiDaSo, WiYeBrSoSo	—	—	—	—	—	1	1	1

32. Hu, Wi, umCh, HumElSi, HuElSiHu, HuElSiumCh	—	1	—	1	—	—	—	1
33. Hu, Wi, umCh, mDa WiMoYoSimSo, WiMoYoSiSoWi WiMoYoSiSoumCh	1	—	—	1	—	—	—	1
34. Hu, Wi, umCh, mDa, Wi (d) ElBr	1	—	—	1	—	—	—	1
35. Hu, Wi, umCh, Hu(s) ElSi, WiYoBr, WiYoBrWi	1	—	—	1	—	—	—	1
36. Hu, Wi, umCh, Humo(w) Si	1	—	—	1	—	—	—	1
37. Hu, Wi, umCh, HuElSiDa	1	—	—	1	—	—	—	1
38. Hu, Wi, umCh, HuElBrumSo	1	—	—	1	2	—	2	3
39. (w) Mo, umCh, mDa, DaHu, DaumCh, DaHuMoSiSo	1	—	—	1	—	—	—	1
40. (w) Mo, mDa, DaHu, DaumCh, (w) Da,(w) DaumCh, mSo, Sowi, SoumCh SoWiumYoBr, SoWiumYaSi	—	—	1	1	—	—	—	1
41. (w) Mo, mSo, (w) MoumYoBr	—	—	1	1	—	—	—	1
42. (w) Mo, umCh, mSo, SoWi, SoumCh, SoWiumYoBr	—	—	1	1	—	—	—	1
43 (w) Mo, mSo, SoWi, SoumDa, SoWiumYoBr	1	—	—	1	—	—	—	1
44. (w) Mo, mDa, DaHu, DamSo, DaSoWi, DaSoumSo, (w) Mo-	1	—	—	1	—	—	—	1

45. (w) Mo, mSo, SoWi, SoumCh, MoMoSiDaSo	1	—	—	1	—	—	—	1
46. (w) Mo, umCh, mSo, SoWi, SoumCh, (w) MoYoSiDaDaumSo	1	—	—	1	—	—	—	1
47. (w) Mo, umCh, (w) YoBr	—	—	1	1	—	—	—	1
48. (w) Fa, mDa, DaHu, DaumCh, DamDa, mSo, SoWi, SoumCh	—	—	1	1	—	—	—	1
49. (w) Ma, mDa, DaHu, DaumCh, DaHuYoSonmSo	—	—	—	—	1	—	1	1
50. Hu, Wi, umCh, HuSiDa, HuSi-DaumCh, HuSiDamSo, HuSi-DaSoWi, HuSiSoSo, HuSiDaSa-WiumBr, HuMoMoSiDa (W) Da, HuMoMoSiDa (w) Da Da, HuMoMaSi Da (w) Da DaHu, HuMoMoSi Da (w) DaDaumCh	—	—	—	—	1	—	1	1
51. Hu, Wi, HuYoBr, HuMoBrSo	—	—	—	—	—	1	1	1
52. Hu, Wi, (w) Da, (w) DaumCh	—	—	—	—	—	1	1	1
53. Hu, Wi, Wi, umCh	1	—	—	1	—	—	—	1
54. Hu, Wi, Wi, umCh, WiElBrDa, WiYoBr	—	—	1	1	—	—	—	1
Total	107	35	40	182	54	59	113	295

Code : Fa=Father, Mo=Mother, Br=Brother, Si=Sister, So=Son, Da=Daughter, Wi=Wife, Hu=Husband, Ch=Children, Yo=Younger, El=Elder.
m=Married, um=Unmarried, (w)=Widowed, (d)=Divorced/Deserted, (s)=Separated.

APPENDIX 4

THE RABHA KINSHIP TERMS

Original Rabha Terms	*English abbreviations*	*Bengali (Raj bansi) Terms as used by the Village Rabhas*
1st ascending generation		
Aoa buda	Fa Fa	Burabapu
Achu	Mo Fa	Aju
Ayebudi	Fa Mo	Burima
Oai/Ambudi	Mo Mo	Aiburi/Abo
2nd ascending generation		
Etei	Fa el Br	Jyato
	Mo el Si Hu	,,
Akay	Fa el Br Wi	Jyatai
	Mo el Si	,,
Eiti	Fa yo Br Wi	Kaki
	Mo yo Si	Masi
Mani	Fa el Si	Pishi/Pishai
	Fa yo Si	,, ,,
	Mo Br Wi	Mami
Mama	Fa el Si Hu	Pisha
	Fa yo Si Hu	,,
	Mo Br	Mama
Hau	Wi Fa	Sasur

	Hu Fa	,,
Nei	Wi Mo	Sasuri
	Hu Mo	,,
Bou, Aoa	Fa	Baba/Bapo
Amai	Mo	Mao/Io
Dadi	Fa yo Br	Kaka
Bongtei	Mo yo Si Hu	Mansa
Ego's generation		
Adagada	el Br (ms)	Dada
	el Br (ws)	,,
Ajong	Yo Br (ws)	Bhai
Ajong	Yo Br (ws)	Bhai
Aya/Jenou	el Si (ms)	Bai//Didi/Baio
	el Si (ws)	Bai/Didi/Baio
Aya/Jenou	Fa el Br Da	Jyeto Beti Boin
Aya/Jenou	Fa yo Br Da	Khura Beti Boin
Aya/Jenou	Fa Si Da	Pishi Beti Boin
Aya/Jenou	Mo Si Da	Jyeti/Masi Beti Boin
Aya/Anou/Jenou	Mo Br Da	Mama Beti Boin
Aya	Wi Br Wi	Didi/Bain
Jenou/Anou	Yo Si (ms)	Bon
	Yo Si (ws)	,,
Jenou/Sodmaram	Hu Yo Br Wi	Didi/Bain
Ada/Ajong	Fa el Br So	Jyeto Beta Bhai
	Fa yo Br So	Khura Beta Bhai
	Fa Si So	Pishi Beta Bhai
	Mo Si So	Jyeti/Masi Beta Bhai
	Mo Br So	Mama Beta Bhai
	Hu Si Hu	Baio/Dada
Anang	Wi Br	Sala
	Hu el Si	Bhoujhi/Nanad
	Hu yo Si	Nanad
	el Si Hu (ms)	Ano/Bonu
	Yo Si Hu (ms)	Bonsugat
	Yo Si Hu (ws)	Bonou/Bonjamai
	el Br Wi (ws)	Bhoujhi/Boudi
Jyeg	Hu	Swami/Bhatar
Jyog/Michik	Wi	Stree/Bou

Biyai	So Wi Fa	Biyai
	Da Hu Fa	,,
Biyani	So Wi Mo	Biyani
	Da Hu Mo	,,
Janai	Wi el Si	Jyeithani/Bhoujhi
Nousil	Wi yo Si	Shali
	Yo Br Wi (ms)	Bhausani
Bhasur	Hu el Br	Bhasur.
Deor	Hu yo Br	Deor
Sodgada	Wi el Si Hu	Jyetpoth
Ayagada	Hu yo si Hu	Bain/Didi
Sodpumar	Wi yo Si Hu	Shalpoth
Kabak	el Si Hu (ws)	Bonou
Jakak	el Br Wi (ms)	Bondi/Bhoujhi
Bhousami	yo Br Wi (ms)	Bhousani
Bhousani/Anangsa	yo Br Wi (ws)	Bhousani/Bhoujhi

1st descending generation

Bagnai	el Si So (ms)	Bhagna
	yo Si So (ms)	,,
	Hu Si So	,,
Jenousamichik/Eitisa	el Si Da (ws)	Bhatijhi
Jenousamichik/Akaisa	Yo Si Da (ws)	,,
Bongteisa	el Br So (ms)	Bhajya
	el Br Da (ms)	Bhatijhi
Bongteisa/Eteisa	Hu Br So	Bhajya
Bongteisa/Eteisa	Hu Br Da	Bhatijhi
Eteisa	Yo Br So (ms)	Bhajya
	Yo Br Da (ms)	Bhatijhi
Akaisa/Eitisa	Wi Si So	Bhajya
Akaisa/Eitisa	Wi Si Da	Bhatijhi
Bagnaisa	el Si Da (ms)	Bhagni
	Yo Si Da (ms)	,,
	Wi Br So	Bhajya
	Wi Br Da	Bhatijhi
	Hu Si Da	Bhagni
Monisa/	Yo Br So (ws)	Bhajya
Ajongsamichik	Yo Br Da (ws)	Bhatijhi

Eitisa	el Si So (ws)	Bhajya
Akaisa/Jenounisa	Yo Si So (ws)	,,
Sa/Miasa	So	Chaoya/Beta
Samichik/Michiksa	Da	Beti
Adanisa	el Br So (ws)	Bhajya
Adasamichik/Bateisa	el Br Da (ws)	Bhatijhi
Kilang	Da Hu	Jamai/Jangoai
Namsa	So Wi	Bouma

2nd descending generation

Achusa	So So	Nati
Achusa/Samichiksa	Da So	,,
Aoisa	So Da	Natni
Aoisa/Samichiksa	D Da	,,

APPENDIX 5

A Short Note on the Janjogi Rabha of Paro Forest Bastees

Janjogi, the Originator, propagator and preacher Baba of the *Janjogi religion* was born at Mirik in Darjeeling district on May 22, 1928. In his boyhood days he was known as Dharmaraj Lama. In order to save the people of this country from miseries and in order to establish a socialistic society Dharamraj started his ascetic life in 1956 and after ten years of meditation on Saturday, October 30, 1965 at 10.00 hours he attained emancipation and became *Param Pita Tribouddha Gnandhari Janjogi Baba*. He then started preaching his ideology. At first he started preaching his ideology in his birth place Mirik but he was not successful there. But he became somewhat successful at North Mendabari and Paro where he could convert some Rabhas into Janjogi religion.

In the year 1966 a section of the Forest Rabhas who were mostly the inhabitants of the Purodha and North Mendabari *bastees* embraced this religion through a very interesting incident. One day two Rabhas met with *Param Pita Tribouddha Guandhari Janjogi Baba* the originator, flag-bearcr and the preacher of this religion. When they first met with the Janjogi Baba, they were taught of accepting the new religion. In spite of Baba's persistence they disagreed to be baptised. But the Baba told them that the world would soon come to an end and everything would be destroyed, so also the Rabhas. Then these two got scared. Hearing the assurance from the Baba that he had been sent by the God Almightly to save his disciples the two Rabhas for the fear of destruction, agreed to follow *janjgoi* religion. After they were baptised to *janjogi* religion they spread the story of the distruction of the universe among their own fellow-man and were able to pursue some of them to accept this religion. Later on when a good number of the Rabhas accepted this *janjogi* religion they constructed an *asram*, near Purodha Dakshin *bastee*. But a couple of years after these Rabhas, who were converted to *janjogi* religion and gave up their own religion, did not find anything wrong and they were alive and the world was not destroycd. They lost their faith to this religion. It is a pecularity that only the Forest Rabhas were converted into this new religious faith and not the village Rabhas.

About twenty years ago, in Purodha *bastee* only 34 out of 107 (31.47%) households were baptised to this religion and they were also willing to give up this region. The total population of this section was 207 individuals. Out of total of 207 *janjogi* Rabhas 45.80% were males and the rest 54.11% females. The *janjogi* Rabhas covered only 4.56% of the total population of five settlements which were studied under this research project. This section shared 31.03% of the total population of the Purodha *bastee*. Like the other population they were also distributed in different age-groups. The age-group 10-14 years had secured the highest frequency. The size of households varies from single member to as big as ten members, the average size being 6.09, The households with five members had the highest (26.47%) frequency.

At present there are only a few *janjogi* Rabhas in the Purodha *bastee*. Their mother tongue is Rabha but most of them can speak in local Bengali. Majority of them are illiterate like the non-*janjogi* Forest Rabhas.

The *janjogi* Rabhas are also primarily dependent on agriculture like the non-*janjogies*. In Purodha *bastee* out of 81 household having land, 26 are *janjogis* 24 of which have 3.50 acres of land each while other two, being headmen (*mandal*) of the *bastees*, have 7.0 acres of land each. Seven *janjogi* households are share croppers without their own land. One janjogi household, that of awidow, lives on, doing work on other's house. Regarding the rules of inhheritance they also follow the female line.

In case of marriage a *janjogi* Rabha is allowed to marry a non-*janjogi* Rabha. Generally they prefer community endogamy. They cannot marry within the same *husuk*, because they follow the rule of *husuk* exogamy strictly. Monogamy is the general rule of marriage, though polygyny is not prohibited. Sororate, levirate and cross-cousin marriages are also permitted by their religion but of rare occurrence. Marriage by service is the common mode of acquiring mate though marriage by exchange are also in existence. Majority (70.83%) of males has married within the age-group 25-29 and majority (61.02%) of females has considered the age-group 15-19 as the most preferred age-group for marriage. Regarding the marital status the unmarried (48.31%) population dominate over the married (46.86%) one. The frequency of widowed and divorced is comparatively very low like that of the non-*jonjogis*. These are 3.86% and 0.97% respectively. The number of married males (50.53%) is slightly higher than that of the unmarried males (49.47%). But the frequency of unmarried males (49.47%) is comparatively higher than that of uamarried females (47.32%) Bride price or dowry is not prevalent in their society. Majority (62.50%) of them prefer village endogamy. After marriage, the rules of residence is matrilocal. They consider the full-moon day of the month of *jaistha* (May-June) as an auspicious day (the birthday as *Parampita janjogi*). This particular day is the most suitable day for the marriage of their children. Marriage ceremonies take place neither in the bride's house nor in the groom's house but in *janjogi ashram.*

On the date of marriage, both the bride and groom along with their marriage party assemble in the *ashram* in the morning and decorate the wedding booth with flowers and leaves. Then both the bride and groom exchange their garlands in the presence of their relatives, neighbours and well wishers. They also exchange *pan-gua* (betel and nut) within themselves in the similar fashion. Thereafter the father of both the bride and the groom garland the bride-groom, similarly the mother of both the bride and bride-groom garland the bride. Before and after the wedding ceremony all assembled persons sing *janjogi* songs, praising five reverential objects (*Pancha-Praolkriti* or *Prakriti Puram*). In their marriage feast *chakat* is never served because chakat is prohibited in their religion. In their marriage ceremony both the prafessional priest and barber have role. Divorce is permitted in their society and for divorce they do not have any particular ceremony. Both the husband and wife have equal right for divorce. Remarriage of widowed and divorced persons is also allowed. For remarriage they do not observe any ceremony.

Among the *janjogi* Rabhas during the pregnancy they pray to the *Parampita* and five *gurus* through the *janjogi* songs for quick and safe delivery. After the child birth women sing *janjogi* songs to cxpress their joy. They do not observe any pollution period. Within a few days after child birth shaving of hair ceremony is observed by them. They observe name giving ceremony on the 5th, 7th or 9th days after the child birth. First rice feeding eeremony is not observed by them.

Like the non-*janjogi* Rabhas when a *janjogi* Rabha child attains 10 or 12 years of age, he gets the permission to enter in the dormitory (*naksa*) untilol he gets married. They do not observe any adulthood ceremony.

Among the *janjogi* Rabhas when a death occurs in the house, it is indicated by a loud wailing of the women and children. After the death the janjogi Rabha women and children sit together and sing janjogi chorus in a low voice. The usual nature of disposal of the dead is burial for which they do not have any fixed burial ground. Preparation of bier and disposal of dead is similar with the non-*janjogi* Rabhas excepted that the Dhami has no role in the disposal of dead. In the funeral procession they continue singing the *janjogi* songs. After thc funeral party reaches the burial ground, the members start digging the grave. When the pit is complete they first of all keep the personal belongings of the dead man in the grave. Then they place the dead body in the grave and cover it in the similar fashion like the non-*janjogi* Rabhas.

No offering is made, but the prayer is uttered. Then they take purificatory bath and come back to the deceased's house by singing *janjogi* songs. The *janjogi* Rabhas do not observe any rite for invoking the departed soul nor do they observe any pollution period or obsequial rites and rituals.

In the level of social control there is no much difference between the *janjogi* and non-*janjogi* Rabhas.

The *janjogi* Rabhas are the followers of *Parampita Tribouddha Gnandhari Janjogi Baba*, the originator and preacher of the *janjogi* religion. They do not worship any deity or idols. The *janjogi* religion prescribes five reverential objects for homage. The devotees only pay their homage to the five reverential objects, whom they call *Tribouddha Gnandhari Guru*. These five *gurus* are the Sun, (Surja), the Moon (Chandra), the Air (Haoa), the water (Pani) and the Earth (*Jagimaya Amai*). They celebrate only one festival i.e., the birthday of *janjogi Baba* on the full moon day of thc month of jaistha (May—June). Every Thursday they observe fast throughout the day and in the evening they sing *jonjogi* songs (*bhajan*). No offerings or sacrifices are made.

The followers of this religion are prohibited from taking any alcoholic drink, narcotics or intoxicants. This religion has also inspired its followers to become self-sufficient economically. They should not allow to sit idle and spent time by mere gossiping.

APPENDIX 6

A Brief Note on Christianity among the Rabhas of West Bengal

The conversion to Christianity among the Rabhas of West Bengal is a recent phenomenon. Though the history of the activities of the Christian missionaries is very long in the Western Druas, the Rabhas were so long resisting the temptation of becoming the Christians. One of the reasons for their movement for Hinduization which started in 1939 and continued onwards was to prevent their people to embrace Christianity. Only recently some of the Rabhas failed to control them from becoming Christians. But the impact of Christianity is only found among the Forest Rabhas.

The Rabhas in some forest *bastees* are mainly converted to this alien faith. These evangelical works are primarily done by two Christian missions—The Seventh Day Abventist and the Rabha Baptist Church Union. The latter plays the major role in conversion of the Rabhas to Christianity. Both organizations are actively working for the spread of Christianity since the late 1970's.

The Seventh Day Adventists are active in the forest *bastees* such as Kodal *bastee*, Gadadhar, Shillong, Panbari, Paro (South), Latabari and Kathalbari. All these forest *bastees* except Kathalbari are located under the Buxa Forest Division of Jalpaiguri district while Kathalbari is under The Cooch Behar Forest Division. Like the former activists the Rabha Baptist

Church Union is working among the Rabha of Mendabari, Kurmai, Khayerbari, Gossainhat, Mela, Kuklung, Gadadher, Paro (North) and Dhumshi forest *bastees.*

The first proselytization activities by the Rabha Baptist Church Union (R.B.C.U.) took place in 1977 in Mendabari, a forest *bastee.* Altogether nine forset *bastees* were brought under the jurisdiction of R. B. C U. The headquarters of the R. B. C.U. is located in Debitola, a village of the Parbatjowar tract of Dhubri District, Assam. The following table highlights the statistical account about conversion to Christianity among the Rabha of West Bengal.

Sl. No.	*Name of the bastee (village)*	*No. of persons converted*	*Year of conversion*
1.	Mendabari	248	1977
2.	Kurmai	?	1977
3.	Khoyerbari	137	1978
4.	Gossainhat	107	1979
5.	Mela	?	1979
6.	Kuklung	?	1980
7.	Gadadhar	?	?
8.	Poro (North)	10	1981
9.	Dhumshi	35	1981

Source : Rabha Baptist Church Union, Debitola, Assam.

To facilitate the spiritual activities of the converts the R.B.C.U. has extended fincial and meterial help to the newly converts. They have established churches in each bastee. The authorities of the Mendabari church coordinate all activities relating to administration, evangelical works and financial matters of all the churches located in the *bastees* inhabited by the Forest Rabha of West Bengal under overall control of the R.B.C.U. Debitola, Assam.

Impact of Christianity

Though Christianity is a new religion to them and they have embraced this religion only recently, yet this religion has some impact on them. In their case though descent is matrilineal yet the males are now liking patrilocal residence after marriage, if not, at least a neolocal one. Some of them are not preferring parents-in-law's house to reside after marriage. In case of immovable property (a few Forest Rabhas have purchased land outside the Reserve Forest, it is reported) and also movable ones the sons are also keen to get share of property equally with the daughters. The son wants his name should be forwarded to the forest authority as the official labourer instead of the name of the daughters' husband after the death of his father. Though such changes are not clearly perceptible right now, but that some Christian Forest Rabhas have keen interest on such changes, is marked when one discusses with them. They are also trying to bring some such changes with the help of the missionaries. The Rabha living in forest are very simple, timid and poor. Almost all of them are illiterate and their exposure to the outside world is too limited. But their congeners in Assam and in other areas of West Bengal is more advanced. To integrate and to ameliorate the condition of the Rabha of forest *bastees* of West Bengal the Christian Rabha started visiting different forest *bastees* where their tribesmen live in deplorable conditions. They felt that the Rabha of forest locations should be first converted into Christianity in order to ameliorate their deplorable conditions. When the opportunity came they began to preach Christianity among them, and in first instance, they provided free ration, garments, free medical help, etc. With a view to attracting such alien faith provided they should give up some of their old customs which were thought to be harmful to their daily life as well.

The converts on conversion to Christianity, have given up their age-old habit of addiction to *chakai* (rice-beer) and also various superstitions, etc. Now they are being trained up in general cleanliness, health care, family planning methods etc. The authorities of the R.B.C.U. have provided medical help by establishing dispensary in their localities. Their children are now getting formal education, and a self-consciousness has developed among them. Now these people are trying to improve their economic conditions as well.

Conflicts between the Christian and non-Christian over the adoption of Christianity are very negligible. No blood-shed, physical assault, excommunication and even fine took place during or after conversion. In general being very peace-loving people, they were not involved in any major conflict. No major incidents were noticed between the converts and the non-converts who are found to inhabit one beside the other in a neighbourly mood. Conversion to Christianity could never prevent the close inter-ethnic and intra-ethnic interactions.

INDEX

ILLUSTRATIONS

1. Late Shri Debendra Nath Das : A Rabha Leader.
(*Courtesy : Shri Sunil Pal, Kamakhyaguri*)

2. A Forest Rabha Woman with traditional costume and ornaments.
(*Courtesy : Director, Indian Museum, Calcutta*)

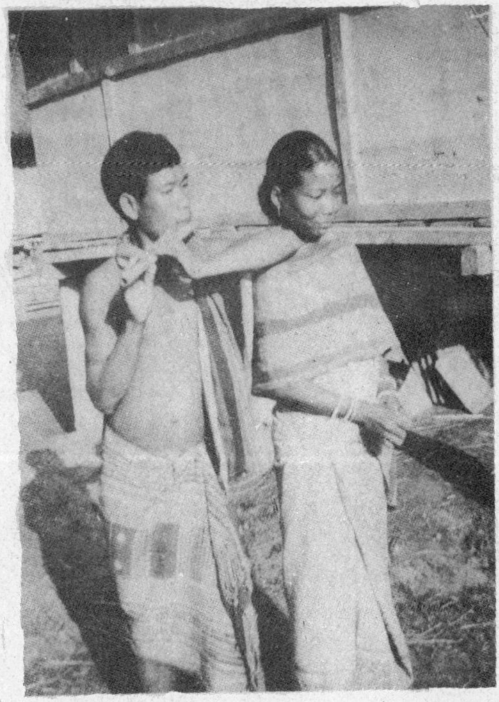

3. A Village Rabha couple.
(*Courtesy : Shri Sunil Pal, Kamkhyaguri*)

4. A Village Rabha family.
(*Courtesy : Shri Sunil Pal, Kamkhyaguri*)

5. Musical instruments of the Village Rabhas.
(*Courtesy : Shri Sunil Pal, Kamkhyaguri*)

6. Preparation for war dance by the Village Rabha girls.
(*Courtesy : **Shri** Sunil Pal, Kamkhyaguri*)

7. A Forest Rabha male.
(*Courtesy* ; *Director*, *Indian Museum*, *Calcutta*)

8. Forest Rabha Mask Dance.
(*Courtesy : Director, Indian Museum, Calcutta*)

9. Forest Rabha Weaving Technique.
(*Courtesy : Director, Indian Museum, Calcutta*)

10. The Forest Rabha fishing basket operated in strong current.
(*Courtesy : Director, Indian Museum, Calcutta*)